# The Edward Dahlberg Reader

# The Edward Dahlberg Reader

edited and with an introduction by

## Paul Carroll

New Directions

# Contents

# Note to the Reader

Three major themes distinguish Mr. Dahlberg's writings: his dialogue with the body; his criticism of other writers; and his condemnation of the modern world. The first three sections of the Reader contain selections embodying one or another of these themes. Section I presents the dialogue with the body. The title of the section *"Omne Animale Post Coitu Triste"* is the commonplace out of medieval Europe which reminds us that "After intercourse every animal is depressed." The phrase "Our Mother Eve" used for one of the subsections comes from an anecdote told about St. Jerome. After having returned from ten years of solitude and mortification in the wastes of the Chalcis, Jerome would often stand in the thronging streets and markets of Rome, pointing an ominous, lean finger at some well-groomed patrician lady, and shout: "Behold! I see our Mother Eve approaching." Section II "On Writers Faire, Foul, and Full of Variation" includes selections in which Mr. Dahlberg attacks some of the masters of modern literature as well as selections in which he discusses those writers and artists whom he has admired. The phrase in the title of the section "faire, foul, and full of variation" was used by Robert Burton to describe the Roman elegiac poets. The titles for both subsections come from phrases by Mr. Dahlberg: "Bawds in the beauty parlor on Mount Ida" occurs in his essay on James Joyce; "My tutelary Muses and woodland Seers" appeared in a letter written in 1958 to Jonathan Williams. Section III presents his condemnation of the modern world. Its title *"Quomodo Sola Sedet Civitas"* —"How doth the city sit solitary, that was full of people"— comes from the opening of the Lamentations of Jeremiah.

Section IV includes selections from his correspondence. Deletion has been made only to avoid repetition or to eliminate material of little general interest. In several instances, a correspondent requested that some passage of a personal nature be excluded: the editor has honored these requests. In one instance, I deleted a vituperative allusion to a man of letters who later became one of Mr. Dahlberg's close friends. Deletion is indicated by the usual . . . . Brackets contain what editorial information seemed necessary to clarify reference to a person or to a book or poem or article. I wish to express my gratitude to all of Mr. Dahlberg's correspondents for their cooperation in making his letters available, and to the Newberry Library of Chicago, and especially to Mrs. Amy Nyholm, modern manuscript librarian, for making available the Dahlberg letters in the Sherwood Anderson Archive. In all, I had the opportunity to study some 200 letters, but I was unable to examine the extensive correspondence with Alfred Stieglitz and William Carlos Williams, which is deposited in the Yale Collection of American Literature at the Yale University Library, nor was I able to read the letters in the Special Collections section of the Library of the University of California at Los Angeles.

# An Introduction to Edward Dahlberg

## "After Intercourse Every Animal is Depressed"

For his patrician prose that seems to come from another century, his savage and often cantankerous condemnation of most of the masters of modern literature, his handling of the old myths as if Agamemnon or Quetzalcoatl or the Sorrowful Mother were our real contemporaries, and his sibylline call to abandon our civilization lock, stock, and barrel and return to an Arcady of "the sheepcote, the threshing-floor, and the augur's timbrel," Edward Dahlberg has become one of the scandals of American Letters, although a distinguished one. He is one of our own. Yet his stance appears so absolute and odd that anyone with a conventionally solid knowledge of American literary traditions can be disarmed or exasperated when first exposed to it. The first time I saw the stance and heard Dahlberg talk I was astounded. During the winter of 1958 the poet Isabella Gardner gave a party for him at the Cliff Dwellers Club in Chicago. Miscellaneous poets, book reviewers, English professors, and other members of the local intellectual community sat over cocktails, many of us aghast as Dahlberg—tall, dressed in Harris Tweed and silk foulard ascot, handsome with white hair and trim, regimental mustache—fascinated and outraged by his high, bitter invective against most of the idols of contemporary American writing. What he said about Hemingway, Faulkner, Eliot, Edmund Wilson, Pound, and, I believe, the New Critics was univocal, brilliant, sour, erudite, and unanswerable. Good words were given only to Sherwood Anderson and grudging respect to Dreiser, both of whom Dahlberg had known and respected when he was learning how to write in the New York City of the 1920s. At one point I remember feeling that we were not in the Cliff Dwellers Club overlooking Michigan Avenue but were instead in the study of Robert Burton at Christ Church, Oxford, the late Elizabethan sunlight trickling through the windows, the large, worn calfskin folios of Tertullian, Plotinus, Dionysius of Halicarnassus, Paracelsus, or the gossip Diogenes Laertius within easy reach if the speaker had need to check some recondite allusion to score his point. Only the cadence of his sentences and cultivated accent seemed to keep Dahlberg's words from becoming a scream.

Long one of the heroes of the literary Underground because of his early proletarian novels, his jeremiads, and his elevated conception of the vocation of the writer—for which he has spent most of his 65 years in poverty, lack of "respectable" recognition, the recipient of no major literary award—Dahlberg has also earned the admiration of several of the leading men of letters of the Establishment, some of whom, like Sir Herbert Read, have called him a lord of the language, the heir of Sir Thomas Browne, Burton, and the Milton of the great polemical pamphlets. Still, Dahlberg has passed his literary life as an outcast—an

Ishmael come out of the Midwest as if the fertile prairies of his native Missouri were barren as the ancient Thebaid or the wastes around the Mareotic Sea, the home only of scorpion, owl, and Egyptian devils.

## II

Certainly there is no prose like Dahlberg's prose in all of American literature. At its best, the Dahlberg style is monumental and astonishing. Decades were spent in its evolution. Limited recognition came early when Dahlberg published the novel *Bottom Dogs* in 1929 with a shrill, chilly introduction by D. H. Lawrence. Two more novels followed —*From Flushing to Calvary* (1933) and *Those Who Perish* (1938)—both written in the hard-bitten, bony, slangy style of *Bottom Dogs*, which the author later discredited. The great Dahlberg style first appeared in the collection of critical essays *Do These Bones Live; Sing O Barren* (1941), later republished as *Can These Bones Live*. Ten years later *The Flea of Sodom* appeared; the style had become supple, bizarre, a weapon of rage and authority. The flowering was to come in Dahlberg's masterpieces *The Sorrows of Priapus* (1957) and the autobiography *Because I Was Flesh* (1964). What commends this style are the cadence and dignity of its sentences and the rich, queer erudition. What is most memorable is its treatment of myth.

Myth is as natural to Dahlberg's sensibility as air, earth, water, and fire. He never uses myth simply as a literary device; instead he lives myth, experiencing his deepest feelings and life in terms of myths.

In *Because I Was Flesh*, for instance, Dahlberg renders his mother Lizzie, a melancholy but Breughelian peasant grasping at the shards and patches which were her life, as the embodiment of the Sorrowful Mother; at other times as the Magdalene or the sister of Lazarus; and finally, through the strength of his prose, she becomes a kind of myth in her own right. Early in the book he makes this passionate, fanatical confession: "Should I err against her dear relics or trouble her sleep, may no one imagine that she has not always been for me the three Marys of the New Testament. Moreover, what I imagine I know is taken from my mother's body and this is the memoir of her body." To call one's mother the three Marys of the New Testament is either to invite ridicule (which the author never encourages) or to insist on a dimension which could prove a disaster in the hands of a lesser writer. But as the events of Lizzie Dahlberg's life are told—how she abandons a doltish husband and two infants to run away with a dude barber, and how later, alone, she bears Edward in a Boston charity hospital; how she eventually settles in Kansas City, Missouri, where amid shabby respectability, greed, and vice she labors as a lady barber and strives to raise her boy and to acquire a new husband; how rotten luck dogs her as suitor after suitor disappoints her, including the last one, a dotty, stinging, rich merchant named Tobias Emeritch, whose wooing of Lizzie provides one of the high moments of comedy and pathos in our literature; how she dies old and alone, in pain, half-crazed—as these events unfold Lizzie Dahlberg *becomes* the three Marys of the Gospels. She becomes Mary the Virgin Mother in that the author, like Jesus, feels that no man really possessed her but himself; Mary the Magdalene in that a stable of suitors actually copulated with her; and Mary the sister of Lazarus in that the author by conjuring back the ghost of his boyhood is her brother, and during the hobo wanderings of his young manhood he is always dead, like Lazarus, until he returns home to her.

One of the commonplaces of modern criticism tells us that the people of myth are contemporaneous with the present. Tiresias broods in the room of the London typist as she submits to the mechanical seduction of the young man carbuncular in *The Waste Land;* Circe, Aeneas, and Thetis appear, disappear, and appear again in the American Army prison camp among Ezra Pound and his fellow prisoners, Snag and his buddy, and the "little coon" and the "big black nigger" in *The Pisan Cantos*. But Dahlberg possesses that rarer gift of being able to resurrect by means of his prose, which is another thing from having the literary imagination to introduce a mythological person into one's poem or novel, or from having the talent to create a memorable fictional character or to write good biography about someone dead. Finding in the events of Lizzie Dahlberg's life echos of the three Marys resurrects these dead women. Much like Odysseus slaughtering sheep to provide blood for the shades in the Cimmerian Underworld, Dahlberg seems to offer the Marys the blood of his mother, a woman as each of them was before becoming a legend among the faithful or a statue in a cathedral or an abstraction to whom one prays—a woman who bears children with her body, who aches, laughs, weeps, defecates, loves, ages, lusts, who wants "to walk quiet and slow among soft dusk" but who dies in pain. The deeper meanings in the events of Lizzie's biography assume shape through the lives and significances of the three Marys; they, in turn, exist once again through her.

When *Because I Was Flesh* ends with an unforgettable and medieval description of Lizzie Dahlberg's death rattle, suffered in a cold-water flat on East 96th Street in New York City, and the final sentence turns into a scream of eloquence, the final metamorphosis occurs in which Lizzie, like the Marys before her, becomes myth through the mystery of words. "When the image of her comes up on a sudden—just as my bad demons do—and I see again her dyed henna hair, her eyes dwarfed by the electric lights of the Star Lady Barbershop, and the dear, broken wing of her mouth, and when I regard her wild tatters, I know that not even Solomon in his lilied raiment was so glorious as my mother in her rags. Selah."

Another use of myth, especially when sexual feelings are involved, exposes one of the origins of many myths. Recalling one of our most tenacious, infantile fantasies, Dahlberg writes in *Because I Was Flesh:* "Once, at daybreak, he [the boy he was] suddenly awakened, hearing his mother let out a cry of pain. Harry Cohen was covering her, and he knew that the cause of her pain was carnal. The baker was one of the issue of those giants who, in the Ethiopic *Book of Enoch*, were said to have had the monstrous privy members of horses." To be reminded of an esoteric text while describing a Kansas City baker helping to make the beast with two backs, and remain bone-serious about it, could lay open the author to a suspicion of unintentional silliness if it were not for the intimation that one of the darker roots which create and nourish certain myths might lie in our reluctance to face raw, shocking events in our immediate emotional lives. Myth, in this sense, distorts emotional fact by displacing it; and by distorting permits us to retain and live with those facts. Who wants to think directly about his mother engaging in sexual intercourse? If her lover is some giant out of Ethopia, then he—like the Paraclete who inseminates the Blessed Virgin—comes from another country: he is more fairy tale than human. Transformation of sexual feelings into myths occurs continually throughout Dahlberg's writing and accounts for some of his finest passages.

*Can These Bones Live,* on the other hand, transforms the books of an entire people into myth. The central, brutal intuition of this reading of classic American literature revolves around a retelling of the myth of Genesis, the Fall, Salvation, and Apocalypse, with one significant variation: the Salvation is perverted. Whereas Whitman becomes "the pioneer Cosmos, before him nothing," and Poe "the Adamic Evil," and *Moby-Dick*, "the allegory of the disincarnate Ahab seeking after his own flesh," the Messiah is the Puritan Christ—the Logos stripped of hair, skin, bone, anus, guts, and genitals. American literature, Dahlberg declares, is the Doomsday Book of a people who have never known the body of the Incarnation except as a nightmare of incest, paranoia, homosexuality, fear and hatred of woman, violence, and masochism. This Doomsday Book, in fact, is one long, insane epithalamium to the effeminate Christ without a body. By way of contrast, Dahlberg invokes a composite, secular figure of Incarnation whom American writing has failed to create: Don Quixote and Sancho Panza, the spirit "with windmills in the head," and the body, all good belly and groin. Although no Salvation or Second Coming can be expected from the perverted Christ there is an Apocalypse. At the other end of time the Whore of Babylon appears as the Dynamo of Henry Adams "that has taken us far underground, where we wander over flowerless and treeless plains of macadam," inhabited by the shades of Hemingway, Faulkner, and the proletarian novelists. Despite the efforts of these writers, in Dahlberg's reading, to resurrect the body that the Puritans like Poe and Hawthorne and Melville tried to bury, they are shown as the other side of the same bad coin. Either they write merely of "the kidney, the prostate gland, and the intestinal tract," or they catalogue no more than the Drama of Bread. Apocalypse, in short, is contemporary American literature.

In an America where myths—except the usual chauvinistic type or those celebrating Herculean muscle or Horatio Alger success—have seldom been part of how the citizens experience or comprehend realities, Dahlberg is our one mythological poet. During forty years of writing he has performed the lonely ritual of recalling to a pragmatic

American world, with its chaos and hearty vulgarities, the fact that men once found grandeur and tragedy in myths that embodied some of the bedrock realities of this life and of the life of the imagination.

## III

Dahlberg despises contemporary America. In his condemnation of it, no American writer since Thoreau—with his stubborn Yankee contempt of the business world, culture, manners, and religion of the 19th century, which he dismissed as "restless, nervous, bustling, trivial"—has worn the cloak of Diogenes with such conviction, day in and day out, decade after decade. Because of the rigor of Dahlberg's hatred, frequently couched in Old Testament vocabulary and fury, some critics and fellow writers have hailed him as a prophet. He is not. His condemnation is grounded neither on an ancient morality, such as that of Jeremiah or Isaiah, based on the tablets of the law given by the god of their fathers, nor on a new morality, a new delineation of what it could mean to be human, the arrogant, virile transcendence of the old gods called for by the Zarathustra of Nietzsche. Instead, the moral energy with which Dahlberg hurls anathemas at our world comes from a peculiar kind of reverence and from a calendar of literary saints of his own making.

His reverence, rooted more in the heart than in the head, is a reverence for the archetypes from the childhood of the race. Throughout his books and letters Dahlberg bestows an almost religious honor upon the Greek heroes out of Homer, Plutarch, and the tragic and comic poets, and upon the Old Testament patriarchs of the cow pasture, the plain of Sharon, and the cedars of Lebanon. At other times, his piety honors the gods of maize, squash, and rain, the reptile, animal, and bird gods of the Incas, Aztecs, Potowattamies, and the nomad tribes of the Western plains. Invoking these heroes and deities Dahlberg condemns out of hand "this immense mortuary cartel," contemporary America. This is not prophecy. This is piety for the elemental, the primitive, the genesis which is each sunrise; and it is hatred for all that is mechanized and sophisticated which separates men from the natural world. "I think you are potentially right," he writes in a letter to Sherwood Anderson in 1939, "in believing that it is the machine that has rifled man in this country of talk, sexual communication, the human companionable touch. As for myself, I'm a medievalist, a horse and buggy American, a barbarian, anything, that can bring me back to the communal song of labor, sky, star, field, love."

Still at other times, Dahlberg renounces the world and all its pomp by invoking the authority of his literary saints. Villon, Pascal, Poe, Baudelaire, Nietzsche, Dostoyevsky, and, when he is not angry at him, Herman Melville—the names change from time to time but the reason why Dahlberg bestows sanctity remains. Inclusion in the calendar seems to be predicated on three attributes: the man must have written well, suffered in his life, and died before this century began, which was when Dahlberg was born. Contemporary man with his newspaper prose, cars, offices, telephones, income tax returns, and political causes is measured against the lives and works of these saints and found wanting. This is not prophecy. This reflects a search—at times desperate, at times deeply moving—among great dead writers for metaphors with which to present and explain oneself to oneself and to the world; and it is hatred of human follies and virtues which are foreign to one's own nature.

# IV

I suggest that Dahlberg's achievement rests primarily in this: he is the Job of American Letters. His lamentation calls not on the god who speaks out of the whirlwind; nor does it call on this American century with its poverty of reverence for the elemental deities. His lamentation is a quarrel with the body—its Sophoclean birth—"never to have been born is best"—its bestialities, maladies, winds, its affronts to the spirit, and most of all, its sexual torpors, its sexual absurdities, its incessant, droning sexual demands.

A certain immemorial quality (which only Melville, among the Americans, has also achieved) pervades this quarrel. It is as if Dahlberg's dialogue with his body could occur in any culture and in any century, as far back perhaps as the origin of man's harsh, sore dialogue with his flesh: "I was naked," Adam said, "and I hid." Sometimes when I am reading Dahlberg I indulge in the reverie that the author, his face half-concealed behind a medieval hood, has stalked the narrow streets "twisted like a sheep's gut" of the Ile de la Cité in the Paris of Abelard, bitter at the spectacle of the dance of flesh and death surrounding him, knowing, too, that he is an actor in it; or I see him standing in the Agora, his sympathies with the sayings and bizarre antics of the Cynics, "the dogs of philosophy," murmuring with approval the famous passage at the beginning of *The Republic* where Plato has old Cephalus say: "How well I remember the aged poet Sophocles, when in answer to the question, How does love suit with age, Sophocles—are you still the man you were? Peace, he replied, most gladly have I escaped the thing of which you speak: I feel as if I had escaped from an insane and furious master."

What strikes the unmistakably indigenous American note about Dahlberg's dialogue with the body is that he never celebrates or documents the ecstasies or even the animal delights of the flesh. In *The Sorrows of Priapus* and *Because I Was Flesh* the body is put on trial, prosecuted with a sustained rage and occasionally with droll, acidic wit, as in this passage in which Dahlberg gives clear statement to his central theme—man's old bafflement over the daemon of his own sexuality.

> The penis, despite the fact that it is attached to each person, has its own disposition; it goes where it will, and though the spurious owner wants to think, it wants to urinate, and if its helpless landlord desires to read or to sow grass it wants to lie in bed . . . A man may want to study Mark, or Paracelsus, or go on an errand to do a kindness to an aged woman, but this tyrant wants to discharge itself either because the etesian gales are acerb or a wench has just stooped over to gather her laundry. The whole matter, when one thinks of it reasonably, is bizarre. The head is so obtuse as to go absolutely crazy over a pair of hunkers, which is no more than a chine of beef.

To say that Dahlberg's central theme consists in a prosecution and an exorcism of the body is only to suggest that despite his classical and biblical allusions and the gorgeous, Elizabethan vocabulary, he works at the core of one of the most persistent traditions in American writing—a tradition which he was among the first to define. I allude to the tradition of the morning after the Fall into sexual consciousness: the body, now the adversary, is viewed with suspicion, anger, contempt; violence against the female or against oneself often erupts; the cultivation of an exacerbated state of frustration usually begins. *Omne animale post coitu triste:* this melancholy dogma informs the American classics from the *Tales* of Edgar Allan Poe,

*The Scarlet Letter, Moby-Dick, An American Tragedy, Winesburg, Ohio, The Sun Also Rises* to contemporary novels like William Burroughs' *Naked Lunch* and Norman Mailer's *An American Dream.* How deeply rooted this tradition is may be seen by looking at the other side of the same mirror. There we witness that longing for a lost, bucolic summer world: the days of Huckleberry Finn upon the raft, Nick Adams hunting and fishing in Northern Michigan, the winter nostalgia of Holden Caulfield for the ducks of Central Park, the bumptious exuberance of Jack Kerouac and his buddies in *On the Road:* an Eden where the adolescent boy forever retains his purity and sexual innocence. Few American writers worth their salt have not contributed to this tradition, and in this tradition Dahlberg is one of the masters. In Edward Dahlberg we have a classic on our own back porch. One reads him at one's peril. At its best his prose asks nothing less than Cardinal Newman's motto: *cor ad cor loquitor,* "heart speaketh to heart."

PAUL CARROLL

# I Omne Animale Post Coitu Triste

## But to the Girdle Do the Gods Inherit

from *The Sorrows of Priapus*

# Prologue

*"Man is eager after knowledge, and the love of legend is but the prelude to it."*

STRABO

*"He laught also at those who spent their studies in the contrivance of curious entertainments; affecting unknown sauces, and variety of dishes, and putting themselves to so much charge and trouble for the love of a short transitory pleasure. For he made it a clear case, that all their paines were laid out upon the bredth of four fingers, which, said he, is the measure of the longest throat . . ."*

LUCIAN

Sing Venus Hetaera; Priam had fifty wives, and Darius went to battle with three hundred and fifty concubines; sing Venus the Courtesan who has sunk the Theban towers. Aspasia sacked all Hellas, and Gnathaena pillaged the pockets of the poet Diphilus.

List the courtesans as Homer catalogues the ships at windy Ilium: Chrysis, Corone, Ischas, and Antycra, who quelled many Argives, and relieved Pericles, Aristotle, Aristippus and Sophocles; let them be recollected, and savored once more, and thrice again as an ox's chine.

There were Telesis, Dippthese, and her whoring mother, and Theolyte who grew rotten hands and hunkers at her trade; the dearest thighs of virgins came from Ithya and Hellade. At Abydos, one of the four great towns of fishy Hellespont, there was a temple of Venus the Prostitute. When Solon saw it was impossible to bridle the youths of Athens he imported tarts from Corinth and Megara, and employed some of the revenue which the women earned to erect a statue to Venus the Strumpet. Aspasia and her college for whores are as necessary to Athens as abstemious Socrates.

Pious Greeks bring cakes and sesamum and the orchites of stags and wolves to chaste Artemis the Huntress who rules Ephesus where every year they hold a Whore's Festival called Aphrodisia. Lacedaemon has given us Cottina whose name is a rumor of pleasure throughout the Levant, and she is immortal, for a brothel bore her dear name. Give homage to Phyrne, for in her heyday, when she gathered capers, she was worth the thirty keels Nestor commanded at Troy.

At the rising of the Dog Star the swordfish go mad for the female; boars propagate their species with joy; vipers take a long time when they are intertwined. Consider the snows of the Alps; Eudoxus and Euclid winter all lechery; the intellect is a hot plague, loud with boasts. The cephali have large heads; cuttlefish have as much ink as Euripides; skin is slime and sand. Men at first, says Empedokles, were eels, graylings, polypi, seathrushes.

Avoid cucumbers, gourds, violets, watercress, and the soft blows and amatory kicks from the Marathonian women. Boiled torpedo done in oil and wine is indigestible and inflammatory; one bed and one wife is philosophy; age withers all wives; the sea-cuckoo has a dry rump which lames the tribe of fish; 'tis best. Copulation is a dangerous pastime.

Darius promised any man who invented a new pleasure a large reward. Cotys, King of Thrace, prepared a marriage feast for Artemis, and waited for hours for her to come to his bed. The sole testament and bequest of the physician Nicostratus was a huge quantity of hellebore which he left to his whore. The great Stagirite named his ethics after his son Nicomachus who was the issue of a harlot. Ptolemy Philadelphus lay with Didyma, Billisticha, Agathoclea, and Stratonica, for whom he built many monuments along the seashore. Clito, Alexander's cupbearer, wore only the lightest tunic, and held in her right hand a cornucopia, which is a sign of seminal wealth. Many splendid houses in the ancient world bore the names Myrtium, Mnesis, Pothina, although Mnesis was a flute player and Myrtium a notorious doxy. Agathoclea was Ptolemy Philopator's prostitute; she ruled him who was supposed to govern Egypt, and ruined both. Hieronymus, the tyrant, fell in love with a common bitch he met in a house of ill-fame, and he made her queen of Syracuse. The king of Pergamus was the offspring of a flute player. Ptolemy, one of the Hundred Companions, was the issue of a whore by Alexander's father Philip.

Greek worship was a theology of bawds. The statues of Demeter, the hymns to Persephatta, and the paintings of Daphne were a scholium on venery. Alcman invented the first songs of lust, and Nicander, the poet, called the goddess of amours Aphrodite Kalligluttus, the strumpet with the marvelous rump. Praxiteles thought the bitch of love resembled the figure of his mistress, Cratine, and all the painters, who paid visits to Phryne to copy those parts which send men to Tartarus or to the almshouse, were patrons of the *muliebria*.

The nereids, nymphs, hamadryads, naiads came out of the sporting houses of Elysium. Aphrodite, the lover of virilia, sprang from the scum of the sea; others say from the gore from the genitals of Uranus. The masculine gods were whore-mongers; Hephaestus, the humpback brazier, as licentious as a fuller, tailor, weaver, potter, was miserable until he married Aphrodite who forsook him for Mars. There was Zeus the Ant, so named because he assumed the shape of that insect in order to have intercourse with Eurymedusa. Jove could never empty his testicles; he lay with Europa, and threw the orchites of a ram upon the breasts of Demeter because he had raped her. Every watery image aroused Poseidon, who deflowered Amphitrite, Anymone, Alope, Alcyone, Hippothoe, Chione, who are sea foam, breakers, tidal waves. The titans were insatiable; Hercules gathered fifty maidenheads in one night. He had at least fifty offspring and was not regarded as exceptional in copulation.

The rituals of these gods and goddesses are mystical sexual bouts. Semiramis, another title for Astarte or Ashtoreth, slew every man after she had enjoyed him. The Athenian women celebrated the rape of Persephone, which they called the mysteries of Thesmophoria; the frenzied women at this ceremony carried the sacred chest of Bacchus which contained his prepuce. They baked sesame cakes, pyramidal cookies, and brought lumps of salt which were emblems of Priapus. In the orgies of Cybele the drums were beat, there was the sounding of cymbals, and the fig branches that were held aloft resembled the phalloi.

The comb, marjoram, and lamp of Themis represented her secret parts.

Beauty is the tomb of the race of men who crave ruin. There was no wanton running after women when Numa and King Tullus Hostilius ruled, for justice and the character of woman were held in higher regard than her navel or licentious toes, though the Sabine maids were most appealing. "Beauty is... a short-lived tyranny," remarked Socrates. Theophrastus called it a silent deceit. Each person has a deity in him which is ravaged by a frump.

Socrates said that nobody ought to be in the company of beautiful persons. Gorgias, the Leontine, lived eighty years, and said that the reason he had all his faculties was that he never did anything solely for pleasure. Before the average man reaches fifty his intellect is a senile carcass. Men of talent lose their minds earlier, for they compose their iambics for money to bring to Venus. Archytas of Tarentum said that no more deadly plague than the pleasure of the body was inflicted on men by nature. Lycon, the peripatetic, came to Athens for an education, and he learned first of all what each streetwalker costs.

The mind is as easily thrown down as the senses. The Greeks said Eros was the son of Isis and Zephyrus, which proves that erotical love bends under the softest wind. Aristophanes informs us that Eros goes as far back as Chaos; Plato in the *Symposium* asserts that Eros has no father or mother.

Pleasure is intractable, and it is told that Semiramis, called the wild pigeon, was the first one to castrate women, because people are mad for what is new or dangerous. Men spend their lives swallowing anchovies, polypi, onions and plebeian carrots, which either make them diuretic, or give them the potencies of pigeons, who are said to require the longest time in their hymeneals.

Man used to wipe his hands on the crumbs of bread and he was safe. Adam passed water and thought nothing of it. He defecated in a clump of leaves and had no lawless sensations. Now voiding is ecstatic and every one perishes for the stroke of a hand or a foot. One should wive an unsociable she-dragon, or a sloven who won't sit, or stand up, or lean, or lie down, for everything raises up a host of profligate longings.

A man may have the testicles of a newt, or wear the rugose coat of a she-frog to be repulsive, or persecute his gullet and abdomen to kill all desires until he weighs no more than one obol, but he is likely to be inflamed, attract a dowd, or have enough concupiscent skin to want a tittle more.

No matter how we long for virtue who wants to be a spado? Even the bull, just after he has been castrated, mounts the heifer once more showing that habit masters nature for at least one copulation. Nor should we give credit to the cold; Alexander never touched the daughters of Darius, because he had little inclination for women. Olympias, his mother, gave him the Thessalian courtesan, Callixene, hoping to cure him of his indifference toward woman, as she thought him to be quite impotent. After the sack of Troy each monarch returns home with a concubine, except Menelaus, who had wasted his genital powers in Asiatic orgies and so required none.

Why does this sadden the abstemious? Does it really matter whether a man can raise his pudendum or not? We are gluttons, greedy, inconstant, and wild asses, for no other cause than this ludicrous exercise. A legendary swan lives three hundred years, and a goose to be eighty, and though some only live long enough to be a goose, the longevity of the former would not diminish lust. What would the multitude do with a longer life except ask for a longer gullet or penis? All the feasts for Persephone, Daphne, Cybele, and the frantic, mystic shouting of *Hevoi*, which is the pagan Eve, or fornication, is nothing else but begging useless idols to give us the ability to rear up this ugly tyrant at the sight of any chit, girdle, or cestus. Since all is lost what harm can there be in a quick perusal of the whore's register of renowned Hellene?

There were Neaera and Phila who wore out her teeth in service, and Nais who had none; and Anticyra who only drank with crazy men. Glycera was the universal friend, and Nanium cheated her customers, for she was astonishing in her garments, but without them showed a listless navel and a brace of turnip legs. Phryne, who razed every husband to the ground, and put to the fire and sword his household, bore herself in public like a sibyl, only disrobing for the whole of Greece on the feast of Posidinia. Had she not observed all the holy days of Venus, that jealous goddess would have slain her, because there was no flesh under the moon to glut men like Phryne's. It is told that Lais of Corinth, who had kindled the fury of that deity, was beaten to death by a footstool in the fane of Aphrodite.

Olympia assuaged the rotten fever of Bion, the Philosopher; Theoris served Sophocles in his old age; Homer gives Phoenix as a mistress to the aged Nestor; Archippa, the heiress of his plays, lay with Sophocles when he was skull and wrinkles. Once when her former lover was asked where Archippa was, he replied, "Why, like the owls, she is sitting on the tombs."

Nicarete satisfied the bed of Stephanus the orator, and Metanira coupled with Lysias the Sophist, and both these courtesans were enemies of all mankind, one solacing an orator and the other a sophist. Philyra, Scione, Hippaphesia, Theocles, Ismathe, Lagisca, and Anthea forsook their occupations, after which time husbands became greater adulterers, going to other men's wives instead of harlots, and stealing out of windows in bags of chaff. This larded deceit, falsehood and cant, for nothing good ever comes of the virtue of a whore. Herodotus praises Naucratis for its beautiful wenches; it is said that Stilpon the philosopher had as his pupil Nicarete of Megara, but she should have confined her metaphysic to his sheets and pillows. Billisticha came from the house of Atreus, and her favors were dear. Leme could be had for two drachmas, and her name means the matter that gathers in the corners of the eyes, a poor name to be purchased for money.

But here is the wind in the paunch of Falstaff, and some filberts for Caliban. Consider the operations of the testicles; will you be Solon or tread a thousand whores and live to die senile? What is copulation that man should be tickled into dotage? Are we born solely because the red mullet and the sea perch have wombs? Shall we eat honey and locusts, or be Agrippina?

# I

Man must be classed among the brutes, for he is still a
very awkward and salacious biped. What shape he
will assume in the future is vague. There are many traits
of early man he has lost, and it is plain that he is much more
given to falsehood, robbery and lawsuits than the primitive.
The first two-legged man scratched himself because he had
an itch. Men now lie and steal for pleasure. Primeval natures
wallowed without thought, but soon as men began thinking how pleasant it was to rub themselves and to have de-
liriums from mud, they employed their minds to achieve
what paleolithic mankind did without being lascivious.

Men lie, not alone for profit, but to root in Circe's
mire. No pigmy or cave-dweller wears more bizarre or
dirty raiment than present-day man. He is often as of-

fensive as the gland on the back of the Brazil peccary. He would rather tell a lie than the truth because his sole purpose is to be a grub.

He is the most ridiculous beast on the earth, and the reason for this is his mind and his pudendum. He sacks nations, or throws away his reason to see the petticoat of Aspasia or Helen empurpled by murex or the lichen at Madeira. The procreative organ in the camel is behind, but in man it is in front, and unless he is too fat to look over his belly, he pays more attention to this gibbous organ than to his arms, his talus, or anything else. He frequently forgets how his arms look, and is surprised to find a wen on his jaw, and he rarely knows whether his pupils are brown or ochreous, but he is always mindful of his testes hanging between his legs like folly.

In the *Book of Enoch* the scribe says that the first two-legged creatures had the private parts of great studs, and it may well be that Methuselah and Jared and Mahalalel were mountains and that from their middle hung hills which were their organs of generation. Otherwise, it is impossible for one to imagine how they could live for nine hundred years without wearing out their genitals. It is known that Og, King of Bashan, had an iron bedstead seven cubits long, and that the giants of Anak had six fingers.

Adam bare stones long before he begat Seth. Human life began as procreative mud, and later man was a shark with a human face. There was a human species with a lion's mouth and the legs of a giraffe, for anterior to the neolithic period diverse animals mingled. Many of our traits are found in the countenance of the bear and in the lip of the pard. The story that the pigmies were chased from the River Strymon by cranes is also a fable of our bird origin.

The old gods were ocean, rivers, animals, fish, birds; Noah was a fish, and Plato supposed that Oceanus was the father of Saturn, and there is as much natural history in this as mythology. Men and rivers are demigods and beasts;

the Scamander is the river's mortal name; Zeus called the fierce water Xanthus; in the *Iliad* it is reported that the bird, said to be named *chalcis* by the gods, was Cymindis among men. This is the heroic conception of human fate.

Pleasure brings about the most violent transport in men, and of all the animals in the earth none is so brutish as man when he seeks the delirium of coition. Democritus of Abdera, unable to bear being stung by any female foot in sandals, or round skirt, was said to have plucked out his eyes. He was as mad as a boar for the shape of Venus; when the testicles of the boar are swollen he is at times so beside himself that he rubs them against a tree until he is castrated. The female deer hates copulation because the penis of the stag is as tough and spinous as a palm leaf; the pain the stag gives her is considerable but she cannot overcome her passion for him.

One marvels what man will do to have his skin scraped. Antony lay with Cleopatra at Daphne for this foolishness, and though he gave all his force to her, his delights were not as long as those of the ordinary fly. One cannot submit a little to sexual excitement without hankering after more such raptures. When birds are continent their testes are internal, but after sexual intercourse the penis is very conspicuous.

Whether man is more lecherous than the partridge is doubtful, but he is not as chaste as the raven, who bleeds from the eyes during coition. The man of sensibility is not satisfied with ordinary coupling; all the arts of Lais of Corinth cannot furnish his skin and veins with the infinite sensations he demands. Pain affords him infatuate happiness unknown to four-legged creatures. He is almost the only animal that cohabits at all times. With the exception of the pigeon, a bird which abstains only a few days in the year, man has the most lickerish tail of all beasts. This has made him very unruly, and double in his words and deeds. Unlike the elephant he has no seasons for his venery. This pachyderm, after impregnating the female, avoids this excitement for two years.

The elephant is an exemplary teacher. It is in many respects a rational animal, and repents of its anger, which is rare among men; when it kills its master, it grieves and sometimes starves to death. The dam suckles her young six years, and many elephants live as long as people. When an elephant is sick he is given wine to drink, and when he has an eye disease, these warm, friendly orbs are bathed in cow's milk. His wounds are healed by butter. These are the simples that the Homeric heroes gave to each other at Troy, and the poet of the *Iliad*, as well as Plato, would have paid the tenderest regard to this superior beast whose diet, medicines and habits are far better than those of the vast multitudes in the earth. The elephant, doubtless, was no less a monitor than the heifer which is so often seen beside the seated Buddha.

Countless adulteries are committed without lust, and with no thought to the peril which attends this folly. Animals do not give each other the pox; when men attempt to lie with a beast it rejects the malady that is said to be the companion of human genius. The adulterer is more senseless than the earthworm who keeps part of his tail in the hole he inhabits when copulating so he can disappear at once should he see an adversary. The tibulae hide in the hedges all day, and seek the delights of the female at dusk.

Most people are furtive, but very few are ashamed; the elephant prefers to copulate near an obscure river bank, and the camel retires to the desert to rut. Modesty has been undermined because it is not generally known that the camel, more continent in his thoughts than a modern vestal, requires a whole day to complete such exercises.

Few labor for anything else but to exchange their sexual properties with blowsy dowds, or to rival the fox which has a bony penis: even the impotent are like the aged boar who waits for the tired female to lie down before he will risk his feeble appendage.

When the camel opens its mouth it looks like the greatest ass, though the ancients made the strongest bow-strings out of its pudendum. The egg of the *sepia* pretends to be black myrtle seeds; the vine the polypus deposits is its ovum.

The rhyades remain quiet until the equinox, and the grasshopper is said to sit upon the olive and reeds when it casts its skin, but man now stays in one place only long enough to void or feed. His irregular habits and haste make him the inferior of the polypi which unite only in winter, and these creatures conceal themselves for this reason for two months.

The tortoise gives a month to coition. The moose cannot have commerce with a red deer that is too short, but men and women of sundry sizes are suitable to each other. Andromache had too long a body, but not for Hector. Nubian dwarfs were ravishing morsels in Egypt. The pigmies who rode on the backs of partridges, which was a way of saying they were concupiscent, satisfied the giantesses of the Thermodon.

The puma never utters a cry when he mingles with the female. Bucks and does herd separately after the rutting season; man is incontinent whenever he has the occasion.

Men are more obscure to themselves than the elm or marine shells. The *solens* perish after they have been taken away from their borning place; the fir is comely in the sun, and the cedar is a Saul in the mountains. Man does not know when he should plant, or from whom he can glean, or what town is his stony Medusa. The *sepia* deposit their ova near the river Thermodon, for its waters are warm and potable; the eels seek reedy ponds, and the pregnant red mullet lies among the rockweed. Paul the Fourth was an ascetic until his eightieth year, but when he became pope, he sported for hours at table as any mare in heat.

Men are too unstable to be just; they are crabbed because they have not passed water at the usual time, or testy because they have not been stroked or praised. The habits of animals can be ascertained better than the mien of a philosopher. When stags are bitten by the *phalangius* they eat crabs and are healed, but if a man has had a poor or dour sleep, he is waspish the whole day, and is likely to curse his parents.

There are certain fish that only breed in the Pontus, and many of the tunnies run to the Pillars to spawn. The *halcyon* appears only at the setting of the Pleiades and during the solstice. The crocodile is a modest brute whose penis and testicles are internal, and he could be regarded the peer of saints did he keep these members there. The polypus hides its ova in holes which is a lesson for modern women who, when they are with child, go through the streets showing the results of their shame. When the mare wants to sport with the stallion she makes water. But this lubricous mammal is continent compared with man, and he eats herbs, barley and oats which is a diet similar to the sacred table of Pythagoras. One has to travel to India to find a savant as herbivorous and savory as this extraordinary brute.

We scoff at Alexander for burying his horse Bucephalus, but the stone of that stallion shows that he had the separate toes of a human being, and this monument stands in front of the temple of Venus Genetrix. Bucephalus was so named because of the breadth of its head. Plato means wide forehead, and it is interesting to add that the philosopher came of the family of Hippias who were horsemen. The horse is so marvelous to behold that Semiramis was seized with the wildest passions when looking upon this carnal beast.

The horse goes mad pasturing by himself; separated from the human flock man loses his reason. Nietzsche, the wildest intellect of his century, lived in solitude, a Dionysiac disease which in crazy horses was known as the hippomania. In his last Bacchic throes he flung his insane arms about a horse standing in the gutters of Turin.

No one but a perverse person takes exception to horse manure. Droppings of many animals are more healthful than those of people. Human dung, except that of primitive races, is unclean. When the stag's horns are most perfect he has a very offensive odor; unlike man, who wears the same skin all his life, the stag casts his horns, the bird moults, and the despised python sloughs off his vile coat; man's despair is that he smells; he is garbed in the same skin until he rots in the tomb.

The Aztecs sold pots of human excrement for working their leather. Civilized nations regarded primitive man as a savory beast. The ancients, having the highest esteem for the offal of kine, said the oxen of the Sun were stalled near the Ocean where the seascum resembled dung.

Man imagines that because he stands on his legs he is intellectual, but the penguin is a biped who feeds until he can scarcely move; the bear too can stand up. Man's passion for disorder, upheaval and bedlam explains his greed. He attempts to prove that whatever man does is for his advantage. This is not true of him, and sometimes quadrupeds, generally reasonable, are demented or perverse. It is fabled that the mongoose breaks the eggs which the crocodile hatches in the mud though it does not eat them nor derive profit from this act. Man's neck is as long as Plutus: Solomon said, his eyes cannot be filled with seeing nor his ears with hearing. He is so bored that he seeks the naive existence of the sow. Having devoured all the experiences possible to the biped, he now wants to be primitive which he thinks is the same as being chaotic, torpid, or supine the whole day. Baudelaire asserted that he had the wildest desire to be aboriginal, because standing on two legs was too trivial and average for him. Man imagines that could he crawl again as an infant or as any brute in the field, he could recapture a primeval existence. Others are only content with the testicles of animals. Could man moult his skin as the bird its feathers, and have new flesh, he would be innocent. The stag casts his horns every year, and the horse may lose his hoof, but each acquires what he has shed. When the teeth or the hair of men decay, they do not grow the tusks they show whenever they desire sexual frenzies, or the hair that makes them prance and sport and neigh. Were it possible for man to shed his feet or his hands he could have a naive heart.

Man pines to live but cannot endure the days of his life. The learned, crouched over their inkspots, covet the customs of the savage who cohabits with a Lais or Aspasia of the Amazons whenever he pleases, or envy the panther. The poet want to be an animal. "Submit, my heart, sleep the sleep of the brute," said Charles Baudelaire.

Men have more sorrow from their entrails than animals; except backward people or ancient races they have fewer rites pertaining to their ordure. They excrete when they are bored or want a savage pleasure. The father of Beatrice Cenci drew the close-stool over to the fireplace and voided in the presence of his wife and daughter.

The Mohammedan of the old order wipes his buttocks with his left hand since he uses the right one to handle food, plant vines, or to greet people. A Moslem woman can divorce a man with a reeking breath, a fault unkown among the natives of Otaheite. Modern man rushes to the water closet, and after the most summary ablutions, extends his hand to the first person he meets. The ancient Essenes had strict tenets regarding defecation and its burial in secret places. Man at present dungs in his own house and considers himself a delicate creature.

The anthropoid is arrogant, and when he finds a remedy for a malady that is the consequence of a cormorant throat he is elated. Tantalus can never eat or drink enough countries, rivers, or carcasses, and this gluttony is the cause of nearly all human woes.

When the sow has a certain disease, it goes to the mulberry for relief, and when the horse falls into a declining melancholy, the sound of the flute will assuage this fever for which men have found no nostrum. The river horse, after overeating, comes ashore and presses its hide against the sharp rushes until blood flows from a vein in the leg. When ill the stork sups upon marjoram; and stags also, in failing health, graze upon wild artichoke. The pigeon has exquisite revulsions, and at times disrelishes his table as much as men, and then turns to bay leaves for food.

Despite all the spital houses in the world, if a man suffers from strangury, can he do much more than the Sudanese who entreat their idols to let them urinate without difficulty? If it please Zeus may we pass water; to prevent chafing, if Cato be true, put a small branch of Pontic wormwood under the anus.

Socrates described love as the sting of a tarantula. We see that desire dominates the old as well as youth; the senile forget to button their clothes, and leave the door of their trousers ajar, showing what is no more than a relic of a quondam tower. Men lose their goatish powers long before their minds; Montaigne complained that when he was somewhere in his fifties he could not raise that sleepy animal more than three times a week.

The anthropoid is more luckless and unintelligent than animals, and the remedy for his ills is not progress, going forward, which is always to his grave, but turning backwards. He has extirpated most of the beasts which he no longer has as tutors. As a result he does not know whether to cohabit with woman, with man, or with sheep, and there are some who are enormously aroused by the sight of a mare. There is a breed of dog that will copulate with a wolf, and it is believed that a species of dog is derived from the tiger, and there is the Babylonian cameleopard; but, for the most part, the stallion seeks the female of its kind, and the elephant hankers after the same sort of animal that bore him.

Man is more incoherent than any beast in the earth.

Schopenhauer has said that pleasure is the absence of pain, but it is not true. Man is not content with negative delights or even with positive transports. Some of his immoral deeds lacerate him, and he finds much satisfaction in being wounded. Man hates what he does, and that is what is moral in him, but he continues to do it, which is why he is Euripides, a spider, or the *Dryophis fulgida*. Man lies in ambush for all creatures, for he is the hunter; the Psalmist cries out that he is the turtledove about to be devoured by the multitude.

The whelp is most greedy for the soul that has fallen down to the ground. In the *Psalms* the soul flees to a hiding place in the mountains. The prophet rides upon a Cherub who is one of the fowls of the air. Man who is the master of the sheep and the oxen has the tender feet of the hind. He crouches before the bulls of Bashan and dreads man continually. But a little while he is a tree planted by the rivers of water, for all lurk in lairs to harm his branches.

Man is either too stupid or vain to know himself, and too self-loving to understand anyone. He cannot endure his own vices in others, and he is least just when he is railing at the faults of people.

Man is the tragic brute because he can never be as sure of others as the ass or the bull who knows that he is the booty of the wolf. A strong foe is better than a weak friend; the heron is always on guard against the eagle; the *anthus* is a reliable opponent of the horse since both covet the pasture. The deer when it has produced the fawn hides, for she knows what beast will hurt it. The wolf is the enemy of the ass, bull and fox; a mountain cat will embowel a porcupine; in a narrow defile the panther will leap upon a small dog instead of a human being. Men have no such certainties, and the more erudite they are the fewer companions they have. Aristotle in his old age said, "O my friends, there is no friend."

Everything in man is double because he has testes. The old Nile god had the form of a man with a woman's breast wearing a cluster of water plants. The Egyptians extracted from the meanest worm the paint to design jars and the sacred, funeral amphorae. In the time of the Pharaohs dense thickets were said to be the resort of malefactors. This was a proverb, and yet among the Quiché Mayans the gods were seated in the ravines, the forests and among the mosses. Not everyone that goes into the wilderness is Elijah or John.

If one considers the acts of his youth he wonders why he was ever young; or if he ponders his later vices he asks himself why he is still alive. In what manner is Messalina superior to the puma, or is anyone any better than a beetle which takes such pleasure in the fungus, called the English phallus, which has a most odious smell. The testicles of the American lizard give off a musky odor, and the monkeys in Brazil when stroked have as pleasant a scent as Alexander of Macedon. Priam had fifty bedchambers, and despite such opulent amorous experiences had no more sense than to select as his consort the termagant Hecuba. Solomon's bed linen was fragrant with Sheba and the perspiration of a hundred concubines, but were they any dearer to the nostrils than the musky testes of the lizard? There is a paradox: the Egyptians claimed that their land was infested with scorpions until it was settled by Apis. The serpent in Eden gave Eve knowledge of the phallus, and this is the source of art, science, poetry, wisdom, and perfidy.

We weep because the human race is no better than it is. The aquatic frog has the tail of a fish until he makes a twig or a blade of grass his house, then he loses his tail and grows legs. Nature advises the frog far better than man; a noddle endeavors to employ faculties he does not possess, and the eunuch burns for Jezebel.

Where is Apollo who rested his foot on the skull of an ox; where are the wild horses, the fawn, the roe, the cubs of bears that were brought to the altars of Artemis? Shall we wed, or woo, or tremble?

# II

It is obvious that we must imitate the habits of many quadrupeds if we are to be gentler.

The animal is still crudely limned, and this is also true of viviparous man. Though he is the one mammal that thinks, the embalmers at Abydos passed his brain through the nostrils. He is much more inconstant than animals. The eyes of the goat and the stag are of one color, and only in men are those two unstable pools of various hues.

He is altogether a double nature, having two lips, two eyes, a pair of feet, and a right and left hand. Man is a congenital hypocrite because he asserts that his purpose is simple. Should he aspire to be apodal, at least, he would have no feet to hasten him to evil.

The pouch between his legs is divided into two, but it can never be asserted that one testicle is the adversary of the other, but the two have one sole purpose. No one then dare be a disciple of a hedonist for the simple reason that it is hard enough to accomplish any idea or good work so long as people have two limbs, two crooked lips and double eyes which devour whatever the mind considers a benefit to others and a deeper nourishment of one's own nature. It is better to try to be continent and to fail than to be an epicure. Antisthenes, the pupil of Socrates, said that when he had any sexual needs he took whatever there was at hand, a trull, a slut, a vendor of vegetables in the Agora, and that she was exceedingly grateful.

Man is double, and who may know his heart: he is a moral hermaphrodite. When Zeus was asleep he dropped his seed on the earth from which grew a demon with the genital organs of a man and a woman. The gods cut off the male organs of generation of this androgynous fury, which produced an almond tree. After the daughter of the river Sangarious ate the fruit of the almond she conceived and bore a son who was suckled by a he-goat. Concupiscence and force are the source of all our actions, Pascal wrote. We eat the almonds and conceive, and all our sons are reared by goats.

Most people are satisfied in shoals, their noon is night and shame, and their dreams are the garbage of their days; man fetches his dreams with the same fetid food he baits the purpurae. All his members are arrogant; the hands, the feet are terrible tyrants.

Man is born wanton, wild, and asinine; he succumbs either to good fortune or to evil tidings, being the toady of both, because he does not know what to do with his head or fingers, or what his mind or hands can do well. The loon uses his sharp head to pierce the water, and his broad, palmated feet as oars. The New Testament is the gospel of the hands, and few can comprehend the homely adage about the tares and the wheat because they have not the manual intellects of the lowliest publican or carpenter in

Bethlehem. The muleteer desires to be Virgil, and the goat licks the olive of Minerva which was said to render it sterile.

The human hand, though it is divided like the foot of the panther, can write, and tenderly touch a child or a mother. The hand, still a residual talon, and when meanly made more predatory than the claw of an eagle, is a marvel to behold. Ezekiel's four Cherubim have an ox in one cheek and an eagle in the other, and though they are feathered, they have human hands. Unloving hands are avaricious horns; unable to caress they are too puerile and deformed for morals or sensual delights.

The Coaita is a large Amazonian monkey; unlike human beings he confines his sojourn, dwelling in the valleys and uplands of the Amazons. His prehensile tail is as close to a human hand as the New World has produced among the higher forms of mammals. Hands in America are strong and cunning, but loveless.

It is abominable to have the same hands and feet throughout one's life, because there is so much vice and shame in the old hands. What cupidity there is in each finger, and in what unclean places have they been, and how often they skulk or hide in pockets because they are parsimonious or debauched. Men with women's hands are often preferred, but long, narrow fingers and nails are more suitable for malign ends than for affection.

Sometimes, the hands of men are the parables of the body. No lion, pard, pelican, or heron has the head of Euripides, or Paracelsus, and one may surmise what a god was the occiput of Amos who was a gatherer of the Sycamore Fruits. The loins of the Angels are of burnished brass or of fire, and men when they are not hirsute are not entirely base. The ears of Aphrodite are small, rotund, and toothsome, but the lobes of the male are a wallet into which he stuffs his greed, gossip, and carnal stupidity. Ears, often no better than the sow's, have a sluttish aspect; they root on the sides of the head, and like the pig can be fed mire and almost any filth.

The ears are worse than the navel because they cannot be hid. There are two kinds of ears, one which is a scale of justice in which all human pains are weighed, and there is the voluptuous ear which is a flute or a lyre, and which is always trembling; every man can play upon it, and receive some tune for his effort. One with fluted ears has eyes for wonders and marvels, and he is able to watch a poor man swallow stones and regard it more as a prodigy than a cause for pity.

The foot is far less wise and good than the hands or ears, and the toes are not so savory in aspect as the horse's hoof. Often human arms and feet are no better than the feet and fins of the cephalopod, and the mouth of the un-intelligent is the tubular siphon of a squid. It is said that man alone has a face, though if one goes abroad this statement is likely to be denied.

The dolichocephalic head is wonderful to behold, and one can have some certainties regarding the cranium of a great faculty. It is easier, however, to recognize the head of a pompion or a gross churl than to discern a wise head. Homer informs us that the head of Thersites is peaked at the top; Thersites employs scurrile words, and is always reviling Odysseus, or Agamemnon, or Achilles for no other reason than that they are superior to him in understanding.

There is no greater ruse than the human physiognomy; the eyes, the nose, and the hands are subtle snares, and the most practiced observer is not sure whether the genius of the person is in the general expression of the entire char-acter, or whether it is to be viewed in the behavior of the neck, or the shape of the nose. He who relies on the testimony of his eyes is very likely to be duped. The char-acter of a person is as much of a riddle as the substance of the soul or the Intelligence of the Universe. In the Cherubim of Ezekiel the ox in one cheek is the ruminative side of the face, and the eagle in the other signifies power. Frequently one sees only the predatory eagle, for men employ their force for booty rather than as angels.

There are countenances which at first blush look like wisdom, but upon closer acquaintance turn out to be vacant. This is particularly true of the large proboscis on the face. Most men of considerable intellectual strength have a conspicuous nose resembling a potato, a squill, a testiculate cucumber, for the nose is the second phallus in the male. Besides that, it is the messenger to the testes, for virile olfactories not only take much delight in the *Analects* of Socrates or in the *Dialogues* of Plato, but they also revel in good weather, inhale the seas and fruits, and are very quick to capture the fragrant skin of Nicarete of Megara or the adulterous uterus of Clytemnestra.

Agamemnon had a heavy rather than a strong nose, and he was a coarse rustic soldier with women, for warriors are not acute in amorous matters, and for this reason was of little worth to Clytemnestra.

The small nose is regarded as more comely in a man, and though it is handsome in a face at table, it generally goes with a short, miserable penis in bed. Lascivious women run after men who have a nose the length of the small finger, but are grievously disappointed when they cohabit with them.

Although the elephant uses its nostrils as a hand, it cannot be said that an animal has a nose, which is the sign of a higher creature. The nose is not entirely intellectual, and though it is better formed than the testes, it is a residual privy organ, and in the prehistoric age men very likely used their noses for erotical labors. Today the nose is more inclined to scent the female than the *Nicomachean Ethics*. As Aristotle remarks, it is good to take pleasure in the smell of apples, but it is intemperate to dote on unguents and incense.

Next comes the mouth which when open is as gawkish as the blowhole of a fish. So long as man has a tongue he cannot be likened to the feathered tribe or with the majority of mammals. What ascetic can compare with the grasshopper which has no mouth and lives on dew?

24

Man is the animal that talks, but the Cosmos is an Act, not a word. Thoth is the alphabet god, and he is the first month of the old Nile year when the funeral papyrus was placed in the hollow wooden figures of Osiris, between the legs of the deceased. Since words have fallen into disrepute we will either return to glyphs or to the simple neighing of the river horse.

The tongue is even less covered than the scrotum, and can hardly ever be called a secret part since few men have enough character to keep it in their mouths. It is difficult to know whether the tongue or the phallus is more harmful to men. The panther and the lion remain in their lair far longer than the tongue will stay in the mouth. This member is the foe to the whole of mankind. Hermes has empowered it with speech, and its utterances are sometimes oracles. Still, there is no galled tail so hurtful as this organ. It is a thorn, a stone, and also a witling, for when it is not a thong, it is a fool, and man spends the greater portion of his life reprehending himself because he could not be silent. If he has nothing to say, he speaks it, and sometimes this adder stings and poisons a friend, without cause and, particularly, to express ingratitude to one who has been kind or bestowed upon him a benefit. Even when it is hid in either jowl, it is said in the *Book of Esdras,* "The stroke of the tongue breaketh the bones."

There is no other part of the body that is so busy; the secret parts in the middle are often lame, but the tongue is rarely dormant, or lying content in its cave except when it has made a huge boast, or has encountered another asp that can wound more, is quicker in guile, or in unjustly assorting words together. Silent people are more prudent than the garrulous, and, though their tongues think rather than speak, they are untrustworthy. As man is not very intelligent it takes him a long while to recognize either his foe or his patron, and he often praises the man who is preparing his ruin, and has an insolent face for one who would give him prodigal affections.

Litigations, courts, legal documents and countless laws have been spawned by the tongue. The tongue of the fish is thorny, but not free, and the sacred Nile crocodile has no tongue, though it devours men, but it is still a more enlightened creature than human beings, because men eat men, and have tongues. The bird is said to be able to put its tongue out as far as the width of four fingers, and that is a very dispiriting fact. The reason that the tongue is hidden in the mouth is that it can hardly be proud of its vile labors.

Far worse than the human nose, often well-made, and the tongue, are the testes, the most ugly and ill-shaped member. The phallus is a slovenly bag created without intellect or ontological purpose or design, and as long as the human being has this hanging worm appended to his middle, which is no good for anything except passing urine and getting a few, miserable irritations, for which he forsakes his mother, his father, and his friends, he will never comprehend the Cosmos. The *balagrus* are without ova or semen, but the Cherubim on the walls of the temple of Solomon were painted copulating.

The tail has grown weaker in apes and men. This is the fifth hand of both; it does as little climbing for some of the Cebides as it does for Pale Face. The scarlet-faced monkey inhabits the forest, and though it is never known to descend its short tail is no sign of terrestrial habits. Man, the fifth-handed climber, is weak; he is not among the branches, or on the ground, and where are the apples and olives of all flesh?

The phallus has always been considered an unkempt beast. Though matrons and virgins brought fillets and hyacinths to this rude, homely god, it was never his face, but rather his abilities that were worshipped. Ptolemy Philadelphus had a priapic image made that was one hundred and twenty-five cubits in length, and the effigy of this lewd brute was carried in the festivals either to Isis or to Osiris. Nearly every ancient idol was priapic. This was the god that protected the garden and seed-time, and who was associated with the melon, the leeks, the mandrake, and the apples of Haran which were aphrodisiacs. The onion was supposed to inflate the courage of the weak and the nervous. Hercules, the patron of the stoic, because he purged the Augean stables, and extirpated the robber Cacus, was at first commended because of his astonishing prowess in bed. This is not too likely. Giants are clumsy with Venus. One can hardly conceive of six-fingered Anaks as having amative wisdom. In neither the *Odyssey*, nor in the fragment of Euripides does Cyclops have any progeny. No women are seen in the monster's cave or island.

Man-eaters, giants, or the well-favored males have less skill with Aphrodite than gnomes or ugly men. Ovid asserts that cripples perform best. The Pythagoreans called lettuce the eunuch of the vegetables, and Adonis hid beneath a head of lettuce. Narcissus is an enervated lover; he is too vain to care for anybody, and so self-loving that he is not likely to have an erection, for nature will not allow anybody to get that excited about himself. He goes to a woman to have two admirers and not for other indecencies. Narcissus, or his Semitic forebear, Ham, has no shame, and the wisest and best men in the world are those who are ashamed. The conscience of Saint Augustine and Tolstoi came from their shameful parts.

Meanwhile, since man is not going to be different for a thousand millenniums he should select certain animals to teach him to be just, eat and gender at regular intervals, and blush. A learned nature never ceases to be revolted by his privy parts which remind him of his nose and his tongue, that second illicit organ of the human being.

When people have been lawless for a half a century, they cannot master themselves at all. Plato may say that the pentagram is a symbol of the good, but all Euclidean shapes and abstractions and Pythagorean diet are no more than the avoidance of the troublous testes. Besides this, what is known as the creative organ is droll and as foolish as the visage of a mule, or a thumb, or a navel, could they smile.

The prepuce is a fatuous appendage, and the entire tribe of pudenda and scroti have the heads of pigmies and the wrinkles of stupidity, decrepitude and mirth. This race, for the penis, despite the fact that it is attached to each person, has its own disposition; it goes where it will, and though the spurious owner wants to think, it wants to urinate, and if its helpless landlord desires to read or to sow grass, it wants to lie in bed; since it is only given to us as a loan or is leased to each one, man has little control over it. A man may want to study Mark, or Paracelsus, or go on an errand to do a kindness to an aged woman, but this tyrant wants to discharge itself either because the etesian gales are acerb or a wench has just stooped over to gather her laundry. The whole matter, when one thinks of it reasonably, is bizarre. The head is so obtuse as to go absolutely crazy over a pair of hunkers, which is no more than a chine of beef. Of course, the whole of human appetite is ridiculous, and although we are delighted to hear that after Ajax has returned from a furious battle with Hector, and has been lucky not to have been killed, Agamemnon gives him a leg of an ox as a reward. Naturally, Ajax is a very stupid man, but who is any better?

There is nothing more outlandish than the necessities of the scrotum and the anus. Lewd men are almost always eccentric; Charlemagne kept the prepuce of Jesus in a box at Chartres. Though good men often abhor their lascivious desires, the wether is also likely to be obscene; spados stood at the side of Phoenician Jezebel, who was a votary of Priapus; however, a eunuch came to the aid of the Prophet Jeremiah. Nothing can be foreseen because all men are unstable.

The saint cannot endure his skin; he is overthrown by his sense of smell, and pleasure lows in his ears all day. He is the prisoner of the least sound or touch; during the season of coition the male fish is in such a state of excitement that if the female strikes his abdomen with her mouth he has an orgasm. The voice of the locust is produced by rubbing himself with his legs. What an odious thought for the seminal male. Origen yearned to be a fish or an apodal animal which has no testicles; but eunuchs burn and fish have young.

We are residual beasts, and though the Cosmos inspires the deepest awe and prayer in mortals, this satyr between the legs is the crudest in shape, and the Creator could not have given serious thought in its making. The Ocean is our father, and the Earth our mother, but the penis is an afterthought.

The will is the deity in man, but it sows its seed in stony places; Philo has remarked that where gold and silver grow naturally, grass and fruit do not. When the will dwindles, the spirit stinks. By soft rivers and willows men lament and love, and small waters produce legends; capes, streams, and promontories take their names from Venus, Adonis, and Sarpedon, for whom Zeus wept; but Aspasia and Helen putrefy. After summer has left her cheeks can Paris or Menelaus understand why Ilium was burnt? The Ethiopic soldiers revolted against their king because he scorned their valor. Quitting family and homeland because fate nourishes the heroic faculties more than the household hearth, they rang their spears against their shields, and lifting their garments above their genitals, said that so long as they possessed such weapons they could secure a new country and other wives.

# XV

Primeval potherbs send their roots down far; the manna ash run deep into the earth. The Indian is a forest people; the deity of the Tupí tribes is called Caypor, a sylvan god who dwells in the woodlands where he hunts pacas and deer. The baboon of the Old World lives on the ground, but the apes of America are arboreal. The Stone Indian sits in the branches and chants to Keetche Manitou before the bison hunt.

This is wild land, undomestic; the natives have a legend of a shaggy tree-Esau, called Curupira, unmentioned in Genesis. The Para estuary is a wild water hymn. How long does it take savage ground to produce the damsels of Jerusalem, or Dido? Praise be Linnaeus for calling a butterfly Hetaera Esmeralda; man is the thrall of an amorous name.

Sow soft fruits in crabbed weather for etesian winds

roughen the furrow of the olive. Broom flowers in dry places. Fir, hemlock and the yew are mountain wood, dour is their fruit; these are no treason's summer friends. Gall-oak, sea-bark, hilly ash and poplar were the names of deities and hewn tree-men. Forest is the hope of the disciples; more learned than the fig is wildest ground.

The *Cedrela odorata* of Brazil is the cedar of Lebanon; of jasper, onyx, and garnet are the hues of the Papilio, which Linnaeus has called the Trojan. There is the Morpho Mene-laus whose wings are the garments of Asia. The cigana who pecks the arborescent Arum near lagoons is no bird of Proverbs. We know the parbales of the wheat and the tares, but the genipapa, the goyava, the mandioca remain unsung.

The holm oak, pond apple, and sumac are Indian. Pale Face is a waif amoung the Sierras and the mesa, a trespasser upon the savannahs. Bog-moss swaddled the Indian infant; the Mechasipi is savage Virgin Mary; the Great Lakes are the five tribes of the Iroquois. The red men of America were not amorists; they had no vehement passion for women. Man is sun, water, earth, air, or depraved; head, arms, feet are ground, sea water, woods, or emptied of them, loveless. Unrelated to the desert, the rivers, the forests, man is feeble and a random fornicator.

Amidst a plethora of oak, maple, streams, hummocks, Pale Face is famished for a tree, a little hill, a foal, a clump of sod; utterly sterile, he begs for the Nature he has warped and killed. He cannot be a thinker, a moral animal, until he returns, as a lover, bringing the peace calumet and the grains of tobacco, as a votive offering, to the cliffs and the wilderness which he threw away.

Every country contains the minerals of Paradise or is the barren ground for rough annals. Art without austere weather emasculates the American. The roots of bed-straw washed in a kettle, with the juice of the moose-berry, and pistils of the larch, provide dyes for the Stone Indians. The

*31*

bark of the aspen and birch is the food of the beaver; these are Laconian arts and meals.

The bison, red deer and antelope crop the meadows near the sources of the Missouri and Assineboine rivers, which are the pastures for congealed American philosophy. Snow and ice are the grazing grounds of North American metaphysics. Want is the god of the North, desolation is his child; the otter, beaver, and the musquash were the Buddhas of Thoreau. The hardships of explorers were vast moral experiences; Franklin and Parry opened northern straits, Canaan was fathoming the limestone strata of the Saskatchewan fringed with purple dogwood and dwarf birch, and populated by the pelican and the brown fishing eagle. The marmot carried the seeds of the American vetch in its pouch; the head of the geographer contains the Nelson River, Swampy Lake and New Waters.

Lichen and moss sang in your heart; the forest was your brother, poverty the chaste girdle of your bride. Be hardy, and ashamed; modest birds cover themselves with chaff after pleasure; the goose bathes, and others shake their feathers.

Ariel lies to the south; when the pampas is a cocoa orchard and the vintage of Israel—Brazil, Peru, Uruguay, Chile, will be the timbrels, the sackbut, and the harper of the Americas. Quito, Lima, and Cuzco are handlooms; the Mexican valley shall be the home of Apis; emerald and turquoise are the stones of Rahab.

Why does the gillyflower, resembling the spindle which has the scent of Abel's blood, allure us? Give me marl, or rotten leaves which delight the oxen; so that I can be frugal; or hellebore, or danewort, fenugreek to quell all riot, and everything impregnates men. Anaxagoras says that the air contains all seeds, and each time men take a breath they are fornicators; for rain, sleet and flesh are the planters.

Man is water and parched land; fire and rock are his hopes; desire is the Trade Wind; the fruit of the Tucuma palm is the Arcadia of the macaws, and the ruse of mortals. Pumice stone in the Amazons carry the seed of plants, and spawn of fresh-water fish as they come down from the remote volcanoes, Cotopaxi and Llanganete of the Andes; four hundred miles from the Atlantic the throb of Poseidon is felt in the Tapajos river. For many weeks' journey one cannot find a pebble in the regions watered by the Solimoens. The lower Amazon is hilly; on the shores of the Teefe are groves of wild guave and myrtles.

Where are the little hills which shall bring justice, or the fruits of Lebanon? O forest spectre, ferns, lichens, boleti contain Eden. Be primordial or decay.

# Heart Speaketh to Heart

## from *Because I Was Flesh*

I

> "What moved you to 't?"
> "Why, flesh and blood, my lord;
> What should move men unto a
> woman else?"
>
> *Tourneur*

Kansas City is a vast inland city, and its marvelous river, the Missouri, heats the senses; the maple, alder, elm and cherry trees with which the town abounds are songs of desire, and only the almonds of ancient Palestine can awaken the hungry pores more deeply. It is a wild, concupiscent city, and few there are troubled about death until they age or are sick. Only those who know the ocean ponder death as they behold it, whereas those bound closely to the ground are more sensual.

Kansas City was my Tarsus; the Kaw and the Missouri Rivers were the washpots of joyous Dianas from St. Joseph and Joplin. It was a young, seminal town and the seed of its men was strong. Homer sang of many sacred towns in Hellas which were no better than Kansas City, as hilly as Eteonus and as stony as Aulis. The city wore a coat of rocks and grass. The bosom of this town nursed men, mules and horses as famous as the asses of Arcadia and the steeds of Diomedes. The cicadas sang in the valleys beneath Cliff Drive. Who could grow weary of the livery stables off McGee Street or the ewes of Laban in the stockyards?

Let the bard from Smyrna catalogue Harma, the ledges and caves of Ithaca, the milk-fed damsels of Achaia, pigeon-flocked Thisbe or the woods of Onchestus, I sing of Oak, Walnut, Chestnut, Maple and Elm Streets. Phthia was a bin of corn, Kansas City a buxom grange of wheat. Could the strumpets from the stews of Corinth, Ephesus or Tarsus fetch a groan or sigh more quickly than the dimpled thighs of lasses from St. Joseph or Topeka?

Kansas City was the city of my youth and the burial ground of my poor mother's hopes; her blood, like Abel's, cries out to me from every cobblestone, building, flat and street.

My mother and I were luckless souls. She strove fiercely for her angels and was wretched most of her days in the earth. Moreover, if she failed, who hasn't? If she prayed for what she thought was her good, and none heeded her, that had to be too. Each one carries his own sack of woe on his back, and though he supplicate heaven to ease him, who hears him except his own sepulchre? Night covers the acts of man; could he lay his follies on the ground and in the light of the sun as he committed them, he would shriek like the owls for his tomb. We know nothing and understand nothing, and this is no boast. The trees are tender and the voices of the many rivers are pleasant, yet our bones quake every day.

She never desired to be miserable, and neither did I, but it is just as important to be unfortunate as it is to be happy. She sighed as often for the wheat as she pined for the chaff, not knowing one from the other. "Many cry in trouble and are not heard, but to their salvation," declares St. Augustine.

My mother had two miserable afflictions, neither of which was she ever to overcome: her flesh—which is my own—and the world, that cursed both of us. "Let me, O Lord, be most ungrateful to the world," comes from the mouth of Teresa, the Jewess of Avila.

There was no angel in Beersheba to comfort my mother or to take pity on her unquenchable thirst for the living waters: "What aileth thee, Hagar?" Nobody heard her tears; the heart is a fountain of weeping water which makes no noise in the world. The Kabbalists claimed that when man cries out, his voice pervades the Kosmos; stones are sentient and tremble for us when we are heavy with trouble, and the ground is our brother and keeper though man is not.

A tintype taken of my mother in her early twenties showed a long oval face with burning brown eyes and hair of the same color. She did not have thick features, and her hands had the soul of the pentagram, which Plato considered the geometric figure of goodness. There was much feeling in the appearance of her mouth, although most of her teeth had been removed by a quack dentist of Rivington Street in New York. Perhaps no more than four feet ten inches in height, health was her beauty. Lucian affirms that "there are some who will be admired for their Beauty; whom you must call Adonis and Hyacinthus, though they have a nose a cubit long." My mother's long nose sorely vexed me. I don't believe I ever forgave her for that, and when her hair grew perilously thin, showing the vulgar henna dye, I thought I was the unluckiest son in the world. I doted on the short up-turned gentile nose and imagined myself the singular victim of nature in having a mother with a nose that was a social misfortune. Aside from her unchristian nose, what troubled me enormously was her untidiness. She slopped about the rooms in greasy aprons and dressed more like a rag raker or a chimney sweep. I was ashamed when we walked together in the streets, and when she showed a parcel of her winter drawers as she sat I suffered discomfiture.

This book is a burden of Tyre in my soul. It is a song of the skin; for I was born incontinent. Everything has been created out of lust, and He who made us lusts no less than flesh, for God and Nature are young and seminal, and rage all day long. I shall sing as Tyre, according to the Prophet Isaiah, like a harlot, and for seventy years.

It is a great pain to divulge the life of a mother, and wicked to betray her faults. Why then do I do it? I have nothing better to do with my life than to write a book and perhaps nothing worse. Besides, it is a delusion to believe that one has a choice. If this book is a great defect, then let it be; for I have come to that time in my life when it is absolutely important to compose a good memoir although it is also a negligible thing if I should fail. Fame, when not purchased, is an epitaph which the rains and the birds peck until the letters on the headstone are illegible.

Would to God that my mother had not been a leaf scattered everywhere and as the wind listeth. Would to heaven that I could compose a different account of her flesh. Should I seem to mock that *mater dolorosa* of rags and grief, know that all my laughter lies in her grave. *Mea culpa* is the cry of all bones. I have always blamed myself for everything except when I was idle and had the time to find fault with others. Our errors, I pray, save us from being dullards; what other salvation have I since I am gross, vile, licentious, stupid, and withal am so peevish that when I lose a pin I suppose I am dropping my blood and sweat in Gethsemane.

Should I err against her dear relics or trouble her sleep, may no one imagine that she has not always been for me the three Marys of the New Testament. Moreover, whatever I imagine I know is taken from my mother's body, and this is the memoir of her body.

My mother was utterly separated from the whole race

of mankind save when she was concupiscent. This woman suffered immensely from solitude—and what eases the lonely so much as sexual pleasure? Unlike Hamlet, I cannot accuse the womb that begat me; however, I am his bondservant when he sobs, "Mother, mother, mother!" for this is Christian grief.

My mother's family came from outside Warsaw, and there were as many Catholics as Jews among my ancestors. I have high Slavic cheekbones, and I am sure my mother and I have Polish blood. How I came by the name of Dahlberg, which is Swedish, I do not know. Often Jews assumed the name of the district or province where they dwelt; they also sometimes took the appellation of a neighboring prince or burgher. The predatory Swedish hordes overran Europe and they came to Novgorod as traders as early as the eleventh century. My maternal grandfather's name was written Dalberg and my mother used this spelling, which was printed in black letters on the cash register of the Star Lady Barbershop in Kansas City, though later through error I added an "h." I always thought this name was apocryphal and from the time I was a child of eight I was sure that my mother had no parents. When I heard a boy speak of his brother or sister, I ran back to my mother and wept: "Mother, have I no uncle, aunt or cousin? Are you an orphan, mother?"

On rare occasions she mentioned a deceased one and whispered in German, "Selige Mutter," and I could not believe that she spoke the truth. When she said that her father had been educated and rich I was certain that she only wanted to comfort both of us.

I had lost even my name, and was as much a pauper in this as those exiled Jews who were not entitled to engage in the occupations of their forefathers because the Prophet could not find their names in Ezra's register.

The Jew is a confusion of tongues and peoples, and though once his language was referred to as the "lip of

Canaan," the Jews were separated from their alphabet, which is a tragedy to a nation as well as to a family of two. My mother's family spoke and wrote Polish and German; she used both languages and muttered Hebrew in the synagogue on high holy days: but I doubt that she understood her prayers.

My grandfather was a timber merchant who traveled back and forth between Warsaw and London to do business and to visit relations who had lived and flourished in London. He also wished to avoid his wife, who was an unleavened mass of Jewish orthodox shibboleths. Many years later I saw an oil painting of my grandfather; he resembled Robert Browning. There was a tintype of my grandmother, whose solid dour jaw dominated her physiognomy. My great-grandmother was a matriarch who locked the pantry and never relinquished the key lest any of the nine surviving grandchildren should filch the black bread. Ordinary aliments were imprisoned and hoarded as much as love. My mother, Lizzie, and her fair-haired sister, abhorring such parsimonious fury, fled to Warsaw and found refuge in a Catholic nunnery. Their father brought them back from the convent, but both refused to remain any longer under such a loveless roof.

There had been fourteen children. Alexander, the eldest brother, killed a Pole over a woman and, after my grandfather secured his freedom by bribing the local authorities, he married a Polish farmer's daughter and reared Catholic sons and daughters in that land. The sister who fled with my mother took a Polish officer for a husband, and two of their sons were Polish aviators in the first World War.

Solomon, who had a tender consumptive face, came to America with my mother when she was fifteen. Herman, another brother, who had mattress factories and sundry properties, and was at one time the wealthiest man in Toledo, Ohio, was supposed to provide for her. He had an evil miserly skull and placed Solomon in one of his sweat shops but did nothing for my mother, who found employment in a button factory in the New York ghetto. Still another brother, vastly inferior in pecuniary importance to Herman, was a chemist in Toledo. He read many books—which makes a man lickerish—and was never able to keep his hands from the hunkers of any chambermaid that happened to be near him. He died of a cancerous prostate at the age of seventy-seven, the reward of countless bawdy thoughts and acts. One of his daughters was given in wedlock to a professor at the University of Moscow, where she went to live.

My uncle Herman, anxious to be rid of his sister, but still moved by some niggish filial feeling, came to New York to see whether he could peddle her flesh. He found a stocky fur operator who was eager to wed her. This man's only virtue was that he had no conspicuous vices. My mother would have preferred to make buttons than to lie in such an arid marriage bed; though she was only sixteen she knew that he could provide her with food but not with fuel. Nevertheless, she obeyed her brother and married the man. Jacob, according to Philo Judaeus, means the performer, which my mother knew before she married him could not be the name of the fur operator.

There were three sons by him, three feeble seminal accidents. In the Kabbala it is said that when a woman has conceived, the Angel of Night, Lailah, carries the sperm before God. But does God see all human semen?

She disliked his nose and thought he grubbed up his soup with it because he kept it so close to his plate. Her days were larded with tedium, and her body was like the salamander, which cannot live unless it burns.

My mother always carried her head high to raise her hopes and to show that she had no reason to be ashamed of her life. After the death of one of her infants, she took to passing a barbershop on Rivington Street, which was on her way to the carts loaded with vegetables, goose feathers for pillows, cotton chemises and corsets. One day she noticed a man leaning against the red and white striped barber pole. He had the soft, crooked locks of Absalom and vain white teeth which he showed her; he wore a dude's vest the color of deep brown eider and patent-leather shoes. He carried a gold watch and chain in his showy vest pocket. She had never seen a sport before; he had a quick, teasing manner, clever and nimble rather than jolly. Wholly deprived by a lubber in bed, she could not resist Saul the barber. He was not that Saul who was king in Israel, or the other of Tarsus, but she had not been born to gratify a monarch or tempt a saint.

She abandoned her two sons and fled to Boston. There she bore a child in Charity Hospital. She had been lying in a cheap rooming house where her bastard would have been born had not her groans attracted the attention of a neighbor. She gave me her father's name to hide the fact that I was as illegitimate as the pismire, the moth or a prince.

When I was six months old she sailed steerage for London. An uncle of hers had died there who was far richer than Herman. She expected—without any reason at all—that there would be a handsome legacy for her. True, securities, much cash and blocks of properties had been left—but to one of the Protestant churches. Penniless and with an infant in her arms, she found work as a scrubwoman and then as a parlormaid, and when she had enough money to secure passage on a ship she returned to the United States.

Then Saul and she went to Dallas, Texas, where they opened a small barbershop in a clapboard shack. There were two barber chairs in front, and in the back of the shop was a pallet and one chair. The customers had to stand and wait for their turn.

Saul taught her how to trim hair, hone a razor and strop it, how to stand with her feet together as she waited for a cowpuncher or a rancher, and how to speak: "Good morning, sir; you're next. Will you have a close shave, a light trim, or a feather-edged haircut? Don't you think a good massage would ease the strain of the day?" The customers were big, fleshy men—joshers, triflers and mashers who ran livery stables or shipped horses and mules to Omaha, Kansas City or Chicago. She knew how to keep her place and give a customer a chin-scrape without using too much alum to staunch a wound from a razor or the hair clippers. She had stout, thewy fingers and could give a drowsy cattleman a vigorous scalp treatment and deftly dust his red corrugated neck with talcum powder. It was a pleasure to have a lady barber wait on the Dallas trade, and a man would rather have her cut his throat than sit in Saul's chair. Some stood waiting for an hour on hot horsefly afternoons, chewing tobacco and spitting in the cuspidor to pass the time. No matter how full the shop, Saul's chair was nearly always empty. After working hours he told her that she was a nobody, without even a diploma from a barber college.

Lizzie liked being with the public and listening to the easy drawl about the swapping of a mare or shipments of stallions, geldings and cows to Topeka, Sedalia or St. Joseph. Still hankering for some other kind of life, she thought she would go from town to town as an itinerant hairdresser, give beauty treatments, clip toenails and do a little manicuring. Sometimes a horsedealer would drop by the shop and offer to take her out for a buggy ride. But she had no time for man foolishness; she wanted to make money and establish herself in some city where the men were good spenders and she could bring up her son.

She kept the cash taken in for the day in a cigar box; Saul would take the money and spend it on sporting women in the Dallas red-light district. When he came back he would sit in the barber chair, wax his mustache, brush his curly hair and show her his white foxy teeth. He had all the arrogant airs of a Spanish conquistador who kept his privities in a calabash of gold. After she had saved more money, he stole it and left town with a chippy from Galveston. When he returned she reproached him for spending the money and in a rage he attempted to slap the infant. She placed her strong, short arms around the child, and Saul broke her small finger, which was crooked after that.

She ran away to Memphis, taking the boy with her. She went from house to house selling hair switches, giving body massages and paring the toenails of women. The boy was always at her side, dressed in a Buster Brown suit and collar and carrying a dummy book which a photographer had given him after he had taken his picture. This made a good impression upon customers.

She would go from house to house and when a door was opened Lizzie would deliver a speech that she had patched together from newspaper articles and advertisements: "Good morning, madam, and health to you. I'm a high-tone hairdresser and beauty specialist. What lovely hair you have, but you look down in the dumps; I hope no man has deceived or swindled you. I'm a hard-working widow myself and know sorrow and disappointment, and here is my only son. I restore hair, give enemas and remove soul-grieving calluses. May I step in and give you a demonstration? It's free of charge."

Memphis was a fast town. Soon she had regular clients in what appeared to be a high-class neighborhood. They lived in solid red brick houses, which gave her stamina. She pared their corns, bathed them, and rubbed lotions on their bodies, which relieved them of all their aches. She was very proud of her strength which flowed so easily from her to them. They wore stylish satins and taffeta gowns; they gave her corsets, stockings and gold hairpins and cockered the boy.

She learned that these ladies had a trade not too dissimilar from her own—they relieved the aches of men. But she was too nervous to look down on anybody. When she told them she had to leave town, they wept and each one took the child in her arms. She thought she would do something wrong by remaining and she was worried about her good name. Although she did not know anybody in Memphis except her customers, she was afraid people would talk about her.

Then Saul blew into town. They went to New Orleans and started another barber business there. If Saul were cutting hair or scraping a man's chin and he saw a fourteen-year-old girl pass by, he would drop his scissors and comb, or shut his razor, and hurry out of the shop after her. The sight of a skirt made his blood run mad. Whatever Lizzie earned with her ten hard-working fingers Saul spent chasing hussies. Though she had the tender, full paps of the Ephesian Diana, no woman or town could keep Saul. He vanished again.

Lizzie and the boy went to Louisville, as rich in bluegrass as Homer's Coronea and stocked with the mares of Pelops. After that they moved on to Denver, where she said the people were spitting and hawking from morning until night. The Rocky Mountain city of consumptives gave her a fear of rot and worms that lay upon her dreams and fogged all her days.

In 1905 they came to Kansas City; it was a wide-open town; there were more sporting houses and saloons than churches. The stews were as far out as Troost Avenue. When a bachelor or a stale codger was in sore need of easing himself, he looked about for a sign in the window which said: *Transient Rooms* or *Light Housekeeping*. A brakeman on the M-K-T knew where he could get a glass of beer for a nickel, which also entitled him to a free lunch of hard-boiled eggs with pretzels and Heinz ketchup. The streets were cobblestoned hills, and their names were April songs of feeling: Walnut, Locust, Cherry, Maple, Spruce and Oak.

The town was not a senseless Babel: the wholesale distillers were on Wyandotte, the commission houses stood on lower Walnut, hustlers for a dollar an hour were on 12th and pimps loitered in the penny arcades between 8th and 5th on Main Street. If one had a sudden inclination for religion he could locate a preacher in a tented tabernacle of Shem beneath the 8th Street viaduct, and if he grew weary of the sermons, there was a man a few yards away who sold Arkansas diamonds, solid gold cuff links, dice, and did card tricks. Everybody said that vice was good for business, except the Christian Scientists and the dry Sunday phantoms who lived on the other side of the Kaw River in Kansas City, Kansas.

The great Missouri River on which Kansas City, Missouri, lay, once known as the *Concepción* in honor of the Virgin Mary, was as dissolute as the inhabitants. There was a lusty steamboat trade on the Missouri, and freighters plied between St. Louis, Kansas City and New Orleans. Country boys from Topeka and Armourdale came to Kansas City to get work in the stockyards and in the Armour and Swift packing houses; and chicks, with rosy, jocular rumps, arrived in hordes from St. Joseph and Joplin.

One could take a nickel streetcar ride to Swope or Fairmount Parks; on an Indian summer evening, when the crickets sang in the tall, speared grass or in the oak branches, workmen in trade-union denims and overalls sat on the porches to take the air and say hello to a switchman or an acquaintance who had a job in the West Bottoms.

When business was dead and the Dog Star had parched the melons, dried up the heifers and the white leghorns, and prices were high, many blamed William Howard Taft. In the Teddy Roosevelt days butter had been eighteen cents a pound, milk was five cents a quart and eggs were ten cents a dozen.

When Lizzie came to Kansas City there was one lady barbershop on Walnut which was three doors from the ticket office of the Burlington Railroad. The proprietor of the place was a round-shouldered, cranky man barber who had an interest in the barber college located on Delaware Street. After six weeks of training at the barber college a green farm girl would be hired as an apprentice; she received no wages for the first three months and had to depend upon tips from customers. Usually no more than seventeen years of age, she attracted a great deal of trade. A stockman or a smart drummer from out of town would rather get a manicure from a lady barber than go to the Orpheum for an evening of big-time vaudeville. The odor of witch hazel, hair tonic and face powder, and the motions of the girls, who wore tight corsets, inflamed an old rounder. When a railroader got into the chair of a country trollop, he felt that he would perish from pleasure when she removed the lather from his jaw with her small finger.

These farm girls were as wild as Semiramis; but if they found out that they had a clumsy simpleton on their hands or an indefatigable curmudgeon who had already used up a wife with a hanging udder and five children, they would make him cough up a few hundred dollars. They did not care very much about an ordinary masher or a codger but they would support a curly-haired Adonis who knew how to chew Spearmint gum and smoke Turkish Hassan cigarettes with the air of one who had had enough amours to have set Ilium on fire.

No lecher was so intolerable as a skinflint. A lady barber took the greatest delight in being courted although she had no thought of a wedding. She liked to go to a good show, say to the Gillis Theatre for a wild West performance; if she craved refinement she preferred *Beverly of Graustark* or a swell burlesque at the Grand Opera House. Supper at an oyster house and a night at Electric Park were exciting; when a city alderman or the owner of a big livery stable took a girl out to Cliff Drive for a buggy ride, she talked about it for a whole week.

It was the time when women went to law for heart balm, and when breach-of-promise suits were exceedingly popular. A lady in sound health, who had locked all her hopes of marriage in her breast, had no hesitation in divulging them in court if she felt a man had been so low and rotten as to deceive her. There was hardly a judge sitting on the bench who was so callous as not to have considerable feeling for the delicacy of her heart. If a bachelor was foolhardy enough to be seen with a woman in public, or worse, to take an embittered spinster of thirty to Swope Park, and after that denied he was engaged to her, he was undone. He was sure to be seethed in the marriage-pot, and should he prove too tough for boiling except in some illicit hotel room, he was compelled to pay for the honor of the woman he had never desecrated. A good many such triflers, or just dead beats who had gotten into woman trouble of this sort, vanished or crossed the state line and found employment in Kansas City, Kansas, so that their wages could not be garnisheed. Fast women, and ladies with the subtlest principles, preferred to speculate in men rather than risk their savings in wildcat oil or second mortgages.

There were six barber chairs in the shop on Walnut Street; a cuspidor, shaped like an Etruscan amphora, stood within reach of a man in a barber chair who wanted to spit the brown juice of his chewing tobacco into it. A shave was five cents and a haircut a dime; a good tipper gave a girl an extra ten cents for a close shave.

Lizzie was given the last chair because she had a long, Jewish nose; turned-up gentile noses were very much in style, and a dapper man who wore suspenders and was as neat as a pin and had a fine position in a meat-packing house or at the Union Depot would go mad over a barber girl with a snub nose. Quite a few embezzlers would skip town with a warm, Grecian-nosed trull from Joplin. The prettiest chits were put up front to draw in transients who happened to pass by and who had never heard of a lady barber.

The shop opened at seven in the morning to catch railroaders on their way to the yards or big loafy-faced men who auctioned off horses and mules in livery stables near the stockyards. The girls rushed to their chairs when a locomotive engineer dropped in; anybody who worked for the Santa Fe or the Burlington was rumored to be a good spender.

The barbershop was an emporium for talk, easy, warm joshing, and expectorating in the brass spittoons. Lizzie knew how to keep a customer in his place, and on occasion cut a man with her razor or dug her scissors into his ear because he had his hand on her thigh instead of underneath the haircloth.

Often the shop did not close till nine o'clock at night. She took the boy to a Catholic parochial school to learn German because she wanted him to be cultured. The school did not let out till late and that kept him off the streets.

She had to work on a commission basis, and her wages, including tips, were seven to eight dollars a week. Cutting hair and shaving cowhands, grouches and town loafers for fourteen hours was no picnic, she told her boy. Most of the time she had to stand on her feet. The man barber would not allow the help to sit, even when the place was empty on dull, rainy days. A woman seated in her chair with crossed legs or lounging on the mahogany settee looked bad and attracted the wrong kind of trade. He was particularly strict in July and August, which he claimed were the two worst months for temptation; a man was teased more in summer than in any other season. He warned the barber girls not to spit, wriggle in their bustles as they stood by their chairs and called out: "You're next, sir," or make squeaking, sensual noises with their patent-leather shoes when they stepped over to the basin to soak a towel in hot water. Smoking was positively forbidden; sporting women were easily recognized because they smoked Sweet Caporals. He cautioned the girls not to chew gum and make loud, clucking sounds with their tongues, and he would not keep a lady barber who went to the water closet too often;

he said that flushing the toilet during business hours raised disorderly feelings in the customers.

He expected a barber girl to keep occupied all the time. When no one was in her chair, she had to cut the *Kansas City Star* into small square sheets on which the lather was wiped. She had to sharpen her razor on a hone and then ply it to and fro on the leather strop. There were the shaving mugs and the hairbrushes to be washed out in boiling water and the combs to be disinfected in Lysol.

Some proprietors of the genteel barbershops on Baltimore Street were thinking of raising prices because the cheaper chin-scrapers were giving the trade a bad name. People said that barber tools were dirty and carried such contagious diseases as dandruff, scarlet fever, barber's itch, boils, pimples and water on the knee. Horse swappers and common teamsters who sat on empty fruit crates in the big livery stables and swore and guffawed all afternoon claimed that one could get the pox or the clap from an unsanitary hair clipper, eyebrow tweezer or hairbrush. This kind of loose chatter could start a panic, and the owner of the place on Walnut was so uneasy that he changed the name of it to The Sanitary Barbershop.

The girls were flighty and easily discouraged, and if a lady barber thought she could not please the trade she took off her apron and quit. A lady barber was in the dumps all day if a customer had been short-tempered with her. She liked to coo into the ear of the man in her chair: "Sir, do you part your hair in the middle, or on the side? What a lady-killer's pompadour you have! How about some tonic? Or let me rub pomade into your scalp and give you a stiff hair brushing." But if he gave her a short answer: "Just leave it dry, lady, I'm in a hurry," she wept or took the afternoon off.

Lizzie rented a furnished bedchamber in a rock-ribbed house on McGee near Admiral Boulevard. McGee was a poor humble street, lined with elms, maples and oaks—what bread and meat there is in the sight of a living, green tree. There were many yards and vacant lots covered with tangled grass and rough, acrid sunflowers, and the latticed porches and sun-fed wooden steps were a comfort to people.

On her feet all day, except for a few minutes to take a quick bite or when the owner ran out for a bowl of chili, she would sink into the oak rocker as soon as she returned to the lodginghouse. She unlaced her high-top shoes, worked herself out of the corset, and removed her beige cotton stockings.

The child slept, graved in the large double bed. When she was so worn out she wondered how she would make ends meet, and then she looked about to find something to do so that she could banish such weak thoughts. She hunted for her pince-nez glasses, which she had laid on the floor, picked up a curling iron or tried to mend the yellowing corset cover.

At least she had gotten rid of Saul, and after she had muttered a curse in German, "*Verdammter Saul,*" she repeated "*Selige Vater*" several times. She never used bad language or swore and she feared that if she cursed somebody she might raise some unexpected grief and wrath from out of the past. She wrung her hands when she remembered how she had sweated her shame in Saul's foul bed.

In the shop and with the public she seldom lost control of herself. At times she had been made to feel that she was a lady-barber Magdalene, and though she had many misgivings about her trade, she liked working hard. Hands engaged in good, honest work are seldom mediocre. Was there not something else in her life besides eating, sleeping and the foolish mandrake apples? Her hopes, which she could not bridle and which were as forceful as her blood, redeemed her. Always believing that she would accomplish something, she was almost invariably duped—and he who is deceived often is never ordinary. She was everybody's gull.

There were days when Lizzie assuaged the weariness of

men by easing their dry, sour nerves and massaging their faces; this was as important to her as it was to that Mary who poured the ointment on the head of Christ. It was only when she doubted that she would have that frugal reward from her efforts that her courage flagged. She prayed every day, but still there were the alms that she required for herself and the child. Saint Teresa has said: "For those who pray, God himself defrays the charges." But how many afflicted ones have wept by the waters of Babylon and to what avail? And what profit had they of their tears save the joy of shedding them? Who hears sorrow, disease and indigence?

She offered her petition to the Lord; she rose from the rocking chair, regarding the washbowl and the crockery pitcher that were as empty as the pots at Cana. She was as impotent as the water hen that stands by the marsh and considers its blighted feathers. She cried out, "O Lord God, I quake before everybody, I am such a nervous woman. I'm not greedy, and I beg Thee only for bread and hope; You know my purse is stuffed with sorrow and when I open it all my poverty falls out of it. It is easier for Thee, O God, to shake the wilderness of Beersheba than for a widow to show her need."

She was afraid of the unmercied space around her, and even her bed was a pit. We go to a room to hide grief and shame as though they could be mewed up in walls, and the sleep we take therein to cover our lives bursts into dreams which paint our sins. Hard, deep sleep would have comforted her did she not dream. Dreams came before there was earth, grass, fish or any other living creature. Sometimes she awakened and found that she had wet the bedclothes, and she sobbed because she had a weak bladder, and all that she recollected of her sleep was water.

One sticky July afternoon, when a pair of flies dozed on the wattled throat of a farmer slouched in one of the barber chairs, the boy, returning from school, asked the owner of the shop for a glass of water, and was chased into the street. This was the child of her belly and sorrows, and there was nothing between her and the winds that always soughed the same refrain through her head: "I am alone in the world. Give Thy servant bread and water, and, yea, for my only infant Ishmael, lest we perish."

She saw her child fall on the pavement, but waited for the proprietor to step out for a Bromo Seltzer. She had laid aside a little money to open up a barbershop of her own and she talked to the girls about her plans. Though they called her a Sheeney when they had a poor day and she a good one, they hated the man barber. All the girls packed their tools and quit.

There was a wholesale barber-supply house on lower Delaware. She needed credit but she was afraid to approach the owners. She knew they were two brothers of German origin. Very nervous, she prepared a cultured speech. When she entered this barber's temple, she gazed at the long show-case filled with scissors made of the best Sheffield steel, hair clippers and combs of bone; on the shelves were jars of face creams and bottles with the necks of geese filled with refined hair tonics. One of the Haeckel brothers was standing in front of her. She closed her eyes and commenced her recital: "I imagine I have the honor of speaking to Mr. Haeckel. I'm Lizzie Dalberg, a hard-working widow with a child to support. My family spoke an educated German, God bless them. There's a dandy location on 7th opposite the high-tone Grand Opera House; I'm going into the barber business for myself. You can have a hundred dollars spot cash if you will let me have three up-to-date barber chairs, razors, hair clippers, hones, scissors, brass cuspidors . . . well, everything."

She removed her pince-nez glasses and wiped her eyes with the one lace handkerchief she owned, and continued: "I don't need charity, just a little time. Believe me, I'm reliable, and besides, I wouldn't harm you for the world."

Then she adjusted her shirtwaist to call his attention to the solid-gold watch that was pinned to it, so that he could plainly see that she was no pauper. She wore no powder or rouge, which only chippies painted on their lips.

He asked her to take a seat and brought her a small glass of brandy, which she refused. She believed that only sporting women drank between meals. Making a well-disciplined laugh, she thanked him and said, "No better tonic, Mr. Haeckel, mein Herr, for good health than a hard day's work."

Haeckel took the hundred dollars and asked her whether it would be too hard for her to pay twenty-five a month. He called her Miss Dalberg as a mark of esteem for a respectable widow with a child, for he regarded a woman, married or not, as a maid, if he thought her morals were sound.

She walked up and down in front of The Sanitary Barbershop, handing out cards which read: Lizzie Dalberg, New High Tone Barbershop, 7th and Walnut Streets, COURTESY IS OUR MOTTO.

Business was good for Lizzie and she associated this with the strength of her body. She took a cold bath morning and night, in winter or summer, and after rubbing her stout thighs and solid buttocks with a rough turkish towel she was confident that she would overcome any obstacle. She kept her bowels open and every morning, before she had gotten into a kimono, she held a small gilded mirror in her hand and put out her tongue to see whether it was pink or not. She then raised both arms and bent her face to smell her armpits before dusting them with talcum powder. How often the girls sweated and just threw powder on their flesh. It was ignorant to smell bad when water and soap were cheap and one could take an enema for nothing.

After a year on 7th Street she thought she could afford to move to a better location. A brand-new building had just been put up at the corner of 8th and Walnut. But when she heard that the rent was sixty-five dollars a month and that a five-year lease was required, she was afraid to take the risk. Suppose she failed, what would become of her and the child who was so sallow and sickly?

Nevertheless, Lizzie took the shop on the hilly part of 8th Street; it was underneath the viaduct over which the streetcar ran to the Union Depot in the West Bottoms. On the door she put a sign: OPEN FOR BUSINESS, and on the plate-glass window in heavy, enameled white letters was: STAR LADY BARBERSHOP: 16 East 8 Street. She had bought a round barber pole with peppermint stripes on it which stood in front outside. A fine metal cash register sat on a pine table, and when she regarded her name, Lizzie Dalberg, printed on it, she had no doubt that she would catch the rush viaduct trade. There were five Haeckel Brothers' barber chairs and two mahogany settees for the customers who sat and read the *Kansas City Star* while waiting for their turn. Up front Lizzie had a glass showcase in which she kept five- and ten-cent cigars and a box of Wrigley's chewing gum. On a rubber mat that covered a part of the showcase was a leather cup containing five Indian dice. She was particularly proud of the two electric fans that hung from the ceiling, and when she observed the brass cuspidors, she knew she had a high-class place.

There was a rumor going around town that the Union Depot, a remarkable red-brick building, a fine example of the old-time tradition of honesty, would soon be torn down and that a fifty-million-dollar railroad temple was to be built a little beyond the outskirts of the business district at 15th and Main. Gossips in the saloons and dry-goods stores were saying that Walnut was a tumble-down street and would look abandoned were it not for the Grand Opera House, the commission houses and Jenkins' Cigar Store, where a Stutz or a Buick was raffled every Saturday night.

When Lizzie heard this kind of loose talk she quaked; she had already signed a five-year lease and thought that her landlord, Mr. Wolforth, had taken advantage of her. Whenever she believed she had been misled by someone she ran into the small room at the rear of the shop, took off her glasses and rubbed her eyes on the soiled haircloth. She was easily duped for she had strong, heady blood. Had she had a more dry and shrewd nature, she would have had fewer disappointments—but less hope. Those who pray God for good luck should also beseech Him to deceive them!

If the boy pestered her for pennies, after she was perspiry from shaving too many bristly chins and cutting hair all day, she would become so nervous that she would weep: "Son, you know I've only got ten miserable fingers and that I can make just so much out of them. Do you think I find money in the streets? If I don't work, who'll help me?"

"But mother," answered the boy, "why don't you invest in real estate? You can buy a small lot around 15th and Grand and open up a beauty parlor there, or become a swell optician and get out of the dirty, rotten barber trade."

When a steady customer gave her a big job and then played Indian dice with her and she won a quarter, or when she coaxed him into going up to the corner to buy her a sack of fruit, she was jolly the whole day. She enjoyed shaking dice with a cattleman who had just come in from Oklahoma City. If the stockman won a Havana cigar, he put it up to his nostrils and as he smelled it with genuine satisfaction his craw shook a little. A cattle dealer always relished any game of chance, and playing a game of dice with a woman was, next to horse swapping, the best of sports.

"You start, Miss Lizzie, I'll shake you for a dime Havana," he would say, winking at her as though he knew beforehand she would win.

"Now, don't be a piker, Mr. Bob. Look at that fortune in ponies and jackasses you're carrying in your hip pocket. How about shaking for a quarter? You sure can afford it."

If she picked up the leather cup and threw three aces, she clapped her chubby hands together; her eyes would fill with so much wet glee that she'd have to wipe them on her white barber apron. The man would watch her every movement, taking out a bandanna handkerchief that was a foot square to dry his rugose neck and the dewlap hanging from his throat.

Lizzie was proud of the trade; solid and well-established people began to patronize the Star Lady Barbershop. There was Max Stedna who owned the livery stable; it was built in gothic fashion of roughhewn rock. Besides the viaduct transients, the Star Lady Barbershop was patronized by well-to-do merchants. One named Cromwell had a commission house on Walnut and sold grain and imported bananas and peanuts from South America. He had been a city alderman and everybody looked up to him. He was a spare, gray man who wore eyeglasses and sat in Lizzie's chair every morning at 7:15. He gave her half a dollar for a shave, and she took the greatest pains with him, powdering his face with talcum, seeing that both business sideburns were neat and equal; and if the colored porter were late or had quit, she took a dirty barber towel and wiped his black shoes. His closest friend was Hagen, a wholesaler in eggs and butter, who wore the latest octagonal spectacles with solid gold rims and parted his hair in the middle. Cromwell and Hagen had two bonds that united them: Cromwell looked hungry, while Hagen, jolly and fat, always appeared as if he had just eaten a big meal. Friends nourish one another, and a bald man enjoys the company of one who has a great deal of hair. Both were most loyal Democrats and fell out only when Hagen voted for Teddy Roosevelt.

Experienced lady barbers were now available. Often down and out, they came to Lizzie for work, and she would lend them money and take them in as free lodgers until they were on their feet. Among these was Gladys, who had Indian blood and a large bun of chestnut hair. She was a great drawing card for the shop. Emma Moneysmith, a Mormon with legs that quivered like a drawn bow, had the second chair; her boy, Marion, took violin lessons. The third was Miss Taylor's, whose son, Noah, had the sexual habits of Ham. He claimed that Tisha, the daughter of the prostitute who kept light-housekeeping rooms above Basket's Lunchroom, had put a love potion in his cup of coffee. Sally Muhlebach, a good hairdresser but too seedy to bait trade, served the fourth chair. Her nine-year-old girl, Gizella, had ballooned, dropsical legs and once when she and Lizzie's boy were at the flat together, she told him some of the dark secrets of pleasure while fingering the keys on the Bach upright piano in the parlor so that none of the girl roomers could hear her. The fifth chair was Mrs. Harney's. She had come to relieve a chippy who had left for Excelsior Springs to take the mineral waters. Claiming to be thirty-four, Mrs. Harney had the blowsy, sapless complexion of a woman who has reached her autumn. She had the dry, average lips of one who had been used rather than loved and she smiled only to gain an advantage over somebody else, opening her wide, sour mouth when she wanted a cheap chin-scrape to crawl into her chair. Whenever Mrs. Harney had finished honing her two razors she sat with *Science and Health* in her lap. The girls remarked that she would not even cross her legs just to show a customer a little courtesy.

Lizzie gave little thought to recreation; if she happened to shut the shop somewhat early on a weekday, she walked back to the flat. She doted on the elms and maples as she sauntered up 8th Street on an Indian summer evening. Stopping at the corner to buy a few apples, she was overflowing with emotion when the Italian fruit dealer graciously saluted her. What health there was in a few pleasant words exchanged between acquaintances. The boy at her side was silent, rejoicing in the Pleiades that hung over the Troost Avenue streetcar as it babbled along the tracks.

He carried his mother's straw basket filled with homemade jellies, some ragged morsels of rye bread with caraway seeds, and grapes and apples. Holding a Winesap in the palm of her hand, she broke it into several pieces between her stout thumb and fingers and spat out the peelings while breathing deeply to exercise her lungs in order that she would have a long life.

When business was dull, or if she had lost money investing in a wildcat oil company, the habits of the girls became a trial to her. They were not hygienic. Lizzie insisted that they scour their armpits, and when she was alone in the back of the shop she would say in a low voice, "My God, they smell like a water closet." She told them that bad odors had an adverse effect upon the trade and tried to persuade them not to wear the same sweaty pumps each day. However, there was always a cruddled voluptuary who was excited by their smelly shoes.

Their profligacy also got on her nerves; she did not care to think about sensual entertainments, which disgusted her. Who can bear somebody else's seminal sheets or tolerate his own turpitudes in another person? God had not endowed these carnal chits with a desire to be ascetic. What is the oldest vice in the world? Itching. Had not Adam scratched himself he would never have thought about pleasure.

Lizzie believed it more sensible to work than to consider the lilies that toil not. Not base by nature, she had sufficient deprivations to ennoble her. Up till now she had not been poisoned by that drudgery which produces the gall on which the larvae of all our living feelings feed.

What worried Lizzie was that the barber girls would give her place a bad name, and that she would lose her lease. How could she guard her bread and roof?

One Sunday morning when Lizzie was obsessed by those motions of night which are the contemplative exercises of great angelic birds, she screamed, bursting the seams of her sleep, "O Lord, I have died, and I have no roof over my head except a terrible dream." The boy crawled up to her damp pillow, his nose nuzzling her neck, and kissed her shaking, obdurate arm, but she thrust him aside and turned her back to him so that she could nurse her bitterness.

How many times she wished she had taken a location on 11th Street, hard by the Bank of Commerce, which was a stately pantheon of lucre. Such thoughts came to her mind when a boozer tottered in from the saloon next door. Lizzie did not care to have a drunk in her chair and would let one of the trulls take him. Good for a two-dollar job, he would not know what had happened to him even after he had crept out of the chair. Each girl wanted the drunk's money and two or three of them would rush forward to help him into her chair, and often they quarreled over him. Lizzie disappeared in the back room to drop a piece of stewing meat into a charred pot so as not to be involved in the dispute. A quarrel upset her stomach, and if someone insulted her, she could not put a morsel of bread into her mouth for a whole day. She would allow the meanest sloven to spit on her and call her a Jew rather than answer one word.

By the time an old sot had sobered up in the chair he would have had the whole bill of fare: a shave, a light trim, raw-egg shampoo, massage, every hair tonic in the shop and a manicure. The colored porter, who mopped up the linoleum, washed the spittoons and helped customers into their coats, would have shined his shoes several times. Unsteady on his feet, the drunk paid his bill and found his way back to the saloon.

The Star Lady Barbershop, though not a Bible house, was no den of atheism either. The girls were spiritualists, revivalists, Christian Scientists, and whenever a preacher set up a tent as the Lord's tabernacle beneath the 8th Street viaduct, one or two of the girls would be absent. If a girl was having her period, or an intrigue was at low tide, she was sure to have a religious seizure. By now Lizzie knew the symptoms: all of a sudden a girl became a dowd; her hair was no longer spun fine and silken, and her shift was frowsy and showed beneath her sanitary white apron. Lizzie kept a bottle of carbolic acid handy to revive a girl who had slumped to the floor—and who seldom awoke without groaning for Jesus Christ.

Only a man cankered by his own zeal would crimp Scripture in order to call a lady barber a disorderly Magdala. When the time came she would be a steadfast wife and provide a husband who cherished her with a jolly, bawdy bed and fat gammons. She would look just as legal and righteous as any other female householder. Love restores the blind, the palsied and the virgin, and even if a lady barber smeared her bridal sheet with Heinz ketchup, no bridegroom should be so foolish as to examine it. A man who scrutinizes everything that he does—or someone else does to him—will die swearing or live to run mad in the streets with no other cover for his nude soul but a syllogism. Besides, a woman is a marvelous chameleon creature, for she can cheat, lie and copulate, and still be the tenderest pullet.

A hustler in the shop had to put up with a great deal to earn her onerous piece of bread. She was besieged all day long by rounders. A steady customer was no better than an out-of-town drummer or the transient viaduct trade; he would never say one word out of the way, keeping his true motives in huggermugger for months until he was ready to take his prey. Hardly a month went by that a girl did not receive a marriage proposal or the promise of an oil well in Tulsa. Even Emma Moneysmith did not know how to handle these lickerish strategists. Just as she was beginning to wax warm over a stockman or brakeman, imagining that he chewed a quid of tobacco as if he had the moral cud of St. Luke in his mouth, she would find out that he had a wife and six children on a heavily mortgaged poultry ranch in Roanoke. Emma had no other teacher but her mistakes. We never learn anything, but simply call old errors by new names. A strict Mormon, she knew that when the body had to be relieved, it did not care a rush for Brigham Young.

When business was dragging, the girls pushed the Star Lady Barber hair restorer. This was one of the specialties of the shop, and although each bottle bore the label: Dr. Ignatius Waxman's Excelsior, Vienna, Oklahoma, Lizzie was the author of this nostrum.

Lizzie had clandestine yearnings to be a physician; she thought herself better than an orthopedist at paring a callus, dissolving a corn or prescribing for aching feet. She prized her brass mortar and pestle, which she had bought from the Haeckel brothers. When a girl was too often cozened, Lizzie made a preparation of diuretics, concocted of dandelions and other pissabeds, to rinse out her kidneys and wash out her stupidity. In addition, she had a more astringent catholicon for pregnancy.

She attributed most of the ills of the lady barbers to excessive indulgence in the ecstasies of Venus. An absent barber had usually lost all her strength in bed; on occasion a girl failed to appear for work for several days, and when she was asked why she had not come, she replied that she had forgotten. For persons with such weak memories Lizzie took sunflowers from the back yard, levigated them and when she had soaked them in whisky gave them to the patient. The sunflower, a foe of frankincense, the Arabian spice of love, is an antaphrodisiac.

Lizzie also had a sample case of lenses and a paper sack filled with frames. When a myopic brakeman handed her a ten-dollar bill and told her to keep the change, she gently led him to the settee as if he were carrying a tin cup and a cane, and after he was seated she let him know the mistake he had made. She then advised him either to stand on the corner of Walnut and 8th and give his wages away every Saturday or get a pair of eyeglasses. After trying on several pairs of spectacles, he selected one because he liked its appearance. As he was a steady customer, she gave him a discount and charged him nine dollars for the glasses. However, if a regular client had had hard luck, if somebody had taken his wallet out of his hip pocket while he was riding on the trolley, Lizzie would give him a face massage and trim his sideburns free of charge. She had, like everyone else, a homemade conscience.

The circulation of money in the Star Lady Barbershop was sound though corrupt; currency was always in good health there because it was never stagnant. The lady barbers stole from Lizzie, and she took what she could from them —plus a bit of interest to which she felt she was entitled. One has to have indignation to steal with virtue. When Lizzie thought she could not make her expenses, she took what she could because she believed that if she had to close the shop the girls would not have a job; she had to see to it that they were not cast into the streets. The lady barbers had their fingers in the cash register whenever Lizzie was in the back of the shop. They also robbed one another.

The girls worked on a commission basis, the barber receiving sixty per cent of her earnings and Lizzie forty. Each girl kept checks either in her apron-pocket or in an empty shaving mug; on these Lizzie marked down the amount she had gotten from each customer. If a beau arrived to take a girl out for a plate of chili or clam chowder, she removed her apron and hung it on a peg, often forgetting to put the checks in her purse. Soon as she was seen passing the plate-glass window and waving to the others sprawled in their chairs, the lady barbers ran to get their hands into the pocket of the apron. When Lizzie witnessed such doings, she reproved the girls very sharply. Mrs. Harney was sorely tempted but she preferred to be more dignified and furtive, and only stole another girl's checks when no one was around.

Should the colored porter be snoring on his shoeshine box, Lizzie would wash the clippers and combs, and if she came upon a shaving mug filled with checks she might put some of them in her pocket. On occasion this did not bother her; were she examining a pair of scissors or wiping the mirror, and at the same time denouncing the girls for not keeping their tools clean, she felt indignant enough to take their checks without moral anxiety. At other times she would suddenly awaken from her soporific routine, part of which was pocketing what checks she could lay hands on, and catch herself stealing. This had a very unpleasant effect upon her blood, and she frequently had long arguments with herself, justifying her deed. But all reasons are so useless that even when we are not guilty we cannot prove it to ourselves.

A balding codger had little chance of getting out of Emma Moneysmith's chair without trying Dr. Ignatius Waxman's Excelsior. Had he intended to spend no more than what a chin-scrape costs, he was mistaken. Emma took pains to show him how dirty his scalp was; she took a filthy towel from the wire basket, rubbed it on the floor and showed it to him. If he was obdurate, she took a handful of hair from the haircloth that had just been removed from a customer of another girl and exhibited that to him. She ran one hand through his hair, holding a heavy clump of shorn locks in the other, and then told him that if he did not do something about the condition of his scalp, he would be absolutely bald before the equinoctial rains. That the hair she clenched in her hands did not match that of her customer never seemed to matter. Had he been told that he had just lost his nose, and been shown somebody else's, he would not have recognized the beak as not his own. One must be very thoughtful to know his own face or body.

Lizzie's remedy for all ailments was a purgative, an emetic or a diuretic. When a customer's hair was falling out, or he had bad breath, she advised irrigation. Pythagoras held that no one could be free of sickness or viscid visions at night unless he had been purged. A balding client received a bottle of Dr. Ignatius Waxman's Excelsior with instructions to take an enema every night. The bottles contained a mixture of horehound, ordinary tar soap, Twenty Mule Team Borax, brandy and geraniums that had been brayed in Lizzie's mortar. She thought that a scant man with a dry hip joint should be purged upwards, but that a corpulent patient given to lickerish phantasms, and who belched solely for pleasure, ought to have a far more puissant curative.

Spite of Lizzie's activities as a Galen, she could sometimes hardly pay the rent for the shop; her roomers often quit and left town without paying for their lodgings or repaying the money she had lent them. Though she continued to get a dime for a haircut, she could not understand that the value of ten cents had fallen. What's in a dollar? It has no skin, veins, gut or heart, and though it is said to circulate, it has no blood either. Even the greediest blackguard, who would eat his neighbor or an absolute stranger, would not thrust a dollar down his gullet.

Lizzie could not charge her girls money for her medical labors. She knew when one of them was in man-trouble. She had gotten into the habit of looking over her glasses to observe a girl who ran frantically back and forth to the water closet. When a jillflirt had lost a Pinkerton detective to another woman or when she was dosing herself with castor oil, Lizzie could not stop a smile from glimmering down the flanks of her steep nose. She did not have the cold, hard ability to revenge herself on a girl who had called her a Jew, but it could not be denied that such misfortunes gave her small rills of pleasure.

Gullible persons are the most suspicious; it is not that they are so mistrustful as that they have so little control over themselves that they confide in everybody. Whenever Lizzie lost anything, she suspected everybody; of course, she did not speak out since she was afraid of altercations. But after misplacing her pince-nez glasses, she would often give one of the girls a severe, sly look, imagining that this was a piece of spite work on her part. She would ransack her steamer trunk, searching for her brooch, diamond ring or the gold watch she wore appended by a gold pin to her bosom. If something was missing, there was no doubt in her mind that one of the lady barbers had pilfered it; much of the time she had one or more of the girls living with her. Her glasses sometimes fell off when she looked in every corner of the flat for the missing object. Then she spent several hours trying to find them. She became so upset that her face broke into many rivers of sorrow and, sitting down on the mahogany piano stool, she wept, saying that she was blind, and that there was no woman so unfortunate as she. Why could not God give somebody else a bit of her bad luck? There was no equitable distribution of sorrow or of money.

If one of the lady barbers had been stealing constantly from the cash register, Lizzie imagined that she bore her an immense grudge—until the girl needed her. Then her kindness, which was a parcel of her nervous disorder, was boundless. But we often love our enemies far more than our friends; we are compelled to observe our foes continually, and there springs up such an intimacy between two hostile people that neither wishes to see the venom abate. When Jesus cries, "Smite me on the other cheek," he is not averse to the joy of pain. Like all solitary figures, he would rather be lacerated and touched than avoided. It is the untouchable who is deprived of everyday raptures.

Of all the lady barbers Lizzie liked Emma the best; she had no respect for the giddy heads who wore their skirts stuck up behind them as hens their feathers, but she envied Emma. Miss Moneysmith had thick, auburn tresses, while Lizzie's hair was beginning to fail. When she held up her glass she imagined her hair was nervous and would revive when she was feeling better. The lines around her mouth were also temporary and were caused by worry. These harrowing thoughts came upon her when she was not at the shop. Every workday was a blessing when one could hear the wheels rattling against the cobblestones and listen to the peddler chanting, "Watermelon, pears, lettuce, potatoes." For six days the streets sang in her blood; every weekday was Walnut, Grand, Oak, Cherry, Locust and Holmes Streets, but on Sunday Kansas City died.

Lizzie knew that Emma had been keeping company with a stockman. She could see him scrabbling about to draw up his puling hams from the barber chair as if he were crippled, or worse, impotent. Emma knew how to work a dewlapped horse trader who was a good sixty-five. It was sport on both sides. An elderly, bowlegged, slouchy stockman who forgot to button his pants was simply reminiscing. So long as he had nothing else to do but cough up a few hundred dollars for Emma he had the foretaste of happiness without going through the ordeal of proving whether he could take it. Emma knew this type of rancher who only wanted to whinny and snort since he had put his pair of senile stallions out to pasture in order that they could run with the mares and still imagine they were in the game. A man likes the company of a woman though he is past the time he can enjoy her; he can groan for her just as loudly as the mandrake does when it is wrenched from the ground, though he has nothing else for his labor and delight but the shriek.

Lizzie knew that Emma was a two-timer; while she was taking money from the cattleman she was also having an intrigue with a curly-haired rakehell from 12th Street. When Emma told the rancher that she thought she was pregnant he left for Seattle.

Emma never confided in the common petticoats on the first and second chairs. She did not trust Mrs. Harney's gold-toothed grin either. Emma thought that Bible-reading at the Star Lady Barbershop would hurt business and attract impecunious celibates or chaplains from the Helping Hand Society. Emma did not think she could afford to have any principles. She was good as she could be, and were she to try to be any better, she would be worse. A very pretty woman, she saw no reason why she had to be a dissembler. She refused to smile when she was peevish and showed the teeth of the fox when it was necessary instead of putting on the face of the lamb. Emma would have believed in virtue had she found anybody else who used it. Lying, cheating, stealing, fornication and fleecing were contagious diseases she had caught from the most respectable folk who patronized the shop.

Emma was positive she was in the family way. A fearless woman, she did not know to whom to turn; and she dreaded nothing except to be stabbed in the back by a simper. She had considered her flesh and knew that she was unlucky during the dog days. Among the very few adages in her bosom was: shun pleasure when the flies copulate. The drowsy, opiate months were insidious and underhanded; it was best to avoid any connection with a man from the time of the summer solstice until the season of the Pleiades. She believed she should have smeared sunflowers on her skin, and upon the rim of her secret parts, before indulging in her fevers. She was still wondering whom she could confide in; she did not trust anybody except herself—until she realized that she was just as treacherous a person as anybody else.

But she knew that Lizzie was no gadder or chatterbox and finally turned to her. As soon as Emma opened her mind to her, Lizzie examined her nipples, which were as erect as the cedars of Lebanon. Seeing that there was no time to be lost, she went straightway to her mortar and pestle, gathering together her glass jars filled with pickled melon rinds and orange peelings, which she took as cathartics. She made

Emma swallow these laxative conserves and gave her two dozen cups of hot tea with senna leaves. The two of them were alone at the flat; the boy was playing on Admiral Boulevard, and the girl roomers were either at Electric Park or spooning on the Troost Avenue trolley.

Lizzie shared the opinion of sacred Hippocrates that to open the matrix one has to free the bowels. She had learned of a Haitian resin, a brown, woody substance that in pre-Columbian times was used by the natives as an antidote for snakebite and which was later exported to Oklahoma and there used as a cure for rheumatism. This indigenous American gum had since acquired an underground and illicit fame as an abortive, though it was kept in almost every family cabinet along with Grandpa's Tar Soap, Smith Brothers' Cough Drops, Sloan's Liniment, Argyrol, Unguentine, Twenty Mule Team Borax, castor oil and barley water. Midwestern folk suffering from strangury, constipation, sciatica, neuralgia, the vapors or ordinary household impotence were their own physicians, and if their condition was aggravated by one nostrum, they tried another—which was all that Galen could do.

Moreover, what reason was there to doubt that a resin which could cure the stings from a scorpion was not forceful enough to bring on a woman's flux? It is said by olden rabbin that when Adam lay with Eve, she bit him.

Lizzie took this Haitian remedy guaiacum and put it into the brass mortar, and dropping in anise seed, garlic, horse-radish, geraniums and the pippins of quince, she brayed them with the pestle. After she had made a thick compost, she poured a pint of whisky into a saucepan and lighted a fire under it; she waited for it to simmer, then put the hot whisky and the pharmaceutical conserve together into a large bottle and gave Emma two tablespoonfuls of it every three hours. The blood ran out of Emma's face, and she looked so green the Lizzie thought she had purged her upwards.

Lizzie then went to work on Emma's body; she separated one thigh from another, pulling them as wide apart as she could, as if each leg were a stalk that had to be plucked up by the roots. After that she kneaded the small of her back with her short, healing fingers, next proceeding to the cerebellum. Could she persuade the head to react to the lower spine, just as the mind gasps and dies a little in the moment of orgasm, she could then relax the uterus. She laid Emma on the kitchen table and beat her hypochondrium, where all her stubborn spleens lay, and turning her over gave her great loud thwacks on her fundament until she broke wind, hiccoughed and coughed.

The two women were so wrapped up in this ecstatic treatment that when Lizzie looked at her patient and saw an ichorous discharge coming from Emma she was elated—until she realized that it was only her nose that was running. Lizzie looked upon the expulsion of sweat, mucus, urine or feces as an encouraging symptom. She listened to Emma's abdomen, putting her ear on it until she heard her ululant intestines, an Atlean borborygmus, after which she gave her more guaiacum.

For three days Lizzie fed Emma the resin, and made her take six hot baths a day. She did not go to work, asking Mrs. Harney to open the shop and shut it at night. She knew that when she returned the girls would tell her that they had done nothing but scrape chins since she was away. Whenever Mrs. Harney went to the cash register, wondering whether she should ring up *No Sale* or not, she remembered the line out of Mary Baker Eddy: "There is nothing either good or bad, but thinking makes it so."

When it became apparent that Lizzie could not open Emma's matrix, both women wept. What a woe was the uterus—a great sea trough through which four edenic rivers flow, one of milk, the second of honey, the third of balsam and the last of urine. Both women lamented their uterine ills, and when Lizzie picked up a pair of old man's drawers as a clout to wipe the perspiration from Emma's face and saw the immoral stains, she threw the cloth back into one of the girls' rooms where she had found it. Lizzie told Emma of her own prolapsus; her womb had been torn at childbirth, and now there were days when she dragged herself about as if she were yoked to some heavy disappointment from which she could not loose herself.

Emma had dire cramps; she said her body tasted of salt, bowels and sin. She told Lizzie that there was no sweeter physic to the soul than self-denial. After a long seizure of indigestion, preceded by large plates of mutton and yards of beef and venison longer than the intestinal tract, even the glutton abhors all animal flesh and imagines that nothing will ever content him more than pulse and water. The maggot always comes after surfeit; since love-making has emasculated the race, we are as foolhardy as the domesticated caterpillar in the mulberry tree who devours the base of the leaf on which he is standing.

After Emma was sure that she would have no need of the menstruous cloth, she had her period. She tried to persuade Lizzie to take money, but all that Lizzie wanted was thanks—a word very few can evacuate.

**III**

*For nothing is more easy to be found than be barking Scyllas, ravening Celaenos, and Laestrygons, devourers of people, and suchlike great and incredible monsters. But to find citizens ruled by good and wholesome laws, that is an exceedingly rare and hard thing.*

SIR THOMAS MORE

In April 1912, when he was eleven, the boy became an inmate of the Jewish Orphan Asylum in Cleveland, the Forest City. No Spartan ordinances could have been more austere than the rules for the orphans. The regimen was martial; Scipio, who compelled his troops to eat uncooked food standing up, would have been satisfied with these waifs who rose every morning at 5:30 as though they were making ready for a forced march.

There was a dormitory for the boys on one side of the shambly four-story brick building, and the other opposite was for the girls. The long hall that lay between the two dormitories was guarded by monitors so that the two sexes would be rigidly separated.

The main edifice had been built in the classical style typical of the almshouses, reform schools and charitable penal institutions of the late Edwardian period. There was a separate school building of the same kind of brick with a kabbalistical stairway leading up to an attic above the third floor where the boys played basketball. Two infirmaries were close to the hinder side of the main building. One was for general disorders, pleurisy, rickets, consumption, coughing, appendicitis, impotent intelligence—and dying. The other was a spital house for contagious diseases. Besides that, there was a steam laundry adjacent to the engine room, and behind that a green-house where turnips, kale and kohlrabi were grown; there were no flowers, since these were regarded as the petticoats among the plants and were banished from the sight of the children.

The playgrounds in back resembled Milton's sooty flag of Acheron. They extended to the brow of the stiff, cindered gully that bent sheer downwards toward a boggy Tophet overrun with humpback bushes and skinny, sour berries. Beyond the bushes was a pond close by a row of freight cars on a siding near the Standard Oil tanks. All this was as sacred to the children as Thoreau's Merrimac or Winnipiseogee rivers.

Some of the children were admitted to the orphanage when they were two and a half years of age. These were known as the little pissers and they slept in a much smaller hall; their mattresses were covered with rubber sheets. Miss Price was the head of this dormitory for little boys. She said she could tell as soon as a newcomer arrived whether he was a bed-wetter or not.

At daybreak a governor rushed about the dormitory, followed by a pair of monitors, shouting, "All up now!" They came by the cots and threw back the bedclothes. Nobody wanted to air his bare buttocks on January mornings at 5:30, and often a monitor dumped a boy out of his cot to encourage him. In the washroom were two long soapstone troughs. Each boy, naked to the navel, his blue shirt, drawers and suspenders hanging, stood in front of a faucet, washed his face and body in icy water and scrubbed his teeth with Ivory soap. Adjoining the washroom were the water closets, separated from each other by wooden panels —which had been made without doors to discourage orphans from indulging in self-abuse or sitting too long and getting piles.

After making up their beds and combing their hair, the orphans ran down to the basement. This was the playroom; there were long, rough wooden benches with boxes under the seat. Each box had a number—which became the boy's identity for his whole life in the orphanage. If the boy were talking or giggling, the governor or monitor cried out: "Number 92, quiet now, all in order!" In these boxes the orphans kept shoe polish—and marbles, ball bearings and stale Washington pies or doughnuts stolen from Becker's Bakery on Woodland Avenue. In the morning the boys would get out their daubers, spit on them and dig them into a tin of shoe polish. When a nearsighted 5th-grader, or a soft-witted half-orphan who wore glasses, spat on his own shirt or the pants of the boy next to him, someone would guffaw and a fight would start.

Everybody wore the orphan asylum mouse-gray jacket, lank, straight pants that fell as far as the knees and woollen stockings with thick ridges. They had no overcoats or caps and often ran out to the playground in their shirts, returning, when their ears were blue, to sit on the hot radiator pipes. There were iron bars on all the windows, and two monitors guarded the door so that nobody could leave the playroom except to march to the schoolhouse, or to play for an hour outdoors after 4 o'clock. The grounds were surrounded by a high wooden fence; in front of the brick ramshackle was a fine lawn and a fountain which made a good impression on passers-by; however, this was *verboten* grass, and the orphans were only allowed to walk on it on first and second picnics in summer. Anybody caught going over the fence got a hundred demerits and was kept indoors for a week. If an orphan were good all year and had received no demerits, two dollars was his award, which he could spend on first and second picnics or on the one occasion when they had a day at Euclid Beach.

At 6:30 an 8th-grader read the Hebrew prayers and each boy, standing at the bench in front of his numbered box, chanted aloud the orison. Some said *Baruch atah Adonai Elohenu,* and others muttered any words that came into their heads; two governors ran up and down to discover who was being profane and garbling the Lord's prayers. At 6:40 they marched in double file up the stairs to the refectory; two girls, dining-room help, opened the doors, and they went in and took chairs at long tables which resembled the planks of a house painter. The boys said they were convict tables. Two hundred girls sat at one end of the vast hall, and three hundred boys at the other. There were four governors assigned to rule the boys, but only two for the girls, who were not considered bona fide orphans anyway, because they were good, quiet and were dining-room helpers. No boy could get near the dining hall except for mess, and they had the greatest scorn for those female hypocrites on the far side of the orphanage who received an extra apple or a meat sandwich from Christine, the Polish cook.

The orphan asylum traditions were severely observed, and any boy caught talking to a girl was taken down the gully, or into the basement when the governors were at their meals, and beaten. This had been a custom for seventy-five years, and no older boy was going to allow laxity of this sort; how could they be tough enough to fight the Irish Micks if boys were permitted to hang around girls?

Breakfast began with a short prayer; then there was a tumultuous scraping of chairs, the rattle of five hundred tin plates and cups, or the rancor of somebody who thought he had been fleeced: "Hey, don't go changing mush plates with me, you crook." The children abhorred the breakfast gruel which was served without milk or sugar in chipped, enameled tin plates; they called it mush. A boy who puked at the table was regarded as a menace because they said the mush looked like vomit anyway. The coffee was a slop of stale ground beans and hot water, and also contained no milk or sugar. Each child was given a slice or crust of dead rye bread which was thinly swabbed with oleomargarine. A tin cup of milk was reserved for boys who looked tubercular. It took the orphans about three minutes to finish their meal; then they grew restless and threw bread rolled into hard pellets from one table to another, or, if one were moody, or just starved, he pushed the boy next to him and said, "Meet me in the playroom; I challenge you to a fight."

When Lizzie's boy, Number 92, had arrived, wearing a pink shirt, a Panama straw hat and tan stockings, the 7th- and 8th-graders said that if the trustees had no more sense than to spend their money and ruin the annual budget to support a nut like that, they might as well admit their defeat and close the J.O.A.

Brutality was also an orphanage fetish; the smaller children were bullied by the older boys. They had no manual skill in affections and were sore afraid of touching another except to harm or punish. The hand is a greater revelation than the face, which is always an enigma. The outward countenance can resemble Jacob but the inward one may be Esau. Lizzie's boy was a greenhorn with his fists and was intimidated by the orphanage dialect. Even the names of the inmates seemed as esoteric to him as the *Pirke Aboth:* Mugsy, Prunes, Shrimp, Bah, Mooty, Spunk, Pummy, Bonehead Balaam, Moses Mush Tate, Phineas Watermelonhead, Mushmelonhead, Sachemhead. . . .

Number 92 wrote his mother, begging her to take him back to Kansas City where he could run in the streets, hear the cicadas singing on Indian summer evenings or listen to the Troost Avenue streetcar making soft water-sounds against the tracks as it passed over a trestle twined with weeds and sunflowers. Later in life, Number 92 came to understand Kierkegaard's "The crowd is untruth," for at eleven he had been a spindly, puking weanling in the midst of a fell herd. He pined to be close to his mother. He was no stoic and wept, because he had no choice, and at the age of eleven one of the few illusions that he still had was that one could do what one wanted to do.

Letter-writing day was once a week. Then an orphan could write to an uncle or aunt in Milwaukee, or a cousin in St. Paul, but there were many who had been in the Home since kindergarten and had not a soul on the earth to claim them. The letters received were opened by the Superintendent to see whether they contained a dime or a quarter— which was promptly confiscated. The contents of all epistles were read and censored; if an inmate said that the *weisenhaus* was a reform school, the words were scratched out, and the turncoat who had reviled the Superintendent, the trustees or the meals was given fifty to a hundred demerits. If the offense was repeated, he was deprived of first picnic and lost the privilege of "going out walking," the traditional reference to a day at Euclid Beach with a philanthropic dowager from Shaker Heights or Chagrin Falls.

The commons were always the same: Monday was a goulash day; for Tuesday there was a stringy, tepid stew with a piece of fat as old as Methuselah's toe. Every other Wednesday they got biscuits with raisins in them. This was a dietary blessing and also the cause of much strife among the orphans. Reliable and honest feeders finished their buns and raisins right away, but there were some table-misers who slowly dug the raisins out of the biscuits and piled them at the side of their plates; then they broke the biscuits into tiny morsels to make them last until everybody marched down to the playroom. A meal snudge was in ill repute.

Twice a month a pair of sausages was served to each boy; these were later vended in the basement for a penny each. During the war years they were sold for three cents apiece, which caused a great deal of argument about unjust war prices. On Thursday they got green-pea hash. By Thursday everybody was starving, but one's appetite was always ruined; either it was goulash or green-pea hash day or some boy puked on the table right after the orphans had asked the Lord's blessing. The easiest way to commence a brawl was to dump goulash or green-pea hash into another boy's plate.

Everybody looked forward to Friday evening *kuchen*. A first-grader could buy the protection of a bully for a coffee *kuchen*. There were *kuchen*-hoarders too who walked about the playroom tearing the coffeecake to pieces while the others roller-skated, braided a horsehair chain while sitting on the window sill or counted the days until confirmation, just to forget they were hungry. On Sundays, when there were stewed prunes for supper, all a downcast orphan had to say to his neighbor at the table was, "Think you're much? Do you know you're living?" and there was a prune fight.

The food was boiled, or rather thrown into vast iron vats. Christine, the head cook, was blamed for all the sorrows of their gullets. Nobody would touch the noonday tomato soup because one orphan swore he had seen Christine cut her finger with a kitchen knife and then let it bleed into the tub.

Eggs were served once a year on the Passover. The Pesaḥ eggs, biscuits and *kuchen* were hawked or bartered for special favors from the door-monitors or the good will of an older boy. After sundown of Yom Kippur, the Day of Atonement and a fast day, each inmate got a small piece of chicken. Though Saturn could not have offered them a dearer bounty, the orphans abhorred the high holy day. The ancient Jews went to the wailing wall of Jerusalem to ease their misery; the boys, forced to keep to their benches or sit in the prayer hall, ran in and out of the toilets. It was sacrilegious to drink water, but no one had asserted that it was unorthodox to pass it. Saturday was as obnoxious as Yom Kippur; that morning they marched to chapel, which spoiled a good day. What had the orphans to pray for? For what had they to thank God? For Christine's rotten food, or not having a kin in the earth? Were they always to be kinless and to have dwarfed hearts?

When they were told to open their hymn books to page 98, the boys in the front seats screamed, "God humbles the proud," and when they came to the second line, "and the lowly he raises," Mugsy, Bah, Pummy and Mooty stuck safety pins through the cracks in the chairs, and into the buttocks of religious maniacs like Bucket De Groot and Pinkie the door-monitor until there was a terrible uproar. Doc put his hand on his ailing heart, and Simon Wolkes, the Assistant Superintendent, shouted that he would expel the whole orphan asylum. The girls on the opposite side of the chapel started to snivel. Blanche Reinitz, who was good in composition, called them atheists, and the boys in high disgust said, "Aw, shut up."

The fighters, Max Lewis, Mugsy, Prunes, Hans, and even Pinkie, who had read *Silas Marner*, would sneak out at night when the governors were at their meals, crawl over the transom of the bread-room and steal bread and apples. A rural delicacy was a crust of rye with large holes in it, known as *gimmels*, filled with molasses. They would break into the kitchen and stuff a gunny sack with raw potatoes, which they took down to the gully where they roasted them. Such an excursion was a jubilee, for every nook of the ravine was holy ground.

For the first lustrum after they had been confirmed, former inmates would return to visit the orphanage, and what a pain was in their eyes because the hill, the gully where they had roasted potatoes and the bend that led to the gut of water that lay close to the cabooses on the siding and the Standard Oil tanks had diminished so much in size. Was their childhood so niggard? Why does everything dwindle as we grow into men?

Before returning to the dormitory each one removed the burrs from his uniform; the boys called them "Doc spies." When the governors or the Superintendent discovered these burrs stuck to the pants or stockings of an orphan, he was taken off the honor roll, which meant that he lost his two dollars spending money and had to stay in the basement during first or second picnics. Besides that, he could not "go out walking."

If an orphan were caught too many times with "Doc spies" on his uniform, he was expelled and sent back to Newport, Minneapolis, Wichita or Kansas City, to join a distant relative, or simply returned to a blank, kinless city. The asylum grounds, its cinders, its junky buildings, the *verboten* grass and muted water fountain out front, were in their ruined infant roots. It bruised their deformed minds when they thought of a separation from the Home. An outcast would never cease hearing the governor blow his whistle and bawl out, "All quiet now!" while Bucket De Groot jumped from one wooden bench to another to escape from Bah, Mugsy or Pummy, yelling, "You stop that now or I'll report you." They would never forget the governor's second warning: "All in order now!" as each one took his seat where his number was, folded his hands and tried not to sprawl.

It was an ineradicable infamy to be expelled. From the time they were 5th-graders they began to count the days until confirmation; yet none wept more by the waters of Babylon than an orphan who was about to be banished. Born to be exiled, he would not get his blue serge long pants and stand together with his classmates in front of the Torah and intone the reverential confirmation song: "Father, see Thy suppliant children."

When he was confirmed and had quit the orphanage would that not too be a phantasm? Or was his suffering so pitiless that a whole numb experience had expunged what we call the corporeal? All acute moments are the same. When pain is absolute, or unbearable, it is similar to the most heightened pleasure. But nothing really exists, for nobody can handle his memories, or take hold of a single sensation, no matter how immense it was when he had it.

Each boy cut his name or initials into wooden benches, painted them on the galvanized refuse cans, on the toilet panels and seats, or carved them on the gardener's wagon. Ulysses in his dotage pined no less for a noble tomb than these pariahs did to leave their imperishable names in the laundry, on schoolhouse desks or around the basketball court of the Jewish Orphan Asylum.

When a boy had been expelled, others helped him pack his agates, marbles, ball bearings, a shoelace, a horseshoe and a stale Washington pie, into a bandanna handkerchief or a paper bag. The outcast sobbed or, utterly silent, asked God to pardon him and to bless Watermelonhead, Prunes, Monkey Bergman, Moses Mush Tate, Bonehead Balaam, Shrimp, Bah, Pummy, Mooty, Bucket De Groot and Frank Lewis. They were all beggars but as immortal as Caleb, Gideon and Deborah the prophetess, who came out with the timbrel and sang before the ark.

Nor was it possible for these "gal-haters" to exclude the petticoat snivelers in woollen drawers, crude, ridged stockings and prison blue cottons who resembled the descendants of the wrinkled, squinting daughters of Thersites. How few had a bosom; would not Solomon have said of them: "We have a little sister and she has no breasts." The girls' dormitory was the clandestine Valhalla of the orphan boys. Suppose a male inmate were exiled to St. Paul or Fargo, North Dakota, how could he endure the world without one of these *waisenhaus* Venuses? No girl would marry one who had been expelled. He would always be in disgrace with

Gizella, Mary Brown from North Yakima, Washington, Ida Lewis from Detroit, Blanche Reinitz, the pretty Mann sisters and Beulah Bull, whose quick, bleating paps once lay in the hands of Harry Kato, who was caught by Simon Wolkes, the next Superintendent after Doc, and sent back to Los Angeles.

The J.O.A. boys often climbed over the eight-foot fence to go to Becker's Bakery on Woodland Avenue, which they called Pushcart Boulevard. Five stale doughnuts cost two cents, a Washington pie, three days old, was a penny, and a half dozen day-before-yesterday's jelly rolls were three pennies. Sometimes seven orphans would come into the bakeshop at a time and while two of them pretended that they were at a stationer's or a candy store, and asked for lead pencils, a copy book, ice-cream cones or jawbreakers, in order to exasperate old man Becker, the others would run out with a tray of cakes.

Some of the boys had huge boils on their necks, cheeks and chins and impostumes—which were called "Becker's boils"—on their heads. For years many had sore heads which were smeared with Unguentine and bandaged with white gauze. Lice were a common affliction, and the two nurses at the orphanage infirmary were kept busy with their fine combs. A continual discharge of mucus flowed from the noses of spindly 3rd-graders. Had Gabriel, Michael, Raphael and Uriel forgotten them? Why was Abraham, who saw the angels as he slept beneath the oaks at Mamre, more blessed than these helpless oafs? Howl, O Heshbon, for 'Ai is spoiled; run to and fro in the hedges. I chant the song of the fungus. I am clay, dust and maggots, but I shall not forget thee, O ye who wore bog moss and hunger, until I forget my own crying flesh.

They were a separate race of stunted children who were clad in famine. Swollen heads lay on top of ashy uniformed orphans. Some had oval or oblong skulls; others gigantic watery occiputs that resembled the Cynocephali described by Hesiod and Pliny. The palsied and the lame were cured in the pool of Bethesda, but who had enough human spittle to heal the orphans' sore eyes and granulated lids? How little love, or hot sperm, had gone into the making of their gray-maimed bodies? The ancient Jews, who ate dove's dung in the time of dearth in Samaria, were as hungered as these waifs. Nobody can even see another without abundant affection. Whatever grace and virtue we give to others comes from our own fell needs. We pray for the face we need and call this intellectual perception. Without the feeling we are willing to give to others, the Kosmos is vacant and utterly peopleless.

Though all day long nothing was in the ailing minds of the orphan-asylum Ishmaels but the cry for food, what these mutes asked for was never given. O Pharisee, when will you learn that we never came to your table for the gudgeons and the barley loaves?

Whenever Doc walked through the back yard, a covey of small oafs took hold of his scriptural sleeves and fingered the sacred buttons of them as though they were lipping the rood. The lucky ones who took hold of the hands of this Elohim of the orphanage shook with paradisiacal rapture. He could hardly loosen the grip of a three-year-old wight with a running nose and a sore head who would hang onto his trousers. "The heart is forever inexperienced," asserts Thoreau; "Feed my lambs," says Christ.

The whole day was a Lacedaemonian exercise. Everyone had his daily work; no one was ever idle. There was the toilet-broom boy; and others to clean and Sapolio the troughs and the bowls in the washroom; four sweepers for the playroom, the window-washing platoon, the pick-up boys for the yard, wardrobe boys, laundry helpers, the garbage collectors who emptied the cans of refuse into the furnace next to the chicken coops at the edge of the hill. What the boys had to do every day brought them the reward of heaven, and, on rare occasions, kept them from getting fifty demerits.

They were disciplined for warfare, which is a benefit to the poor in will. Nobody suffered from that malady, velleity, which disables the soul. Any kind of work that does not harm the health or brutify the spirit is essential for children. Epictetus remarks: "For since you must die in any case, you must be found doing something, whatever it be—farming or digging or trading . . . or suffering indigestion or diarrhea."

There were a few lucky ones of the male gender: unprincipled orphans like Bonehead Balaam who had saved his first and second picnic money and invested it in white leghorns. He sold a few eggs to people in the city but he preferred to drink a raw egg himself to settle his blood and increase his weight. Bonehead was such a miser that he wouldn't go "in whack," that is, "divvy up" his eggs and chickens with a boy who was going to be confirmed in a year. One couldn't beat him either, because an older boy was sure to forget himself and hit Bonehead on the head and break his hand.

In January the orphans skated on the frozen pond. Midway between the clinkered hill at the edge of the yard and the bottom of the gulch was a hummock. When a boy on a sled struck this bump he rose several feet, then passed through the dead, mangy bushes and went around the bend as far as the pond and the oil tanks. All the fights with the tough Irish Micks took place in the ravine.

Every winter the Irish Micks came from Kinsman Road and the slums of Superior Avenue to fight with the orphans. These January battles had been going on for years, and though an 8th-grader wasn't afraid of anybody, he was always on his guard with these brawlers who had knives and hid stones inside icy snowballs. Once when a fight with the Irish was about to start, and Mush Tate was waiting for souvenirs—a mumblety-peg knife, marbles, nails or a penny—to fall out of somebody's pocket, he said to Hans, "I'll hold your coat for you so that you can lick that Irish bastard," and he did.

Achilles was no fiercer than an orphan fighter. Hans, who got a glass of milk every day because he was underweight, had merciless fists. He had whittled a broomstick to a fine edge, which he dug into the belly of a timid boy warming his pants on the radiator pipes of the playroom. When he saw a boy mumbling to himself on the window sill, he beat his knuckles until they bled. No one escaped Hans's punitive broomstick except Moses Mush Tate, who made him laugh. Mush Tate was the Socratic dialectician of the orphan home. His words fell out in prophetic order and with such good luck that only a whole orphan with half a wit would argue with him.

On Sunday evenings, when they got stewed prunes for supper, the orphans said Kaddish, the Hebrew prayer for the dead, for Christine the cook. Not even Mush Tate would touch that supper of Hecate. Everybody in the refectory was starved and bored. When the governors were not looking, an orphan might take a prune pit, put it on the handle of a spoon and then strike the bowl as hard as he could with the palm of his hand. The aim was generally accurate, and when an inmate who wore senseless eyeglasses was hit in the head with a prune pit and yelled "Ouch!" the governors, followed by the Superintendent, came running to the table to discover the malefactor.

Not only did one receive demerits for running out into the city, a capital offense, or throwing goulash or green-pea hash at a "newcumber," but he was summoned to wait in the marble hall after supper. If there were seven or eight culprits, they had to stand in this holy alcove and wait for Doc to finish his meal. They would study the names of the deceased donors which were chiseled in gold in the marble: "In memory of Abraham Cornhill . . . $500."

Doc was a stubby, corpulent rabbi with a white beard;

no orphan would have doubted that he was God—had he not picked his nose. He occupied an oak-paneled apartment opposite the memorial slabs, where he slept in a large, downy bed and had incredible meals; broiled fish, spring lamb chops and lettuce and cucumber salads dressed in olive oil were as unimaginable to the J.O.A. boys as ambrosia or nectar.

Doc had a long and seasoned experience with the Old Testament and the retribution of Jehovah. He had many ruses in disciplining the orphans. He would commence in a solemn, gentle strain, holding his hand on his bad heart; he was sorely grieved for the circumcised offenders before him. He took his place in front of the line of boys, usually beginning with a reference to the golden calf or the trials of Moses after he had descended from the holy mountain that spoke. Then, while he admonished an orphan at the extreme right end of the line, he would strike another at the other side. In spite of the fact that these stratagems were well known, Doc sooner or later caught someone off guard because of a poignant allusion to Leviticus.

When Doc asked Mush Tate what need he had to defy the Mosaic dietary laws by running out into the city and eating gentile jelly rolls and Washington pies, Mush Tate hung his head, and as soon as Doc saw he was lost in the throes of meditation, he gave him an uppercut.

It was during the first World War; there were new sore heads, "Becker's Bakery boils" and ringworms every day. On the third day of creation there was grass, but after the Lord had rested the orphans had pimples, spinal meningitis and rickets. But it was the time of the harvest for these gnomes because the physician had prescribed white bread for them. What a benediction were all diseases. Had not the Lord given them measles, mumps, chicken pox, scarlet fever and made them dwarfs in order that they might receive an albic crust?

The lavatory had become more popular than usual;

this was the agora of the orphanage. Mush Tate went to the water closet to meditate and to jot down neologisms he claimed he had received from Mt. Sinai. By five o'clock every seat was taken. Human beings eat to defecate; the orphans dunged as a pastime. When the meals were the most repulsive, both Doc and Simon Wolkes told them to rejoice in their swill because of the famine in Armenia and the floods in China. Their poverty was so equally distributed among all the orphans that no waif, unless he coveted the indigence of another, had any cause for envy.

These children with senile, swollen heads were already as wrinkled as Adam who stood in the River Gihon and wept. When they were unusually hungry, they invented word games, or just relieved themselves.

Pete Kayte was drumming on the wooden panels with his lopsided knuckles. Gabbie, with his trousers spidering down his naked legs and his suspenders dragging on the cement floor, had a harmonica in his mouth on which he was playing a J.O.A. classic:

We'll fight for the name of Harvard . . .

Mush Tate was musing over his prophetic J.O.A. lexicon. Beans Mugsy was howling:

My little girl, you know I love you.

A *Cleveland Plain Dealer* was lying on the lap of Benny Marble's woollen drawers. He was counting the number of Canadian, Australian and English casualties for the week. The boys computed the war fatalities as if they were baseball scores. They made wagers and the one who came closest to the number of soldiers who died on the battlefield during one week won an every-other-Wednesday biscuit or a Friday-supper *kuchen*.

When Simon Wolkes walked by the toilets in his black

kabbalistical suit, he gave Number 92 a brief, prayer-hall face and pulled the hair of Pete Kayte, who was then whittling into the wooden partition: P/K. Conf. 1917. Mugsy went on howling, paying no heed to the Assistant Superintendent, who, he said, would not be earning $6,000 a year, plus his apartment, free meals and laundry, had not Mugsy's mother and father died. Number 92 descended into his legs while the water sang in the urinal with the Jesus-pensiveness of the brook Kidron. The hallowed Adonai had forsaken Number 92. Why must Wolkes make his daily inspection of the toilets when 92 was sitting on the hole and the Lord had fled?

The real Pythian augur of the orphanage was Moses Mush Tate; he would say as he passed a shoal of mites in the playroom, "Lo, I am the living water; for does not Pharaoh's daughter say, 'He is Moses, for I have drawn him out of the water.' " Mush Tate had a great round head like a nimbus. Being of an oracular bent of mind, he did not trust anybody, particularly himself; he carried his pennies, mar-bles, shoelaces and horsehair braids in secret pockets he had sewn together inside his jacket and trousers, so that neither he nor anybody else could find and filch them. Though a liar, a thief and a rhetor, Mush Tate was wise and good be-cause he had never been known to call another boy a perjurer, robber or just clever. But his character was not without unusual defects. During the war he described him-self as a conscientious objector, and the big fellows were so impressed by his vocabulary that they did not molest him.

One day it was noised about that Mush was to deliver a discourse. The door-monitors stopped all roller-skating in the basement, and the 8th-graders bawled out, "All quiet now, bastards and newcumbers." Those who had been skating, or sitting on the toilets and defecating to pass the time, gathered around Mush.

Mush Tate had enough genius to understand that language is as unreasonable as life. He paid scant heed to grammarians, who imagine that literature is the result of reason. The Moses Mush Tate Bible was a two-penny composition book which he had stolen; he also had two hundred lead pencils, ten pencil sharpeners, one hundred erasers, twelve bottles of Waterman's ink and fourteen copy books which he had taken from the schoolhouse supply room. He said that they were the essential paraphernalia of a doctor of literature. Moreover, Mush Tate's playroom box, number 13, was a mystification to Mugsy, Pummy, Sid Corman and Bah; for where did he get the horseshoes, the twenty agates, the Washington pies and stale crullers? No one violated good principles who purloined Becker's stale cakes; Becker was a miser and a war profiteer anyway; but what good was it to send Mush Tate to chapel on the Lord's Sabbath and force him to starve on Yom Kippur when he had no more ethics than to steal the cakes which other orphans had carried out of Becker's bakeshop?

Moses Mush Tate never had an equal. The only reason he had not been expelled years ago was that he studied the Psalms and Proverbs, which pierced old Doc and made his bad heart flutter when he listened to this orphanage Lazarus through whose words flowed the blood of Elohim. The mediocre had no better reply to Mush Tate's Mosaic argument, which he had received on Mount Horeb, than the tawdry, brutish rejoinder of the witless: "Knock this off my shoulder"; but Mush Tate was enough of a seer to ignore that. Besides, there are many ways to sink the Theban towers.

It was his custom to commence his hortatory dialectic with: "God humbles the proud, and the lowly He raises. Think you're much? Know you're living?" Which is unanswerable, as no one really does know. A waif in the Kosmos, who had walked through the Valley of Hinnom and had drunk contempt in Orcus, he went on: "Though I walk in the valley of the shadow of death I shall fear no evil, for Thou art with me."

How many times had Mush Tate climbed over the fence and, going by himself along Pushcart Boulevard, wearing the stigmata of Ishmael, the flat, dusty-gray uniform of the *waisenhaus,* heard a passer-by say: "There goes a poor orphan." What is sealed to the unsuffering—hunger and rejection—had ripened for him; for gall, derision and the world were his birthright. A warrior of ten thousand chagrins and a soldier of sorrow no less than David the harper in Jerusalem and Christ at Golgotha, he knew by heart the hymn of the fallen when he sang: "Say it not in Gath, publish it not in Ashkelon, lest the daughters of the Philistines rejoice."

By now the orphans surrounding Mush Tate were lost in the throes of words no Midian could comprehend, and the body of Mush Tate had passed over into the soul of Gideon as his words marched on: "I will open my mouth in a parable . . . Doc's overalls, Christine's stale drawers, Benny Marble's bungers, Watermelonhead's ringworms, Mooty's dandruff, Doc's marble hall and his stiff-necked Israelites . . . He maketh me to lie down in green pastures, He leadeth me beside the still waters . . . Down the hill, down the gully, around the bend . . . Green-pea hash, goulash, Sunday night's stewed prunes . . . Man is born unto trouble . . . Mount Zion, Mount Carmel, Shaker Heights . . . Who shall ascend the hill of the Lord, and who shall stand in His holy place? He that hath clean hands and a pure heart . . . The Lord is my shepherd, I shall not want Christine's green-pea hash or her Polack Hungarian stew . . . Come on, talk, think you're in school, think you're much, know you're living; fifty demerits, a hundred demerits, you're a sorehead; you're in company, you're expelled, confirmation day . . . Yea, though I walk through the valley of the shadow of death I shall fear no evil for Doc is with me . . . Talk, Bonehead, think you're an orphan? . . . God is our refuge and strength; I drink up the scorn of the world . . . My God, my God, why hast Thou forsaken me? . . .

God humbles the Micks and the lowly Orphs He raises . . .
My soul is weary of my life . . . Psalms, Proverbs, Exodus,
Leviticus, Numbers, the five books of Moses, the asses of
Kish, Saul's dead march . . . First picnic, second picnic,
going out walking, Euclid Beach, Euclid Avenue . . . *Pirke
Aboth*, the sayings of our fathers; Abraham's bosom, Isaac's
bedpan, Jacob's mumps, Isaac's measles, Moses' scarlet
fever; Rosh Hashanah, so's your Day of Atonement, so's
your New Year . . . How's your circumcision? An eye for
an eye, a tooth for a tooth . . . May Jehovah destroy all
mine enemies, lest the board of trustees rejoice; I am thy
rod and thy staff; my cup runneth over . . . Smite me on
the other cheek, smite me on the other ass . . . Kaddish;
*Yithgadal, yithkadash, sheme raba . . . Baruch atah Adonai
. . . Had gadya*, and you got me . . . What is man but dust?
. . . My bowels, my bowels . . . Aw bull, say something;
think you're a newcumber, a Pharisee? . . . So's your uncle
in Milwaukee, so's your illegitimate gentile cousin in
Akron."

When Mush Tate had finished, his face red with the
energy of the prophetic afflatus, he strode through the
door, and no monitor stopped him. He had gone out of
matter into ritual. After which he disappeared from the
home for a week. The orphans were sure he was dead and
that he was secretly sepulchred on Mount Nebo. Doc swore
that before he resigned because of his bad heart he would
expel Moses Mush Tate.

Mush Tate had caught a B. & O. freight, for he
wanted to be free—though nobody can, because each one at
the same time that he aches for liberty also pines as the
ancient Israelites did for the cucumbers, the leeks and the
melons of Egypt. He was picked up by the railroad yard
dicks outside Toledo and brought back to the orphan
home.

As he stood in that burial place, the sacred alcove on
whose walls were the memorial tablets in marble, he studied

the amounts of money each deceased trustee or his relation had given to maintain five hundred castaways and wrote the following in his Biblical composition book: "Fred Lazarus, donated $1,000." He hung his head because he knew Doc would expel him and he would not receive the confirmation blue serge pants, the Roman toga of virilia, and a Bible with his name engraved in gold letters on it: *Moses Tate.* No one would shine his shoes, and he would not have fifty cents to bequeath to Frank Lewis, with whom he had been in whack. He would never sob the confirmation liturgy: "Father, see Thy suppliant children." He would go back to nobody, and the world would be a stranger and a foe to him. Should he cry out as Jesus did. "Oh, I have overcome the world"? Every day away from the Home would be Golgotha because he would be absolutely kinless. Once he left the J.O.A. he would be an orphan.

Doc expelled Mush Tate, and everybody thronged about him; two 5th-graders showed him all the respect due a confirmation boy; they shined his shoes and gathered together all his real estate from box 13: the marbles, the agates, Becker's stale cakes, the plaited horsehair chain which Mugsy and Pummy closely scrutinized, the ball bearings he had taken out of Mooty's box, who had stolen them from Mushmelonhead, but who had the heart to be virtuous now and claim his own possessions.

They walked Mush Tate to the front gate, and he turned about just before passing out of their lives and said, "Mark my word, my address will be 1036 Mark Twain Place, Hamilton, Ohio," and he bequeathed his Mosaic ledger from Mt. Sinai to Bonehead Balaam, who was as illiterate as the twelve disciples. He knew that the word had corrupted the whole earth, and that the Pleiades and Lucifer, the Morning Star, tremble only in the breasts of the fallen.

Soon after Mush Tate was expelled, Doc resigned because of his bad heart and Simon Wolkes succeeded him as the rabbinic lawgiver of the Jewish Orphan Asylum. Salt and pepper shakers were expected any day. Diogenes was able to be a philosopher on the scantiest fare of apples, millet, barley, vetches, lentils and acorns, but filth deforms the soul—Christine's watery mush, green-pea hash and the dead stewed prunes produce Shorty Joshua, Pummy, Shrimp, Prunes, Mooty, Mugsy, Give-eye Newman, Sa-chemhead and Watermelonhead. They expected loaves, as white as the shewbread on the holy table in the temple, to be loaded on porcelain platters. The big boys would wear city knickers and go to the public school, and the older girls were to be clad in white middies and wear blue skirts; they would have ribbons for their hair—as dear to the orphan-asylum Eros as the wimples of the damsels of Zion.

Imagine an orphan, who was not really a human being, wearing a necktie, having a cotton handkerchief instead of a bandanna rag and being able to look at girls without shame. Gabbie, the leader of the harmonica club, gave a symphony in the basement and played three favorite J.O.A. classics: "Und der kuchen schmeckt so gut," "O wie schön es, O wie schön es," and "We'll fight for the name of Harvard."

Everyone in the washroom, latrines and dormitories kept the monitors up after the lights were turned out, gab-bling about the innovations Wolkes was expected to in-troduce. Shortly after he became superintendent, Simon Wolkes summoned the 8th-graders to the schoolhouse. The boys were so rapturous that they kicked each other in the pants and spat on each other's shirts. They sat at the desks with folded hands and waited for Simon Wolkes, who strode up and down the classroom in his hundred-dollar Talmudic suit, to tell about the new orphan-home com-mons. In a long, solemn sermon, he admonished them not to be slaves of their stomachs; he delivered a Levitical ca-veat, warning them never to use public toilet seats lest they come by a venereal disease. Then he told them that they would be gray-haired and senile before confirmation day if they masturbated. After Wolkes' potent exhortation the 8th-graders were crestfallen; many now thought they were no better than fish who rub themselves against something rough, as Dio Chrysostom says, when they have the need to eject their sperm, and they were sure their legs were too hollow and decrepit to stumble back to the basement.

The hopes in the breasts of the orphans were cindered. The fare was still the same dirty Spartan mess. What else could Mugsy consider but food? Shrimp, thinking of Lizzie's boy, asked Mooty what an orphan could get out of puking all the time and walking by himself. Bah, utterly disgusted, went to the court on the top floor, climbed the basketball post and with a knife dug a memorial into the wooden board from which the net hung: "Bah Birnbaum, 307 days before Conf."

Though Number 92 called on the Lord for help, he could not stop retching. After he had vomited on the school desk, Simon Wolkes, showing an underlip upon which the scrolls of the Torah had soured, told him to control himself. And how he did want to control himself—so that he could walk by the side of Wolkes and touch his bony, Jehovah fingers which smelled of Cashmere Bouquet soap.

On various occasions the boy endeavored to gather together the face of his mother; he had not seen her for so long, and though he willed to perceive her he could not. At unexpected moments, she appeared to him, on a sudden, and when afterwards he did his utmost to grasp her image he was unable to identify her, and he wept, and his heart sat down by the River Dan. He knew her eyes, nose, chin and mouth, but each time he tried to put them together, instead of seeing a whole face, he saw nothing. Even when he caught her short, upright gait, which he could clearly imagine, he looked into the palm of his hand for that image of her, but it was empty. What parts us totally from others? Is it that they do not exist? Did he have a mother? Suppose he had placed the six-year-old child alongside the same boy who was now Number 92, would he even recognize him? How many people are sepulchred in us?

Number 92 praised the God of Abraham, Christine's tomato soup, Hans the bully, the Standard Oil tanks, Sunday evening prunes and graham crackers, and accursed *Ivanhoe* and *Silas Marner* because his hair had begun to curl. He brushed and folded his gray, lank pants and wiped the buttons of his shirt with saliva because of the *weisenhaus* Shulamites who now wore ribbons and plaited their tender hair. When young boys are filled with the virile seeds of the serpent Samael, they faint with desire as they hear the April elms and the opening of flowers. Holofernes was overcome by the sandals of Judith; 92 swooned when he saw a black, elastic garter around the leg of one of these skinny, chaste doves, and he rejoiced in the seminal song of Solomon: "A garden is my sister, my bride, a spring shut up, a fountain sealed." But who would notice a puking orphan?

There was at least one hosanna in the hearts of the orphans. Hans was confirmed and for a whole week everybody sang the Sabbath hymns as though they were the little glad hills. Hans had been the defender of the old martial traditions of the Home. He would kick a boy in the groin because he wore eyeglasses. When he saw a crookback warming his frozen pants on the steam pipes his high cheekbones became feverish. His underlip shot out at the sight of a lopsided cranium. His tongue, always lying in wait for the prey, crept out at the corner of his mouth when he beheld the squint-eyed or the sorehead bandaged in smelly Unguentine.

Hans carried a bunch of marbles, ball bearings or a rock in one hand, which he tightly shut as he beat an orphan. A bleeding 5th-grader who said, "I'll report you to Wolkes," had to lie in the dead scabby bushes by the diphtheria stream or run out into the city to escape Hans.

Were he weary of his bleating prey, he would go bare-footed upon the cinders, cross over from one icy window-sill on the fourth story to another or walk in the tin trough hanging from the gabled eaves of the main building. The spoil of the snail is the plant, the hyacinth and the summer leaves of the melon, but man pants for the soul of his brother.

Three months after Hans was confirmed, Simon Wolkes told the orphans to howl for Ḥeshbon and weep for Tyre. Out of the coffined throat of Wolkes fell the funeral words: "Our beloved son of Zion, Morris Hymson, was crushed to death by a freight elevator while perform-ing his duties at the Richman Brothers' warehouse."

Each orphan had to sit in his place on the wooden benches until Kaddish was said in the prayer hall. A former inmate donated an oil painting of Sir Galahad to the orphanage; it was pensively framed in gold leaf, and Mr. Martin, head of the manual training class, made an engraving for it on a metal plate: "Morris Hymson, Con-firmation 1916." It was hung in the venerable oak room of the board of trustees.

Hans was buried in the orphanage cemetery near Cherry Farm. Not even Moses Mush Tate became a greater myth than Hans. The inmates spoke with awe of Hans's Homeric fists, his war with the Irish Micks and his battles with the J.O.A. Skamander. Man is as homesick for the grandeur of Caligula as he is for the prophet Jeremiah. Hans was no less ineradicable in the soul of the orphans than the gully, the measles-and-mumps infirmary and the B. & O. freight cars alongside the Standard Oil tanks. All that is sep-ulchred in the bosom of man is sacred, and nobody will give up a single remembrance of a chagrin, wound, shame or infamy.

Our past is our only knowledge, and, good or ferocious, it is, for sublime or baleful purposes, the sole viaticum of the spirit. We can digest our childhood but never our present deeds, because no one knows what he is doing while he is doing it. The present is an absolute sphinx to men. Had Peter really known that he was walking on water, he could not have done it, for every act, small or great, is a veiled trance.

Now every day Lizzie's boy walked in the wind when the rain scribbled round drops on Bonehead Balaam's chicken coop. Soon he too would receive his blue serge long pants and five dollars—he would be a former inmate. He could return and look into the face of Simon Wolkes without having to drink up the derision and the waters of Marah from his Levitical mouth.

Suppose Simon Wolkes should die and he would never be able to prove that he had walked to Capernaum, and that he had been at Golgotha. Could it be that after he had come to manhood he would still be no more than puking Ishmael, Number 92? He wept and he shook the mountains and the hills and the rivers because he would never be able to say that his miserable orphan dust was anything more than Number 92.

The day of leaving the Home had come. He stood on the stage in the prayer hall and sang the dirge of separation together with the other orphans who were in the confirmation class of 1917.

A boy had died and a man had sprouted. Whatever the child had been, the man must overcome. Would he long for his homeless boyhood? Are there children whose years are watered by the four rivers of Eden? Give us love and justice and the heart to sorrow for others. O heaven, earth and seas! He who is not pursued by the Erinyes has no love or justice or sorrow for the house of flesh. It is an infernal tragedy to be too fortunate. Pitiless is he who has not been harried by the furies.

He left the Jewish Orphan Asylum, but he was never to obliterate its hymn, because all experience is holy unto the heart which feels:

Father, see Thy suppliant children
Trembling stand before Thy throne
To confirm the vows of Horeb
And to serve the Lord alone.

X

*Fortune ruleth in everything: disposing of them according to her will rather than unto truth.*

SALLUST

In 1925, my mother sold the Star Lady Barbershop and moved out to the grassy Missouri village called Northmoor, a short distance from Kansas City. There she had acquired a two-family stucco duplex, one half of which she occupied. It was about fifteen yards from the clapboard cottage Captain Henry Smith had built. Also, in exchange for the barbershop, including the value of its good will, she had obtained a wooden bungalow in North Kansas City. With the help of her son, now teaching school in New York after his graduation from Columbia, she bought four hundred Rhode Island Reds and Plymouth Rocks and sold eggs and broilers, thus adding to the pittance she derived from renting her three small properties.

A very agile woman, mewed up in her four walls, chicken coops and back yard because she feared the galling bigotry and gossip of rural folk, Lizzie resolved once again to improve her circumstances. In order to find a suitable companion, she inserted an advertisement in a matrimonial gazette. She had rewritten this notice, before sending it to the periodical for publication, above twenty times. She requested that the following item be printed as soon as possible: A highly polished widow, a young forty-four, with five languages at her finger tips, as well as an accomplished pianist, desires to meet a cultured bachelor who is a good conversationalist, and a man of considerable means. Object: Marriage.

Shortly thereafter Lizzie received a letter in which a gentleman expressed himself in lengthy sentences that were both emotional and gallant. He described himself as a retired manufacturer, though still in the prime of life, and very light on his feet. Not given to boasting, he added, he had the highest taste for literature. Though neither tall nor short, he had a rosy complexion and was withal not fat nor a skeleton either, and could prove at first blush, and without peradventure of a doubt, that he was a seasoned talker. Although in the middle of life, he had hardly come to the beginning, and if he were not stylish in appearance, he could amend that by his faultless deportment. He said he was not looking for any kind of brutal or cheap amusement, since he had the most elegant and lofty regard for the opposite sex. He wrote that he would call on Saturday.

Lizzie was exceedingly impressed by his educated language, but was confused by the three snapshots of himself which he had enclosed with the letter. In one picture he had wavy, chestnut hair, parted most tidily down the center of his head, and a well-bred though conspicuous nose. The second picture was puzzling to her, for it did not resemble the first: here he had on glasses with thick, bifocal lenses, and his jaw was long and loose. His face was far more sparse, looking as though it had been flensed, and the nose appeared to have spread or grown up since the first picture was taken. With even more gravity and suspicion, she scrutinized the third photograph. In this one he was standing on a front lawn shaded by a large, rock-ribbed house, and either because he was in a shadow or the snapshot was poor, his hair looked more like a January frost than August foliage; he was emaciated, if not wholly dilapidated. More baffling, his mouth was so sunken that it occurred to her that he must have forgotten his false teeth that day. In all three pictures he had on big galoshes, a winter coat, a heavy flannel muffler, and carried an umbrella. Since the pictures were taken outdoors, the sun must have been shining, but what was he doing with rubbers on and an umbrella? She hoped he was not a crank or had weak lungs.

Saturday morning Lizzie wore a freshly laundered kitchen apron and silk stockings that did not match; the evening before she had retouched her hair. Awaiting her prospect with the utmost impatience, she rubbed off the Marsha's Tennessee Face Cream she had smeared on her cheeks and forehead, and sat in the oak rocker for two minutes trying to read a page of *Moll Flanders*. She then hurried out to the yard and stepped into one of the coops to see whether her hens had laid any eggs. She thought about the stature of the gentleman who had not yet arrived. Even if he were short, she prayed that he had not a sickly, sallow complexion borrowed from the tallow of a candle. Still, if a man were no taller than she, he would not be the energetic type; a man ought to have enough ambition to be higher than a woman. Lizzie was also troubled about the effect she might have upon a debonair bachelor. Naturally she had lied about her age; she was sixty, and though her skin was as clear as a babe's, she was worried about her throat, which could have been stitched together by the thread of a tailor. But a woman who is mellowing—and is thus far more serviceable to a mature man than a green bantling—has to cover her neck, which ages first. It was odd: her feet were quick, her torso succulent and buxom (and who could deny that she had young, virile nipples?), but the worst signs and symptoms of failure, disappointment and years, which were otherwise imperceptible, had showed themselves first in her throat. Hurrying to the dresser drawer, and throwing the pincushion, a pair of ragged woollen drawers, a torn pillow-case and a heap of moth balls on the floor, she found a small silk scarf that she wrapped around her neck—but quite loosely, as she felt as if she were suffocating if anything on her were tight.

Then lying on the bed and forgetting the pile of clouts on the floor, she endeavored once more to envisage the retired manufacturer. She did not care to have a miserable stump of a male dragging at her heels; were he skinny he would not be the enthusiastic sort. A poor feeder at the table made her downcast; she had never laid eyes on a man with a mean appetite who was not stingy.

At noon Tobias Emeritch knocked on the door. Lizzie greeted him and took him into the sitting room. After looking into her eyes and prancing about her, he began kissing both her hands. He smelled of cheap hair tonic. The odor was disagreeable, and although she had not yet had time to recover from his triumphal entry and to notice how old he was, she had already come to the conclusion that an old man smells worse than a young one.

Lizzie's ecstasy vanished. She was so overcome by the man's appearance that she fell into a painful reverie. Was this a nation of squat, pasty men with kitchen-garden noses? Circlear had had a low, slouchy stomach that ran into his lap when he was seated, and though this one had a far more frugal countenance, he was no different from her former admirer. When Tobias Emeritch lifted his insufficient mouth from her two hands and stood erect, she thought he was either sitting down or exhibiting only his bust. By now Lizzie herself was fidgety and her forehead flushed; without knowing how brusque her words were, she exclaimed, "For God's sake, sit down, or keep quiet, or stand still. What are you—a young bull in heat?" He sank down onto the couch, altogether worn out.

Having somewhat recovered, Lizzie began to take inventory of her suitor's visible merchandise. What was breathing or even rattling inside his secondhand suit she could rather surmise. His overcoat, which he had not yet removed, had a frayed black velvet collar. He wore a silk cravat with stripes that hurt her eyes, and he had not taken off his muffler or his galoshes. Still lounging, he was shaking the dust out of his umbrella. Lizzie jumped up from the rocking chair, grasped the umbrella as though she had a cat by the scruff of the neck and exhorted him, "Don't make yourself at home so quickly. Give me a chance to get used to a brand-new article like you. Besides, sir, I've just mopped and scrubbed the floor. Can't you see it is still wet?"

Whereupon Tobias Emeritch endeavored to put on his rubbers—which were still covering his shoes.

Lizzie now hopped to the window, drew the curtains aside, and seeing the sun was clear, she ventured to ask him, "Do you wear rubbers because you're cold? We've had a long dry spell, so what are you doing with an umbrella?"

She noticed the sleeves of his undershirt hanging out beyond his detachable starched cuffs, which made her positive that he was extremely wary and parsimonious. Lizzie herself wore long woollen underwear, winter and summer, but that was for her rheumatism, and quite different.

This creature seemed an unusual acquaintance already; if the first impression was hazy and perplexing, what would she make of him later on? The longer you know a person, the more nebulous he becomes; by the time you are friends, you may be strangers to one another.

As though he were speaking to nobody, he began, "You know, lady, it could pour, hail or there might be a sudden snowfall; I simply cannot afford to take chances."

It seemed to her that whatever remark she made he

did not hear it, and though now and then he cupped one ear as if he were hard of hearing, it was obvious that he had no intention of listening to her. Evidently, he also forgot whatever he had said and pursued his own thoughts, whether relevant or not, imagining them far more significant than somebody else's refuse.

"This is a duplex, is it not? Would you say your next-door tenant is in arrears? Without any prejudice to your lofty character, may I ask, do you indulge in foolish recreations, such as a worthless stage show? Are you in the habit of taking cognac or sitting in public restaurants by yourself? Do you go for a walk after six-thirty in the evening when you are sure to be accosted?"

Who but she could have discovered such a specimen? She was quite exasperated, for now he was digging the toe of one rubber through a hole in the rug. He started up again: "What did you do with my umbrella? It has a genuine silk lining, and I picked it up at the Salvation Army. Where is my flannel muffler?"

"Do you take me for a thief? You've got your umbrella in your right hand, and if you don't get out of that suffocating muffler, you'll catch cold. Maybe you're running a fever. Do you ever see a doctor?"

"See a doctor? I'm a discouraged man, but why should I be that despondent? If a physician tells me I'm sick, would it be prudent to give him money just for giving me bad news? A doctor who doesn't tell you that you're in perfect health is likely to worry you to death. Lady, I don't believe I caught your name, but never mind. Every time I meet a new person he gives me such a load of gas on my stomach that I am unable to sleep until I have evacuated him. You must realize that I do not have a sunny disposition; it's better, don't you think, to come right to the point, and not to deceive anybody. Did I not tell you that I was a big reader? I'm a disciple of Arthur Schopenhauer, the pessimistic philosopher. Whenever I have a little spare time I read him."

Lizzie had to admit that this man was no boor; in some vague way she regarded a book as a demigod and she could not help having elevated emotions about a man who had both knowledge and money—a very weird and abnormal combination in this world. Her son always told her that learning and money were never in the same pocket. But why did this guest have to be so melancholy?

Impressed by his mention of Schopenhauer, and now softening her manner, she suggested quite hesitantly, "Do you have to be dejected all the time? One should have a little hope."

"What will it get you but a little more hope? And one expectation weakens the next one, and in a little while you are so disappointed that you have no prospects at all. One's life is absolutely unendurable unless one's outlook on life is hopeless."

Lizzie was rocking and only half listening. She was utterly forlorn and wished she had something to do. So long as she was occupied her skin crowed, and since she had given up the barbershop, solitude hummed around the watery marges of her soul.

Perhaps she ought to excuse herself and get into her loud, geranium-colored dress; scarlet cottons revived her spirits, and made her look plumper. Moreover, red could make a fool out of a passionate man—but she was in no mood for such nonsense.

Tobias Emeritch, seeing that she was remote from him, felt that he had better do something to enliven their colloquy, and he commenced anew: "It must be damp. I've got such rheumatism."

Should she go out and examine her tomatoes?

"It must have cost you something," he went on, "to put up this stucco duplex." Tobias Emeritch was chewing the upper part of his lip and then feeding on the lower one, which he found more suitable to his cogitations. Now that the space between him and Lizzie had increased, he grew moody. Well, it was useless going on in that vein, and he asked, "How much is horse-radish this year? Do you know that during the War you could not buy German sauer-kraut? I wonder what a quart of sour cream brings, or if a barrel of smoked whitefish has gone up since last June? If you are in the market for coleslaw, I could do something for you, or should you be interested in pickles—dill or sweet, wrinkled ones, it makes no difference to me . . . I'm a retired manufacturer of pickles, myself."

How could she collect her own wayward mind? She remembered that another suitor had a ketchup factory in the West Bottoms, and that he had a similar kind of bent-in pot of a head and that his nose resembled a potato. Neither the former suitor nor Tobias Emeritch had enough energy to reach any higher than five feet one. She was sure Emeritch would not be able to extend himself in any other way either.

Lizzie enquired, "Are you in the ketchup trade also? Are you positive, sir, that you don't have an uncle or a distant cousin who's a wholesaler in sauces, relishes or cucumbers?"

"Absolutely not. The reason that I did not mention cucumbers is that they remind me of my youth. After all, I was dilling cucumbers for nearly fifty years and, discontented like everybody else in this world, I wished that I had been pickling beets instead. Madam, I do have a brother who is also retired. He's past his ninetieth year, but still commercial-minded; one could say that he's in the life business, a very dreary and tedious occupation, though I admire brother Ebner. His only thought now is to reach his hundredth year. Imagine, as monotonous as life is, and thoroughly unbearable when you come to think of it, he declares that after his one hundredth year he will aim to reach a hundred and ten. Till this day, I cannot say whether people long more for something acid in a very dry season or in a wet one. With women, it's another matter; did you ever know an intelligent and healthy woman who did not hanker after a cucumber salad? You see, I am in the habit of brooding, though I am no great eater myself, for no matter what food you put into your stomach you're sure to get a disease for doing it. Peas give you gas, cabbage sours your whole system and one plate of spaghetti is enough to rush one of your relations to a dealer in tombstones. Frankly, I would not eat if I could avoid it. It would be more prudent to keep quiet also; almost every word that drops out of your mouth would have been wiser if it escaped through your upper or lower colon. Walking would be preferable if one had somewhere to go. It's terrible to take the air, knowing that nobody wishes to see you, and, after arriving at an inhospitable door, to realize that you would have been more cheerful, with a kinder attitude toward humanity, if you had remained at home and never seen anyone. If I could keep my mind on one thing long enough, I wouldn't do anything at all, for as soon as you do something you're sure to regret it."

She had never expected a miserable bargain like this. Should she pretend that she was a busy woman and that it was time for her to get the galvanized tin pail of chicken feed and scatter it in the poultry yard for her Rhode Island Reds and Plymouth Rocks? What did this acid nature want of her? Lizzie did not have the courage to tell him to go. She had never turned a tramp away without offering him a plate of split-pea soup, some leftover stew or a few homemade cookies. But this stranger paralyzed her and if he continued in this funereal manner, it would raise her high blood pressure or give her a fever. Why was she invariably unlucky?

Surely it was time to gather the eggs from the layers, count her cheeps and see whether the roosters with their erect, seminal combs were treading the hens. Lizzie grinned at that; her mouth parted enough to allow a little quantum of happiness to seep through it. What a compost for human bones is laughter. Oh my God, my God, laughter is a sweet country well. The rain cometh, and May and June come louder; the August corn silks the morning air, and the crickets noising in the evening yard put leaves again on your bare branches. Could we die laughing and sport in tombs, death would only be another season.

Should she put another advertisement in the matrimonial periodical? Maybe she could bait a rancher; a man around cows and horses has more sense with a woman. Certain that she had aged since Tobias Emeritch had arrived, she was having those hot flushes and nervous spells.

She raised her glance from the floor and was about to propose that she make food for him, but before she could open her mouth, he continued with his own ideas as if she were not present.

"My brother Ebner lies in bed all day without even a nightgown on and he can swear that he has not had a hole in one sock or broken a button or lost a sixteenth of an ounce in the fabric of his shirt in twenty years. My sister has Bright's disease. She is in the other bedchamber with its four large, beautiful bay windows, which she never opens as she is afraid that an unexpected draught will settle on her lungs. It is always what you don't anticipate in this life that you have to look out for."

Communing with herself and thinking of getting rid of him—yet afraid to lose him—she did not know what course of action to adopt. No matter where she was, he was elsewhere, and he had prattled so much about pickles, sauerkraut, coleslaw and cucumbers that she wished he would go, so that she could take an enema and lie down. She endeavored to interrupt him but was unable to; he went on as though he were hysterical and had not talked to anybody but himself for years. How could such a piece of skin and bones contain so much conversation?

"You must realize," proceeded Tobias Emeritch

apologetically, "that I feel it would be insincere on my part if I did not tell you everything about myself right away, so that later you won't be able to say that I deceived you. Suppose you got the idea that I was exceedingly cheerful, or that I had many appointments and was really too busy to come and see you—that would be dishonest. If you thought I took persons into my confidence easily, you could then call me a hypocrite. You see, after I gave up the pickle factory, I had a side line buying and selling second mortgages and was interested in foreclosures. Besides that I had an equity in an undertaking establishment. At that time people were dying like flies; it's peculiar the way everybody does the same thing, and generally together. Have you noticed how one week you receive from eight to ten letters, and from persons in different towns and cities though no one has sent you even a card for a whole month? Then, all of a sudden, you lose three relations; people so lack individuality and are so lonely that they won't die unless someone else does it with them. Human beings are only reasonable up to a certain point, and after that you can't do anything with them, dead or alive."

Extremely agitated, Lizzie had her hand over her breast; was her heart weaker or her pulse more rapid? Pensively scratching her nose, she tried to calm herself. How many times she regretted having given up barbering. What confidence she had had in those days; it had made her so high-spirited. Then there had been an agreeable leaven to the whole lump of her days because she was with the public. Frequently she would take close to an hour over a customer, honing her razor to the finest edge so that the shave would ease him. Poor old Cromwell, he had vanished; how could that be? She used to dab powder on his skin with the utmost delicacy and sprinkle tonic on his moral, gray head. He had larded the barbershop with his goodness when he came in, and how she waited on him, sometimes wiping his shoes with her sleeve or the tail of her white apron and, when she had no porter, taking the whisk broom and brushing the lint and the hairs from his coat, or hurrying to the counter for a towel to wipe a bit of lather she had missed when she scraped his neck. Had Mary, who anointed the hair of Jesus with frankincense, been more devoted than Lizzie when she massaged Cromwell's cheeks to relieve him of all the weariness of this life?

Now Tobias Emeritch brought thoughts of death to her. Was death made for everybody? Would not God protect her? Of late, insurance agents had been coming to her door, telling her to make her son her beneficiary. Whenever somebody came to the front porch she was usually ecstatic; it might mean an event or a windfall. Could she only take her hopes and put a leash on them! Oh, where do pleasant tidings come from, from what distant star? After she returned to her senses and comprehended what the agent was saying, and that he was no better than an embalmer, all her dormant force sprang to her words: "Mister, you should be ashamed of trying to convince people they're going to die just to earn a livelihood. Why don't you learn an honest trade? You could be a paper hanger, a plasterer or a union bricklayer."

After that she gently shut the door; she could not push it hard against his face. A man in the dead-business was acting against nature, but she couldn't endure the tumult of an argument.

Tobias Emeritch had gotten up and was frantically hunting for his galoshes and demanding his umbrella. Doubtless he felt that she was neglecting him, and was making ready to go. She had to remind him again that he was wearing his rubbers and that she had placed his umbrella in the tub.

Trying to placate him, she said, "Why don't I prepare a fine borscht with a boiled potato in it? And I could slice a few extra beets just to make it more solid. Then I'll fix up chopped eggs and onions, and for the main course a veal cutlet that will stick to your ribs. For a dessert you can have a glass of tea, Russian style, with a piece of lemon in it and three lumps of sugar, and my homemade cookies. Do me a favor; please talk about something else beside pickles, horse-radish and coleslaw. If it won't offend you, may I say that the business you were in must have soured you. Why don't you visit people on Sundays—a family or some friends?"

"Madam, if I must have others under my feet, or someone around me, I prefer an enemy. A friend will forsake you after a single misfortune, but an enemy will never leave you no matter how great a disaster has fallen on your head. Furthermore, a friend is always pretending to love or admire you for traits that belong to another man rather than yourself. Whereas a foe hates you for what you are and has the canniest insight into the weaknesses of your character that nobody else ever noticed. Did I hear you mention a meal? Why don't I lie down and take a nap while you eat?"

Outraged, Lizzie asked herself whether this was a courtship. So far as she could remember he had not discussed *her* at all. He had not told her what a handsome figure she had, and she was hasty to reproach him: "Did you come here to sleep, or to see me?"

But he was too exhausted to answer her. Should she continue to handle him with kid gloves or should she bring him his Salvation Army umbrella? Obviously, he was no bluffer; he probably had the knack of making money or of turning the worst into the best—while she always managed to turn every advantage into a loss. Even if she could scheme, she pondered, and work on a crab like that, when it came to trimming him she would stop short.

After nodding for several minutes, Tobias Emeritch was sufficiently renovated to start again: "I wish, Madam, I could be more entertaining and that I did not have to repeat myself all the time. The truth is I am no longer fit to be with others. As I always say, the poor are companions of the poor, the rich of the rich—but the wise associate with no-body."

These remarks fell deeper into her wilderness than she cared to think about; but still she hesitated to make it clear that she had no need of him.

"Sir, I'm not detaining you; however, I have the utmost faith in life. Be assured, I have always something to do. In the morning I'm up before six to feed my Rhode Island Reds and Plymouth Rocks. I pour fresh water into the wooden troughs and after that I take a broom and sweep up the poultry yard. If the chicken wire is broken, that has to be repaired; I have to be the handy man here. Then I clean out the coops and wipe the roosts, and put clean straw in the wooden boxes for the hens, and see to it that the roosters' combs are in good healthy condition. During the season for tomatoes, I pick them when they ripen, and they are as red and plump as a farm girl. What a joy it is to look at my patch of corn. My eyes used to be sore and strained, and now I hardly ever use boric acid.

"You can see I'm no lady of leisure. For breakfast I take a bite of toast and a little cup of oatmeal with sugar and cream, but I don't touch coffee, for I've heard it's hard on the arteries, though my digestion couldn't be improved upon. Afterwards I lay down on the bed and use my violet ray machine. You should see the violet electric currents in each glass tube. Let me give you a treatment with this miraculous machine; it would take some of the sores and aches out of your disposition and relieve you of all your despondency. Think it over—it's for your benefit, not mine. There are dishes to wash, and a woman has to be on her feet all day, inspecting the icebox, greasing the stove and filling the kerosene tank. And every day I go to my steamer trunk and unlock it just to give my deeds and legal documents the once-over, to be sure that they're safe. By one o'clock I reheat a stew, or drop a lamb chop in the iron skillet, or make a bean soup. In the afternoon, when there is no rent to collect or I don't have to see an attorney about my properties, I sit in the wooden swing on the front porch and relax my bowels by doing nothing for an hour except look at the green fields. Every week is so full—I could go on and on—but tell me, isn't that a day?"

Tobias Emeritch was chewing his silk cravat and he no longer felt sleepy because what Lizzie was revealing was profoundly reassuring and satisfactory. He said with the gusto of a man who has discovered that others are in no less of a predicament than he, "Madam, that's not a day, it's a whole life, and if you don't object to my saying so, a terrible one. You are always doing the same thing—rummaging through your heavy, tedious hours as best you can—and the only way you can endure the time you destroy is by pretending that one day is different from another. What's so unusual about Tuesday that it couldn't just as reasonably pass for Monday? And as for Saturday and Sunday, aren't they the same as the weekdays, except that they are worse? Be quite frank with me—what is so vacant, tiresome and lonely as Sunday? You take all the slops out of the business days and throw them away, and call it the Sabbath which is the emptiest day of the week."

Lizzie's discouragement had deepened and she scarcely knew how to respond to this crank and pessimist but she had to give some kind of answer. He was looking for a pretext to leave, and this made her stumble, "Didn't God invent the calendar?"

He was ready to go, but he didn't believe that a woman should have the last word. He simply couldn't afford the defeat. Following such a disastrous episode he would not be able to rest easily for a month.

Thank heaven, this time he was quick enough to say what was on his mind, and without delay: "If God divided the week into seven days and the month into thirty—besides inventing a year—he simply made another mistake. Anyway, what's so perfect about God? Didn't He create man also, and He made just as much of a botch of that as He did of Sunday."

Lizzie did not wish him to declare that he was leaving before she had brought him his umbrella. Quite courteously, she stepped toward him as if to help him get into his coat, which he had never removed.

Twilight fell upon Lizzie after Tobias Emeritch left. What was there to do? Her head was compressed. She could boil water in the kettle and lie down with a hot towel on her forehead. Doubtless she needed an enema. Her tenant, next door, was probably primping and getting ready to take the inter-urban train in to Kansas City. Her husband, poor fellow, was a night watchman. Well, that was none of her affair. They were behind in their rent, owed her for nearly two months—and were anti-Semites, too. How many times she saw that chit hanging out the wash in high heels, all painted up and powdered, and babbling with the cheap trash who occupied the Henry Smith cottage. Lizzie would be sweeping the back porch and neither of her two tenants would look in her direction or even greet her. How easing would a "Good morning, Lizzie!" have been. But when a tenant wanted a favor, how quickly would this same chippy come over with her mincing high-heeled steps, pretending that she was getting mud on her feet although it had not rained for a week. She would exclaim, "Oh, Lizzie, honey, do be patient—Emery was laid off a month ago." Then she would stroke Lizzie's crumpled, greasy sleeve or affection-ately pat her on the arm where her torn woollen underwear showed, and Lizzie, melting, would wipe her sticky cheeks and tell her not to worry. Several times a couple who had taken Henry Smith's bungalow or the other half of the duplex would skip town, owing her several months' rent, and cross the Kansas state line to avoid being sued. She knew what these low Northmoor folks said behind her back about a Jew. Still, she could not be hard; it was too much of a strain on her to evict a tenant.

One day Lizzie was tweezing her eyebrows and imagined she saw a wrinkle around her mouth she had never noticed before. Taking the hand mirror, she held it up closer to her face, but she realized that the looking glass was cracked. Where had that brand-new, rueful line come from? Had she not massaged enough customers' faces to understand the beauty-parlor business, and was she not a complexion specialist who knew how to take care of every pore?

Maybe—and she shook her head mournfully—her son would return from New York where he was teaching. Was he not a buffer between her and every cruel mischance? Her own flesh and blood would shield her from old age.

My mother, peeled and ravaged by some trance, had heard, across the distance that separated us, the ghost that was wailing in my throat as I moaned, "Every mother, even while she lives, is the pit and grave of the son." And I wept, calling out to NOTHING, "Who will save my mother? What can I do? Shall I go soft and grovel before God who has mangled His saints and prophets?

"How shall I slumber, and where shall I sleep so long as I tremble for the vine, my mother? O mother, thou art my right hand, but my left is lame, and I cannot lift it up." I cried, "My father, my father! My left hand; half of my seed is spoilt. I am half born and half dead, always one part of two, though never two in one, the father and the mother."

And now I said, "I must guard my mother each moment against that corrupt phantom who is always looking over our shoulders. My mother must not be taken by surprise; I will watch over her with the spear and javelin of the mind. I hear the wings of that woeful archangel whose cry in our waters is like the screaming of a gray gull seeking its prey. We will conspire together against that skulking demiurgic glutton who, although he has devoured all the peoples of the earth since the beginning, yet requires even one more body, my mother's. Though this fat, garbage cherub is swift and comes on a sudden, I will repeat each instant in that mocking dream that is death and not life the liturgy from Luke: 'Thou fool, this night thy soul shall be required of thee.' "

# XI

For the first two days Lizzie was overjoyed at the riddance of Tobias Emeritch. When she was not obsessed with the mournful cypress or thrown down by her blasted hopes, she was not forlorn. She did not always stand in her doleful buskins when she viewed her life. On the third day it was still a benison to listen to the evening noises of the crickets and to the mumbling weeds that lay against the lattices. However, she accepted the fourth day of his absence with less composure and argued with him in her mind as she mopped the rear porch and threw stale bread to the chickens. She had dropped into the habit of reviling people long before they had proved that they were good for nothing.

Lizzie now described to herself how Tobias Emeritch had concluded his visit: he had given her a low leg which shook like the aspen leaf and covered her two hands with so many wet kisses that her fingers felt like sops. Why did he have to place his hand over his moth-eaten vest and swear that he would return to her after he had recuperated from their adventure? Also, the mouldy snudge had promised to bring her a box of chocolates. That exasperated her; did he take her for a simpleton? Lizzie could stomach almost anything—a poor appetite, diarrhea and even mislaying her glasses and keys—but when somebody said he would give her even a package of chewing gum and then did not keep his word, she raged about it for weeks. What could she do with a miserly bachelor who arrived to court her with nothing else but himself?

On the eleventh day she found a letter in her tin mailbox outside the gate. Before tearing open the envelope, she read: Timothy Andrew Smithingate, Counselor-at-Law. She quaked; who was suing her? Lizzie had a mordant apprehensiveness of the law, though she had no reason for it. Shaking all over, she sat down on the wooden steps of the front porch. Maybe she should not examine this epistle. Was this a court action? Was one of her tenants leaving without paying the rent? Why couldn't she drop everything into her saucepan, cover it with gravy, let it simmer and then gulp it down so that she could forget about it? Frequently she swallowed a regret or an insult so that she would not taste it afterwards.

Unable to control herself, she began to peruse the letter:

Dear Madam:
My benevolent client, Mr. Tobias Emeritch, a most circumspect gentleman of venerable means, has requested me to send you his appropriate appreciation for receiving him on the 16th day of September. He wishes also to call to your attention that this was in every sense of the word an informal, and an extra-legal visit. After some somber reflection, he deemed it advisable to make it absolutely clear that he is a retired man, and if you compass my meaning, that he is retired in every respect.

As it is imperative to eradicate any misconceptions you have regarding the social amenities between a gentleman and a lady, he wishes to convey, and without flatulent ambiguities, that he does not have the comprehensive appetites of the ordinary person. Albeit he finds matrimony despicable from almost any point of view, he does not care to give you the impression that he would offer a vehement repulse to such a step, which at this moment he has no intention of taking.

Nonetheless, he would not be averse to calling on you, could he be assured by you that he had no heart in it whatever.

It would avoid any embarrassment for either of you, could you express yourself in a letter, addressed to me, guaranteeing that you will never bring any action whatsoever against him for heart balm or alienation of affections or even, if I do not sound morose or abnormal, for adultery. It is of the utmost importance that Mr. Tobias Emeritch can feel that he is, as it were, sitting easy on his properties, securities, mortgages and sundry investments. After I have heard from you, I shall advise him accordingly.

Very truly yours,

Timothy Andrew Smithingate

While Lizzie studied this document, Tobias Emeritch himself was crouching behind the hedge; his mechanical buggy was parked a little way down the gravel road. Noticing that there was no postage stamp on the envelope, she suddenly looked up—and saw Tobias standing before her. His cheeks were hanging and plaintive, and when she said nothing to him, he cleared the mist out of his throat and, leaning on his umbrella, told her that if she did not invite him to come into her house he would catch cold.

Leading the way up the steps, she opened the door for him. Once inside the house, he wandered about aimlessly until he blurted forth: "If I'm not too bold in mentioning it, would you be so kind as to inform me which is the direction to the public convenience?" But Lizzie had her mind on the missive from the attorney. He became quite excited: "Excuse me, but I'm in a big rush; where's the blue room?" She walked toward the water closet and turned on the electricity, even though there was daylight, to show him how a noble-hearted person should act.

While waiting, she searched each word that the lawyer had written her and memorized his name: Timothy Andrew Smithingate. She wondered whether Tobias would lay out money for an attorney when there was not even a stamp on the envelope.

When he returned to the parlor he still had his hat on, his muffler wound around him and the umbrella in his right hand; his galoshes were on his feet and the overcoat upon his back.

She expostulated with him: "My God, it makes me sweat to look at you! The least you can do is to remove your overcoat—unless you're trying to suffocate me."

All of a sudden Lizzie's head cleared, and holding the letter aloft, her eyes dancing behind the tortoise-shell glasses, she queried him, "Who is Timothy Andrew Smithingate?"

He wet his lips, for although it was damp, he was dry, and hesitantly answered, "Timothy was a well-to-do building contractor who also had a cement factory. He died in 1908 or '12; I'm not positive—it is impossible to keep a record of all the corpses you know."

Lizzie's mouth filled with glee, and she jibed, "Don't you even know your own lawyer's name?"

Her triumph deepened the wrinkles in Tobias Emeritch's face. Momentarily his jaw hung like a bodkin, his nose grew and he whimpered, "Why should a man of my age recollect anything? Soon as something comes to my mind it grieves me to death. Besides, if a counselor-at-law isn't clever enough to remember his own name, what's in it for me to remind him of it."

Seeing that there was nothing to be gained by pressing him further, she suggested that she give him a violet ray treatment. Tobias Emeritch was fidgety; why is it that a man always baits himself and has not enough patience to wait for the woman to do it? Tears of laughter rinsed Lizzie's eyes, and after she had removed her glasses and wiped them, she asked him, "How is it that a man of your mature years has never been married?"

Tobias answered, "I was saving my strength."

"Well," retorted Lizzie, "judging by your appearance, you didn't accumulate much."

That remark fell out of her mouth unexpectedly; she had vowed to be gentle. She hoped she could get somewhere with this parsimonious curmudgeon if she handled him carefully.

Tobias was hoarding his own conceptions; it had occurred to him that perhaps it would be much cheaper to take a wife than to hire a housekeeper. His stale cheeks almost looked hectic. The letter had been a mistake, and now that she possessed that letter, which was doubtless grounds for legal action, the wisest step he could take was to marry her. Of course, it was also exceedingly foolish and improvident. What a harrowing situation for him! He would be up all night, scheming, arguing, passing water and complaining to her, although she was not present, and demanding that she return the letter. He found a tear on his trenched cheeks. What consolation was there in the fact that he had not aged, for he had never been young? It was tiresome to hear Ebner tell him every day that he would outlive him or to listen to his sister Martha complaining that the windows were rattling and that air was coming through them. Could one acquire a legal helpmeet and come out ahead? A consumptive had a better chance of recovering than a married man.

Wondering how long it would take to rouse him, Lizzie asked him again, "Why don't you do something with your life besides saving it?"

That nettled Tobias. She was always telling him to do something. Well, one had to answer a woman or she would master him: "Do you think that the possibilities of life are unlimited? After you've awakened in the morning, you eat, if you're gluttonous, and then, pardon me, no offense intended, you relieve yourself. If Ebner is asleep, because he wants to live longer, and Martha is too tired to ask you to close the windows tighter, you open the door and then shut it. If you have the temperament of Ponce de León or Columbus, you circumnavigate your room ten to twelve times. After that you go out for a walk; there is always, of course, a gross acquaintance who stops you and tells you that the sun is out, and that his doctor has advised him that his prostate gland is in tiptop shape.

"You wrack your brain for a couple of hours and wonder how you can demolish the remaining part of a horrible day. One should postpone every decision in order not to make a mistake; still, everybody is in such a hurry that he cannot wait to get to his grave. But say that it is already nightfall, then I often read the tragedies of August Strindberg, who really abhorred life; think of it, you only get one genius like that in a century."

Thoroughly impatient, Lizzie got a pen and a bottle of Waterman's ink: "Can you make up your mind, mister? This is no romance, and it's not strictly business either; but what's right is right. It may be that you're too cautious and you will discover that nobody in the world will look out for you but me, and if wed, am I not entitled to something? We're a lost couple, worse apart than together. Be noble, please, and set aside a few stocks and shares, a few thousand dollars. Keep most of what you have for yourself. Otherwise, what have you to offer me but your name? What's in Tobias for a woman, or in Mrs. Emeritch? Frankly, I find more honor in being Lizzie Dalberg; it's an educated name, and not common. I was born into my name and I didn't start from nowhere. Make a little contract with me, since you're so hasty to run to an attorney's office after one visit."

At this point, Lizzie felt suddenly reluctant to enter into such a bleak and desperate arrangement. She wished that she had not sold her upright Bach piano, so that she could run over her scales and sing in her high thin treble:

> Beautiful garden of roses,
> Kissed by the golden dew . . .

Had she reached that juncture in her own life at which it was essential to relinquish all her tenderest expectations? Why had it come to pass in this way? She recognized that this lonely old miser with his decrepit hopes was as miserable as she, and that neither of them had anything left. But, O my God, and my heaven, there is my son . . . if he could only come to my rescue.

Tobias Emeritch was oblivious of Lizzie. She might have thought her guest was asleep or dead, had she not seen his heaving hat and ruminative overcoat. At moments he arched his eyebrows, and then he shrugged his coat lapels, as if he thought that no matter what he did it would be amiss. Who knew better than he that a man could do more harm to himself than anybody could do to him?

Besides, why should he heed what she was saying? What had he to do with woman's gaggling? The best conversation is a monologue in which no one else can meddle. He renewed his musings: My watchword is prudence. When a female folds you in her arms, she is winding a sheet around you, and knotting it too. Luckily there's no woman who can feast on my jaw, or gnaw my sunken temples, or dig her rotten, amorous molar into my joints. I am grateful to admit that I have no marrow, and no wife will ever make a chronicle of my anatomy. No, it is positively clear: a bedfellow is a bailiff, a summons, a foreclosure, a pauper's oath and a hearse.

Lizzie was out of patience; she was determined that she would find out what were his views. That she scarcely knew him was not important, and that she might know him better was her corrosive predicament. After all, he had answered her matrimonial advertisement and his second visit, like the first, was already so prolix that again she realized she would be too tired after he left to take an enema.

She had gotten the pen and the ink from the dresser, but he had taken no notice of it. Did she have to command him again? Should she say: See here, Mister Tobias, I just don't have the constitution to wait any longer for you. If you're not old enough to know what you are doing, the situation is hopeless. Never mind your years—for which I forgive you—but speak to the point; are you here for a wedding, or to trifle with my valuable time? You cannot expect me to wait on you—and your brother and sister—without making some reasonable marriage settlement upon me.

Yet he was such a suspicious soul that he might take her for a pickpurse or a hard, scheming woman. At this point she did speak to him: "Can't you see that I don't mean any harm to you, and that I wouldn't hurt a fly unless it fell into the soup? Why don't we settle matters and come to an understanding? I don't care to be disrespectful, but if you're not a good seventy-two, and you should be grateful . . ."

But this was an impure remark, and he interrupted her: "Well, is that the way to address a guest? Do you think I'm such an inexperienced bookkeeper that I don't realize that you're much older than you admit? I write down everything that people tell me. On Wednesday you hear that a woman is a grass widow, but Friday she tells you she never had a lover, and Saturday that her marriage was annulled, and on Monday she's a virgin. People are far more changeable than the weather; no matter what the season is, you know you can expect a storm, a hurricane, a tornado, rain, snow, sleet or hail. That's pretty constant—but can you anticipate what a human being is going to do or say?"

Lizzie looked at him; it was the severest glance she had ever given him. She had already had her secret revenge; taking a silent inventory of his ramshackle frame and habits was sufficient: he doesn't drink, he has no need of tobacco, he won't indulge in an innocent appetizer . . . what part of his body does he use?

True, she might not be forty-four. Well, she did not appear much older than that except when she was fatigued or discouraged. There could be no doubt that he was closer to eighty than seventy, and should she be collecting relics or picking up bones in alleys like a stray dog? This lucid and comfortable judgment assuaged her considerably, so that she was able to become very soothing: "Why don't you step out into the back yard and look at my chickens?"

Tobias Emeritch stated flatly that he did not relish the stench of poultry, and Lizzie, no less positive, claimed that her Rhode Island Reds and Plymouth Rocks were as good as a sedative to excitable people. Prompted by a gentle and good-natured push, he rose and accompanied her. When they were out in the yard, she picked up the bucket filled with chicken feed and cast the grain about the pen like a professional poulterer. Tobias gnawed his tongue, which caused her to reproach him: "Do you have to stare at the hens with your mouth open—and without any color in your face?"

"Is it necessary," he replied, "for me to observe your chickens with the blushing cheeks of a lover?"

The sight of poultry seemed to make him listless. If she were more hospitable, she might open this tomb. Actually, he appeared more somnolent in the open air than inside. She returned to the back porch and looked into the secondhand wooden icebox which contained at that moment a watery squib of butter in a chipped dish and a cup of cold string beans. Still brooding, Lizzie prayed that they could come to terms; she had no intention of pauperizing him, and the thought that anything ill might befall him dismayed her.

Who wants to ride in a limousine following a hearse? Obviously, nobody would marry him for his jocular disposition, and maybe he was not much of a companion, but he was an improvement over the four walls.

While she was busy on the porch, Tobias was at the dresser, picking through her receipts from the electric light company and inspecting a postcard or two; then he noiselessly opened the drawer, looking for love letters that she might be receiving from other correspondents. It was not simply avarice that consumed his skin; he was a profoundly jealous man. He pulled open the door to her clothes closet, where Lizzie stored many of her memorials, and found Captain Henry Smith's Stetson hat. He took it out and turning it upside down put his nose against the sweatband. When Lizzie caught him, she ran up to him with the most startling agility and snatched the hat from his hand.

"What are you doing in my private clothes closet?"

"This is a man's hat," he shouted, "your lover's, no doubt."

"Don't be a fool; it's my son's," she retorted.

He snorted: "It smells much older to me!"

Tobias was already resolved to make an unexpected appearance at her house in the close future. He was determined that although he had no inclination to cohabit with a woman, he was not going to be a cuckold either.

That Tobias Emeritch might be furtive did not surprise her, but who would expect the blackamoor's passion in this almost disembodied figure? She tempered her scolding with majestic courtesy: "Sir, since you are a bloodhound in my house, smelling my oldest receipts, postcards and letters from bygone friends, why are you so backward in other respects? You need not be bashful; please take the pen, and there's the tablet of paper, and write down in plain language just what provisions you intend to make for my security. Since you are a suspicious character and imagine I'm hiding a man in the dresser drawer, why do you want to be the husband of a woman in whom you have no confidence? People must have a certain amount of trust in one another."

Tobias Emeritch did not fail to hear that one. "That's fine," he remarked defiantly, "so why don't you start trusting me?"

But she was not behindhand herself and saw it was imperative to have a swift answer for such a sharper: "Mr. Tobias, you're not the type to have too much faith in; tell me, honestly, do you have any confidence in yourself?"

"Why should I have," was his own rapid response, "when I know I'm likely to change my mind before the day is over? So if I doubt my own word, should I believe that somebody else is any better than I am?"

Endeavoring to divert him, she dropped into her gentlest manner, almost cooing: "Look, the cabbage soup is excellent, and I have a sheep's stomach stuffed with roasted chestnuts, kidney beans, liver and cinnamon toast."

He sat down most unwillingly. Very gingerly she tied one of Popkin's gold-embroidered napkins around his neck. The sound of "sheep's stomach" did not improve his appetite, and he ate the meat with restrained disgust; at the same time he could not keep the napkin out of his mouth and he thought he was chewing moth balls. Beside herself with anguish and desperation, Lizzie did not know how to please him. He was spoiling the meal for her. She admonished him, doing her best to hold herself together and not shriek: "Excuse me a moment, and I can go to the hen yard and get a tender broiler or a fryer for you. In a quarter of an hour you will be the happiest man in Northmoor."

The blood ran out of Tobias' cheeks, and he wished to make a statement, but was unable to do so. Since Lizzie could not understand his mood, she imagined that what he actually wanted, but was too timorous to express himself so boldly in another's house, was a rich dessert. She enquired in a pleading tone, "What about a plate of strawberries with sour cream just to top everything off?"

Tobias Emeritch, in a helpless, queasy voice, beseeched her, "Don't mention food to me—it upsets my stomach."

That raised Lizzie's anger. "Well, you don't increase my appetite either!" she answered.

Apologizing to her, he sniveled and muttered, "Whatever I say is wrong; what kind of a couple will we make? Two persons together should be harmonious with one another. Though I don't get along very well with myself, I don't see how I could put up with two of me. Admittedly, you're different from me, but aren't we all the same?" In a louder voice he proceeded, "Has anybody got a lien on your properties? Are you in arrears? I sincerely hope you take care of the electric bill promptly. All these things count up and are genuine evidence of a person's sound judgment. Who needs an extravagant housekeeper? Frankly, it would pain me deeply to discover later on, when it's too late, that you buy ice in September, or that you put on the lights in the evening when you could save this unnecessary expense by retiring at six o'clock. You hear of people burning gas to take the chill out of a room when they could have gotten into their overcoats or thrown foot rugs over their shoulders. We live in a period of unimaginable waste. What sense is there in sending one's trousers to the tailor's to be pressed; what can you do with a crease? Think of having a suit cleaned; anybody with an ounce of intelligence knows that sooner or later it will pour."

This aimless conversation would never come to an end; it was impossible to relieve this old man of his monetary aches. "Oh, you make me tired," she told him, as though by now she wanted him to go home. "It's sure hard on a woman's nerves to be pestered by a man who is always under your feet, but you worry me sick because even after you arrive—and sit down in your coat—you don't seem to have enough strength to make an appearance. Never in my life and in all my experience did I ever see anybody fade away like you do. After all, this is a courtship, although I must say you're some dandy of the heart. Don't you think you ought to put yourself out a little, so that when you're present I don't feel that you're absent?" And she asked quite testily, "Where are the chocolates?"

Lizzie took him by the arm, pinching his sleeve, marched him out to the front porch, and they walked over to the grocer's. The skies were extremely low; the clouds were black and hilly. Lizzie had let go of him because he moved lethargically. She went on ahead, Tobias trailing behind her, and crying out, "My dear, Madam Lizzie, it's going to rain; let me hold the umbrella over your head."

Turning around, she called back to him, "Let it rain, it won't cost you anything," and she moved faster, while he bleated and begged her to wait for him.

At the grocer's, a wooden shanty down the road, Lizzie asked for three cans of Dutch Cleanser, two cakes of tar soap, five pounds of potatoes, a large sack of granulated sugar, a bag of flour, a box of black pepper, a loaf of rye bread, a package of macaroni, a pound of sweet butter and two quarts of milk. When Tobias Emeritch saw her handling the grapes and feeling the apples to see whether they were hard and had sturdy stems on them, he became extremely agitated and complained, "For heaven's sake, save a few articles in the store for the next customer; are you going into the wholesale grocery business?"

Lizzie moved about to face Tobias Emeritch, who was shaking. This was an ambush; he knew it—she would make him pay the bill. He started for the door but stumbled against his umbrella, and Lizzie pulled him back. She was most emphatic: "I forgot to bring my pocketbook; be so kind as not to keep the grocer waiting; I need a little change."

Pulling out his wallet that had been cooking in his trousers for a year, he cautiously held it and used his free hand to peck pennies, dimes and nickels from his pocket. He managed to lay only the loose change in the palm of her hand. While counting out 68 cents, he stuffed the wallet into his coat pocket. But Lizzie immediately plucked it from that crevice, took out three filthy one-dollar bills and paid the grocer. She kept the 68 cents and the small change the grocer returned.

As soon as they were outdoors Tobias Emeritch said, "Remember, you're a lady of honor, and I expect a receipt from you for $3.68; that's not chicken feed, you know." She was halfway home by then, but he went on, "Is it necessary to inform you that Jeremiah the prophet said we live in a land of robbers and thieves?"

Moving his head up and down ruefully, he paid no attention to the ruts in the road. A heavy storm was coming up, and Tobias stood still to conserve his energies and to gaze with wonderment at the emerald meadowland opposite the duplex, and at a bull of tremendous girth which was looking back at his offending, gaping face with ferocious hostility. The rain began to fall, quickly gathering into a puddle, and Tobias slipped and went down into it. The umbrella flew open and was blown over into the glistening grassy pasture; the bull pranced toward it as it descended to the ground, and butting it first with his head, then gored the cotton material, and after stamped on it.

Lizzie, far in advance, paused and caught a glimpse of Tobias, who was absolutely motionless. She became apprehensive, fearing that he had been struck by lightning or had had a stroke and was now paralyzed. With quick and sure steps she hurried back to his side; at first she searched his sagging and morbid face, and then as she raised her eyes, she saw the bull treading the umbrella. Lizzie took Tobias by the arm, turned him about and led him toward the porch.

Her clothes soaked and strands of her hair matted down, she pushed him up the steps; they entered the parlor and then went into the dining room adjacent to the rear porch. Removing his coat, and then his jacket and shirt, she took a towel out of the trunk and rubbed his shoulders and back;

after that she found an old shirt of her son's that she made him put on. It fitted him like a nightgown. Lizzie lighted the kerosene stove and made him sit down on a varnished kitchen chair in front of it.

Tobias slept, upright in the chair, for over two hours, and when he awakened he felt so tranquil that he parted his lips to smile—but then thought better of it. Quite conscious —which he found a most uncomfortable sensation—he remembered the $3.68 which he would probably never recover. His rheumatism began to bother him, and then he had a cramp in one foot. He whimpered, "You always want me to spend money." But he dropped this thought which unduly inflamed him and asked, "What does your son do?"

At that Lizzie braced her shoulders and standing erect before him as if she were delivering the valedictory at a commencement exercise, she cleared her throat and confided, "Oh, he's way up in the world; he writes books—and he gets so much praise for them."

Tobias Emeritch scowled and replied, "Does he put it in the bank?"

That made Lizzie indignant: "You call yourself an educated gentleman; tell me, would a cultured man go to a bank teller with a satchel full of praise and say to him that he would like to start a savings account with it?" Lizzie fetched a copy of Gautier's *Golden Fleece* and showed it to Tobias—who inspected it and pronounced that it was a French novel.

Tobias had no inclination to bruise himself further over the $3.68 and considered that it would be more convenient to mention something else: "What are your relations with your grocer?"

Fuming at this, Lizzie demanded that he take his coat, galoshes and hat and leave her courteous house at once. Tobias was in a grave quandary; where should he go? He searched the rooms for his umbrella until Lizzie reminded him of the bull.

When Lizzie said good-bye to him, he realized that after he had driven back he would have nobody to see but brother Ebner, who was entombed in his bed, and his sister, who would complain about the rattling windows. He was undecided, and that softened Lizzie; she told him to go home and think it over and, though she made it clear that he would not get back his $3.68, she would marry him if he would only show her a small amount of consideration.

At first she was about to let him go out by himself, but seeing how loosely he filled his shambly clothes, she took him by the arm; after he cranked the car and crept into it, she sorrowfully waved her hand at him.

Now it was February, the month of winds, freezing hopes and lamentations, and the rain gabbled against the windowpanes. Lizzie had not heard from Tobias for five months. Three times he had come to Lizzie's house to drive her to Kansas City to take out a marriage license, but on each occasion they quarreled. He had sworn that he would see his attorney and have him draw up papers so that Lizzie could have title to a little wooden cottage and $5,000 in cash, and though he would press his rigid, empurpled lip against the shoulder strap of her kitchen apron and apologize, he never did anything about it.

Claiming, as he put it, that he was "property-poor," he warned her that he could not afford to give her more than ten dollars a week for housekeeping expenses; after an altercation he increased that amount to twelve dollars . . . but a fortnight later alleged he had promised her only nine dollars as her allowance for seven days. Then he declared that only after she was his wife, would he sign over the bungalow and the cash to her, as a wedding present. She ought to take his word for it, he pronounced; but Lizzie averred that his promises were already overdone, and would be cold meat by that time. Haughtily he let her know that he had no intention of dying a pauper; to which she retorted that she could not see how he could die or live any poorer than he already did.

Then her son returned. By now he had come to understand that his mother was arrayed in broken and forlorn rags because her life was in tatters. When he was alone, or far from her, he vowed that he would never chide her again for her slovenly appearance. But when he peered into the icebox, or gaped at her sick, sniveling stockings, or examined a pile of dishes filled with the leftover carrion of several meals, he still railed at her.

How many times he had rebuked himself. What dotages of books had wasted his nature? Was he not tossed about from one book to another? And had he not strode through the pages of volumes as if he were in the drunken streets of Babylon and wallowed in the mire of novels and philosophy until his eyes were so muddied by vanity and custom that he could not see, hear or feel?

One day, out by himself in his mother's back yard, he was watching a straggling hen peck the rain as it splashed and wormed around in the ground.

He resolved that he would fall at his mother's feet and beg her to pardon him for all his sins. O, miserable, deformed son, your mother has long ago forgiven you; are you not the son of her afflictions, and of her dark, peopleless forests?

The son ate his remorse, but it was mouldy bread. His mother was grieving but near her tomb sat a Gadarene demon, his tongue. Was it not he, rather than his mother, whose days were the sluttish songs of habit, and who had a heart that had died? From the beginning he had been a guilty and fallen son.

Now if he were not bedewed with her sorrows, he would be sterile, and no fire, hail or snow could burn or melt him. At this instant he must go to her and kiss the latchets of her torn, grubby boots . . . but he did not. Worse than the paralysis of feeling would be some mock show of self-abasement, for it is a terrible sin to look or appear humble, or to adopt the lamb's meek visage, when one has not the gift for it.

He panted after kindness, but the waters of his brooks were dry. He said, "I love the good and hate the evil." But a flea sat in the corners of his mouth and it bit him, and when he scratched it, his virtues tickled like vices. And he roared like the bear and mourned as the dove: "That foul act which I have not yet done I have already committed in a wicked dream." Then he made a fell prophecy: all people have the automatic impulse to harm others, and while one is stroking the neck of the beloved he has an involuntary desire to break it.

He had been estranged from the womb and would injure whatever he loved. Having no water within him, he came upon a pool, and in it he saw the visage of Cain and knew that wherever he went, or whatever he did, he would be a wilderness.

Coming back into the dining room, he gently implored his mother to put on a fresh dress. She went to her trunk, which, aside from her meager possessions—papers, letters, a shirtwaist and a watch—was like the holy of holies in the temple, for it contained nothing but manna, which is the remembrance of hunger and past hopes.

She returned in a faded silk blouse and apron. She had pinned on the gold watch which she had given herself when she married Popkin. They sat down at the table in the dining room and played casino. The laughter had long since expired in her; it had been graved since the time that Captain Smith abandoned her. On the rarest occasions, when she heard a laugh rise from her crypt, she listened to the cock crow and it stalked away and vanished like an unclothed ghost. When a smile appeared on her face, it was the wan image of a former, carnal smile.

Although she seemed distracted, and to be paying slight

attention to the cards, Lizzie had already won two games from him. He began to watch her shuffle the deck and on a sudden he recalled that in both games his mother had gotten every point—the ten of diamonds, the four aces, the deuce of spades, and big and little casino. In the midst of their third game she shuttered the cards so nimbly that he reached over the table before she could deal them and turned up the ten of diamonds that she had cleverly put on the bottom of the deck. No matter how closely he watched her, she dealt either the aces or the deuce of spades to herself, and then the other points. Roaring at her, he stood up and denounced her as a cheat; as he rose, the morning newspaper fell from his coat pocket to the table. Lizzie adjusted her tortoise-shell glasses and picked up the paper—simply to do something else, so that she would not grieve over her son's sick temper. Motionless, she read: "Tobias Emeritch, aged 74, a prominent merchant and philanthropist, has died, leaving $50,000 to his brother, Ebner Emeritch, a wealthy retired manufacturer, and to his unmarried sister, Martha."

Her face was immutable, and when her son turned away from the window, she took her hand from her throat which looked as though it were pieces of threadbare woollens she had patched together. She whispered, "My son, I am an old woman."

He stood in her tears and placed his hand over her suffering wrinkles. Then he went out again into the rain. He cast his heart out of his mouth, and although he wept and wept, when he stared at the dirt into which his heart had fallen, it had grown into a stone. Suddenly a cry like a sword passed through his bowels, and he moaned, "Mother, mother, guard me from myself."

# XII

*"Abba, Abba, it is finished."*
JOHN

There are five trash towns in greater New York, five garbage heaps of Tofeth. A foul, thick wafer of iron and cement covers primeval America, beneath which cry the ghosts of the crane, the mallard, the gray and white brants, the elk and the fallow deer. A broken obelisk at Crocodopolis has stood in one position for thousands of years, but the United States is a transient Golgotha.

In 1926, my mother had decided to join me in Astoria, a cheap German borough with grum and gritty delicatessen and hardware stores and the dead bricks of tenements. But after a year in Astoria we moved to Bensonhurst, then a rheumy marshland. A low, squab mist hovers over the bay which damps the job-lot stucco houses. Many months later I found an apartment in a block about ten minutes by elevated train from Queens Plaza. Queens is an immense warehouse for New York cadavers, and I had taken the greatest care to find rooms that were remote from the grave-yards. But after I had signed the lease and was standing at the window overlooking high, shaggy iodine-colored bushes, I found they concealed the cut-rate Virgin Marys and Christs of Calvary Cemetery.

My mother had become an old woman; her apron was much skinnier, and the sleeves of her underwear looked ill and starved. Now she seldom scrutinized her decayed skin. Could her lips really be as faded and sapless as they appeared to her when she thoughtlessly picked up her looking glass? And yet she continued to cling to one belief: others will die but I will not. At moments she could not believe that there was not one person noble enough to say to her: "Here is a morsel of a smile; you are not forsaken." But the world was Pilate who had washed his hands of her.

Too old now for barbering, Lizzie fancied she could become a matchmaker. After she had dismissed this chimera, she considered returning to Kansas City; she still had her houses amidst the chattering weeds and the antiseptic sunflowers of Northmoor. Away from the Midwest, she now imagined her days there had been good. How she hankered for the alder, the tender back yard and the Indian summer crickets.

Poring over the obituary notices in the papers had now become her daily pastime; it was also a specious consolation. When she read: "Samuel B. Forbes, importer of ceramics, deceased in his 91st year," she rejoiced; she was sure she had as many years, if not more, stored away for her in the Lord's garner. But when she examined another woeful piece of tidings: "Jezebel Mullen MacMahon, 47, dead of liver disease," she declared that the woman must have led a dissipated life and worn out her organs. Then she looked at the classified advertisement columns: *Help Wanted Female* was only good pasture for a typewriter chippy, so she turned to *Lost and Found*. Oliver Goodness offered a reward for a ring he had dropped in a Fifth Avenue coach. She could write to him and that might start a correspondence. Speculation of that sort might lead to a partnership in a small broker's office. Perhaps it would be better to go to Canal Street and track down Popkin. She knew his cousin had been a salesman in a haberdashery there. Popkin must now be at least sixtynine, or more, a good seventy-two; that gave her confidence.

Having so little else to occupy her, my mother had begun to brood over the $3,000 Popkin had swindled from her in 1909. Whatever she deemed good or bad had occurred to her in the past. She preferred a galled memory to anything that was now happening to her.

She thought that maybe she did not look so seamy as she imagined; perhaps she could threaten to sue him for damages, whereupon he would remarry her. Had Popkin ever done her any wrong, and what effect had he had upon her life? Had he altered it one tittle? Popkin was weak rather than vicious, and weak people cannot trouble our depths; the heart is indifferent so long as it is not wounded.

One Saturday afternoon I returned to the flat and found there a man in a loose brown jacket; he wore a white shirt without a tie and a faded maroon vest that sagged comfortably below his navel. Bad food as well as a certain style of thinking had given him a lumpish appearance. Was he the same person I had known in 1909, or a dilapidated replica of him? What had happened to the sharp and well-trimmed pate of the jewelry salesman? Was he wearing a new face or a different experience? Obviously, he wished to convey the impression that he was natural and skeptical; his meals bulged confidently in his belly, but his face was seasoned with weariness. I learned that Popkin was now a salesman in a clothing store on Delancey Street.

What might Popkin's thoughts have been as he studied Lizzie after thirty years? He must have been glad that he had left Kansas City. How her throat had failed! What poulterer, he sighed, had plucked her hair? A man like himself could age yet be even more seductive than he was when he was a raw prentice among the ladies. When he sauntered in the evening along Second Avenue amidst the Jewish intelligentsia, it was not uncommon for a smartly rouged widow or a bored adulteress to look at his experienced nose and to appraise his mouth.

Lizzie sat on the metal cot opposite Popkin. She was rigid in the dated lace dress that he had bought for her in Palestine. That was the only concession she had made to him. Otherwise, she was formal and cold—far more than she intended to be. She wanted him to know that she was a prize, and believed that this would be made more plain if both behaved as if they had never been in the same bed together.

The two scrutinized one another and each shook his head. Popkin took a handkerchief from his pocket and flopped it about his face to dry a tear. He tried his utmost not to show that he was weeping a little for her as he mumbled to himself, "What a relic the poor thing is; anybody can see she is rapidly sinking."

Lizzie fastened her eyes on his pouchy neck and then she looked at his stomach. "Why does he eat rotten delicatessen food," she thought. "Look how much gas he shows; a man cannot afford to let himself go like that. If old Popkin had not once been my husband, I would not have recognized the slob. Could you believe it, he used to be as neat as a pin."

Popkin folded one lip over the other and he made some sounds, but she did not catch his remark: "Where did the old girl get that costume? Does she still think it's 1895?"

Lizzie was rancorous; she could hardly keep from blurting out, "You old fool, did you come to pay me a visit or to talk to yourself?" But reconsidering her diatribe, she added to herself; "Maybe he's so advanced in years that his mind's weak; you can't fool nature. Still there's no excuse for acting like a boor; he could at least pay me a compliment for putting on the dress he bought me with my money."

Before Popkin had arrived, Lizzie had been crowing; no mistake about it, she had Popkin right where she wanted him. She would now settle with him—but in a ladylike manner. He had spent the savings account that had come from years of sweating over her scissors and comb.

Their conversation was not going well. The deliberate

aloofness of Popkin nettled her, and she pushed her skirts more closely around her. "What kind of a bargain does he imagine he is? Does he think I am going to chase him?" She stirred a little, moving her nostrils—she was not positive but believed she could smell another woman on him. Maybe, she speculated, she had better pump him and see just where she stood.

"You know," she began, "eating in restaurants will give you a nervous stomach, Louis. It makes a man look pasty and sour. Don't tell me—I'm still from Missouri—that you've become a housekeeper." At this Lizzie let out a small, forced giggle.

Her remarks had such a disagreeable effect upon Popkin that he commenced to taste his mouth and he made a face. This was a furtive attack and most ill-mannered. He knew that he should not have accepted her invitation; he had grown old in one visit. Well, he would have to deal with her in a more candid way.

"Lizzie," he said, "I don't believe in marriage anymore. I admit a man needs a companion, and I've got one—a Lucy Stoner. She carries her own name, and I take care of mine. We're a pair of free lovers."

Smarting from this outrageous disclosure, Lizzie could scarcely control her nerves. What impudence this sloppy codger had! Did he come here to boast about a chippy, a low common-law wife? She wiped her face which was smeared with perspiration and held her throat so that she would not snivel. Then she snorted, "You can't fool me, Louis, love is never free; I guess I've had the experience and ought to know!" And she gave Popkin such a strong and passionate glance that he lost most of his mundane slouch.

Popkin was ready to leave, and when he took out his watch Lizzie stumbled toward the kitchen sink to get a glass of water. She removed her glasses and wiped her eyes with a stale dishcloth. She had been patient and noble long enough. Either he would have to make a cash settlement with her out of court, or she might marry him, but she would be quite outspoken. A woman would have no picnic with such a bilious rounder. But should he be unreasonable, she would be strict and sue him for breach of promise, heart balm and damages. With interest on the money he had swindled from her, and an additional lump sum she was entitled to for the grief he had caused her, she would have about $10,000. When she came back from the sink, she was about to tell him that she had had brain fever after he had gone to Jerusalem and that her hair had fallen out, and not all of it had grown back again, but she restrained herself. It was poor business for a woman to call a man's attention to her defects. Show the average man a few gray hairs or a wart he has never observed before, and he becomes listless and stays out nights.

That Popkin looked like small change did not concern Lizzie; she craved her imaginary advantage. Popkin was still glancing at the doorknob and wondering how he could reach it. Before he had come, he could not wait to air his radical opinions about marriage. He had expected a large glass of Russian tea with lemon, but looking about the room he was puzzled because he could not see a samovar. How differently everything had fallen out. He had wanted to talk about Kansas City—about Delaware and Wyandotte Streets, the Paseo, and Fountain Place, where they had had a six-room flat when they were married.

He got up and went over to Lizzie and, taking hold of her hand, said, "Lizzie, why don't I buy the boy a suit? You know he's like my own flesh and blood." He desired to show himself to be a man who could never forget the obligations he owed to a kinsman.

But Lizzie did not like his hand. "He sweats so much," she said half-aloud, pulling her fingers away from his. Besides, she had no intention of accepting a $25 Delancey Street suit as payment for the $3000 he owed her, and for which she had received only a hand-embroidered bedspread with two pillowcases to match, a table cover with six nap-kins, a lace dress and a Hebrew parrot that cocked his beak and shouted: "*Aleph, Beth, Gimel!*" Lizzie was certain that Popkin had handed over most of the money to his former wife, as she had never seen any of the diamonds he was supposed to have bought in the Holy Land and smuggled into America.

Giving Popkin a cool face Lizzie announced, "If you want to be a gentleman, Popkin, and do what is right, you could give up that chippy." She stopped short; she realized that she had made a narrow-minded remark, and what was worse, she had lowered herself by pleading with him. When her glance fell to the floor, she noticed that his socks had dropped down about his heels. It was hardly refined for a lady to be gaping at a man's nude skin, and what interest could she have in Popkin's leg; still she was so repelled by the sock that dangled and hung over his shoe, and the gray, nasty flesh that he showed, that she was unable to take her eyes from that part of his body. Popkin became so uncomfortable that first he crossed his legs and then he pulled down his trousers and sat bolt upright and prim. This upset her and she detested Popkin the more because he acted as if she had been looking at him. Lizzie had always known how to keep her place, and no one could say she was not polite; but what sort of new fashion was this? By now her indignation was most agreeable, and she felt she had a real advantage over Popkin; she was quite elated and re-marked to herself, "That ugly rounder has no garters on; he's half undressed, just like a woman in a sporting house. In all my experience I never knew a gentleman to show his bare ankle in a public place."

As she glanced up again, Popkin was at the door. She could no longer repress her wrath and, as she wrung her hands, she exclaimed, "I've handled you with kid gloves long enough, Louis. I just can't afford to be noble-hearted; it's too much of a strain on my nerves."

Popkin crept out, and Lizzie sat down again on the cot. She took her revenge and rocked it in her arms. It was finished; what strength had she for a court case? Are there no triumphs? What can one do against a bad act? She always had chagrins which were supposed to be lessons in experience but which never prevented her from suffering another humiliation. Whatever made her think she could overcome anybody? Had she ever won an argument? Besides she had never had the skin for a quarrel; the least commotion boiled her veins.

If I have said little about myself, it has been too much; but I had far less intelligence than the fossil remains of the Testacea. Besides, what is more boring than the sensitive young man who desperately wants to have feelings? I looked everywhere for a Buddha, and found several lizards, foxes and the small rodentia on our venal and barren Patagonia. As for her whom St. Augustine calls the shake-rag goddess Pecunia, I had no luck with her at all. I dreaded useless and brutal drudgery; work that is bad and vulgar warps the hands and the human affections. Sir Thomas More speaks of those "silly poor wretches" who are "tormented with barren and unfruitful labor . . . [which] killeth them up."

I had resolved to be a writer and to clean out the Augean Stables of society, but there is no meat, bread or potatoes for Hercules the stableboy. After I had written three novels my plight was no better than that of the niata which starves to death when there is nothing on the pampas but a few twigs and reeds. Nor was I any more apt with a good book merely because I was in the world. Santa Teresa has said that she read many books without understanding any of them. Reading Plato's *Timaeus* was as squalid a pleasure as the bite of a louse; no matter how I studied the *Dialogues* I was still covered with the vermin of ignorance. And how men love to scratch themselves. After poring over the works of the sages I had no less spleen, bile or vanity, and I was just as vacant as I had been. The crow says: "Give me more life that I may be ever eating dung." In what way was I different from the crow in the *Mathnawi?*

The distance between my mother and me had grown. My life was now so hopeless that I wrote a book. All day I scribbled while listening to Beethoven's *Moonlight Sonata* on the phonograph. My mother staggered about, dropping a kettle or a fry-pan, and finally turned to me, begging, "Please turn that funeral song off. I just can't stand it, my son."

Was there some piteous ancestor wailing in my ribs? What I heard was the hymn of lineage: Ham begat Cush, and Terah bore Abraham . . . but where is Saul? I tried to piece together the image I had had when I was six years old of the man I believed to be my father and I collected his separate features—the licentious locks, the vulpine white teeth and the agile nose—even as the men at Jabesh-gilead had gathered together the bones of Saul, King in Israel, son of Kish. I pined for that other Saul, Paul of Tarsus, and I wept for every Saul that had lived. But Saul the barber was my anointed Anthropos.

On days when nothing filled my sore, raw spirit I went to Hebrew orthodox cemeteries in search of his headstone; could I find his name in an epitaph, maybe I would not be so broken and separated from all flesh. Every burial ground whispered to me, "Waif, stand before the Cave of Mach-pelah and mourn for the FATHER. The perverse son tells his soul that he abhors Abraham, Isaac and Jacob, but all flesh owes the price to the seed that begat it. If you curse your seed, who will quicken your tomb?"

Was I to be a castaway all my days? And could I only plant my ghost in the wilderness and eat my manna in waste places? Each time I have dropped a thought a dark forest has sprung up around me.

One night as I lay in bed, I heard a maggot wail, and it was torn into many parts, and it was Saul. It was separated from other groaning worms that were twined together and who recited: ". . . the sons of Levi were Gershon, Kehath and Merari, and the sons of Judah were ʿEr and Onan and Shelah and Perez and Koraḥ."

I asked, "Am I of their stock?" But Saul did not answer me.

When I bent over to caress the worm, it was piecemeal, and I turned my eyes against my breast and watched the various bits of myself crawling into the ground. Then I heard it say: "I am Saul your father. Though I have sinned much, do not renounce me lest you mangle your own worms; no man can flee from his own worms and not be an evil to himself."

Now in my dream I saw that many maggots were clinging to me, which I thought were Enoch, Noaḥ, Shem and Abraham, and then I beheld Jesus the paraclete. He had a lump on his neck that galled his whole back; the sensual auburn curls of Saul crowned his head, but the face was dominated by the long Nazarene nose of my mother. It was a wild, prophetic nose, and like the olive, the seer of the trees that grow in the vales of Schechem and on the plains of Gilead.

I looked in vain for the hands that were said to have made the oxgoads and the ploughs, but in the place of a rough workingman's hands were trembling feelings out of which he had fashioned the sayings and parables.

I asked the spectre, "Art thou Jesus?"

And he answered, "I am Yeshu of Nazareth."

Then I said, "Was Joseph the carpenter your father?"

His foot shook. I paused, fearing to vex the ghost. But I could not hold back the words from my hungry lips: "Was your mother Miriam the adulteress? Did she lie with Joseph's groomsman?"

The Nazarene spoke: "I think my mother was a natural woman; I always preferred the women who sinned to the foolish virgins who had no oil in their vessels. Tell me, is it

not a rumor throughout all Judea that the women of Nazareth are lovely wantons? Have the Pharisees forgotten that
the daughter of Lamech was called Na'amah, which means
beautiful pleasure, and was she ever denounced in Israel as a
transgressor? My real mother must have been Miriam
Megaddela Neshaya, Mary Magdalene, the women's hairdresser, because I loved her more than anyone in the earth."

These words were nails in my eyes, and they pained
me so bitterly that I could not see the voluptuous ringlets of
Saul. Did Miriam Megaddela Neshaya, the lady barber who
had dressed Yeshu's locks also shave and manicure customers
in Memphis, Louisville, New Orleans and Dallas? Now I
saw her standing at her regular chair, holding the comb and
scissors in her hands, and when she laid them down for a
moment, she folded the curls that hung over my forehead.
Who was sitting in her chair—the Nazarene or I? There
were large seals of bastardy on his chest and loins, and the
gore fell at his feet, and I bent down to kiss the illegitimate
blood.

I could hardly perceive his emaciated and nameless
stem, unfilled by the Father. Had he invented the genealogi-
cal tables in the Four Gospels? Was he the descendant of
David? Does not every bastard allege that he is of royal
seed and of the stock of Jesse? Who was his father? Saul?
Or God? Not once did he call for Joseph.

My cheeks shook because Jesus of Nazareth had no
lawful ancestors. "He has no spermal parent," I wept.

And I was bitter when I heard him address God in his
Aramaic tongue: "Father, Father, it is finished!"

In my dream the Galilean lake continued to pour its
waters through me as I repeated, "Abba, Father," and I said,
"I will walk the rest of my days over the Brook Kidron until
I find Saul."

He spoke again: "I was conceived in a lawless bed, but
I am a Jew of Nazareth, and the pure blood of Israel flows
through my veins. Since I was illegitimate, I was considered

*146*

as defiled as one who has a clubfoot or is blind in an eye, and therefore unfit to stand in holy places. But take heed lest you forget that the law is never the heart."

"But you were not alone," I said, pondering my own deserts. Then I added with a wry mouth, "I don't believe you had twelve friends, or even five as the rabbin claim."

He replied, "I pretended there were twelve disciples because Jacob, the father of Israel, had twelve sons, though not one of them was Yeshu of Nazareth. A waif, I was despised by everyone and taken for an uncouth fellow; for is it not asked, 'Can anything good come out of Nazareth?'

"A beggar in Bethany and at Capernaum, imprisoned in Tiberias, wretched in dissolute and simpering Tyre and Sidon, I was in exile everywhere. When I returned to Galilee, it no longer existed, because one cannot go back to anything. Were it possible to recapture the incident in Jerusalem and to drink the same evening at Gethsemane, I could believe that I had lived rather than died. Do you really think there is a world?

"You have a right to wonder if there were twelve beloved ones who trembled when I was ailing and who were as sudden as the aspens upon my pulses. You have not forgotten that he who warmed himself by the fire and swore that he did not know me went by the name of Shim'on Kefa, Simon Peter or Petros, the Rock!"

"Who are you, then?" I pleaded, and I heard the echo: "No-place, no-time, no-body."

"Are you Jesus Balaam the sorcerer?"

"Why call ye me Balaam? Am I he who knew not even when his ass perceived the angel? Was I so callow in the arts of contemplation?"

"Is it true," I continued, "that with the aid of Beelzebub, who only performs his subtle craft in the dark, you were able to cast out unclean spirits? Did you not go to the land of the Gadarenes to learn how to expel the devils that make swine of men?"

His retort was so waspish that I was certain that he was not spectral: "You are making a mock of my anguish and feigning that you do not know what I meant when I claimed that I walked on the sea. Surely you know that there can be no trance without water; nor are you so ignorant of hydromancy that you have not yet discovered why I am referred to as Jesus Piscis. Call me Balaam, if you like, but the only magic I ever practiced was the sorcery of the dream. When a man slumbers, he can perform miracles. At Caesarea Philippi I did not deny that I was The Messiah, or that I could hypnotize the leper and the palsied; when I raised the dead I only resurrected Lazarus' demons."

I took a drop of compassionate spittle from my mouth to wipe away his illegitimacy . . . and then the vision changed, and I saw a boy standing underneath the viaduct in Kansas City in front of the Star Lady Barbershop. The hot, smutty July pavement was holy ground; and as the flies began to swarm and hum around the barber pole, the boy heard the wings of angels. He could not turn his sun-baked face away from the thick plate glass on which was enameled: *16 East 8.* He started to chant aloud: "16 East 8," and he knew that this was his song of Jehovah, for both the address and the name Jehovah are made up of seven characters.

"Yeshu! Yeshu!" I cried, clinging to the curls of Saul, but before I could open my eyes, I saw that my lips were on my mother's long, Galilean nose, and I whispered in her ear, "Miriam Megaddela Neshaya, the lady barber, oh my mother!"

Then I awakened and sat up on my cot, but the vision of Miriam was still before my eyes, and in my ears I heard the refrain "16 East 8," those seven letters of the dream which were the Kabbala of my childhood. Why was it impossible for me to let go of the misery of my boyhood? I hugged close to my breast the scene of the skinny, narrow shop containing the five barber chairs and the pair of brass cuspidors bespattered with tobacco juice which was as pungent and brown as the saliva of grasshoppers. The two scurvy electric fans hanging from the ceiling and the mahogany settees on which waiting customers sprawled in their workingmen's blue-denim overalls would never disappear from my mind. Did I not also cherish the back room, where the water closet stood no more than a yard or so from the rusted, cockroachy gas range? Would I ever break the terrible image of that table covered with cracked and spotty linoleum, beneath which were two deep, bow-shaped drawers where my mother kept her flour and in which six newborn mice once nested? Even though I swooned with nausea as I remembered this, why was it that I could not part with the recollection?

There was the black, filthy alley behind the shop, festered with four-footed creatures that mangle the imagination. The rear of an umbrella factory gave onto the alley, and there one could find and collect a sheaf of tin spokes, or come upon a whole frame; two doors away was the shop of a wagonmaker, where a child could pick up axle grease with a stick and put it in a tin can. And nearby were large wooden cases that one might sit on and contemplate the steep hill of mustard-colored clay that ran away from Phineas Levi's pawnbroker's establishment. What sticky, amorous secrets there were in the prostitute's rooms above Basket's Quick Lunch counter: the odor of Lysol and potassium permanganate and the sweat of venery came from there, stinging my nostrils. When I saw Tisha, whose mother ran the place— and advertised it as light housekeeping—I thought all the rough, emerald pimples and pouchy boils on her cheeks and neck were the marvelous, occult sores and scabs of Venus.

Would I walk past the shanty commission houses on broken-down lower Walnut Street or loiter about the penny arcade on Main Street all my days? Would I always be looking for a large, pondy mudhole in a vacant lot, hidden behind a signboard, where one could make a raft to float on the water?

What purity there had been in the anguish over a lost orange; how round and carnal was the fruit, and after I had peeled it and was making ready to slice and put it into my mouth, I had dropped the orange in the gutter. And how I wept.

Is there no real revelation after childhood? Can we learn only by remembering what we felt then? Why do we love our vermin? Do our souls need dirt, lice, rats, mud puddles and woe? The sweetest fennel makes us indolent and gives us antiseptic memories. We caress and stroke our rotten, starved years because the dream requires it. You who have pondered Joseph's interpretation of Pharaoh's dream consider this: the seven lean kine that stand in the hot river Nile will always devour the seven fat ones—aye, seven again; it is the sign of pestilence and famine—but there is more food here for the despairing, niggard heart than in the tenderest grass and herbs.

I sat on the bed, holding my head between my hands. With a weary glance, I swept up our penury; there were the narrow iron cot and the mealy bed upon which my mother slept, two chairs, with spindly, sick legs, a secondhand deal table and her steamer trunk which she used as a dresser and on which she set her jars of rejuvenating face and hand creams. A famished cotton sheet served as a curtain between her couch and my sleeping space.

This was in a cold-water flat we had taken at $24 a month in a slum tenement on East 96th Street in Manhattan after leaving Queens. My mother was still determined to occupy herself. Speaking Polish and German enabled her to get a few customers for her violet ray treatments. She still had enough strength in her hands to massage a fatigued woman or a young wife who was agitated because she had not menstruated; she kneaded the flesh of her back, and sometimes she pared the calluses of a patient to relieve her of a toothache or a neuralgic jaw.

The cold-water flat on 96th Street was our desert of

Paran. My mother was a Hagarene daughter from the beginning, and I had inherited her wilderness. I was already as gray as Ephraim. Canoes that are filled with stones to sink them have a pensive quiet at the bottom of a river which every man craves. Would that our thoughts were heavy enough to push us down to our depths and hold us there. "Behold, he drinketh up a river and hasteth not," says Job.

My mother had little left to keep her going but her will. She had made up her mind to live; dreading to make a grave of her belly, she hardly ate any food. She avoided salt, pepper, ketchup, sugar, fats, meats and milk. If she were fatigued, she nibbled two carrots and chewed half-cooked porridge. And she had become more absent-minded; after she had taken a sooty, dented pot and boiled a little water in it, she poured parched cereal over the simmering water, and then forgot about it; by the time she remembered, the pasty oatmeal or farina was spoilt. Often, if she caught herself rushing about, she would suddenly stand still and beseech herself not to hurry, which would only increase her high blood pressure, or, God forbid, irreparably damage her heart.

Aside from other tormenting ailments she had prolapsus, a dropping bladder; she feared to lift a pound of potatoes, as she thought it might be too great a strain on her. Because she was short, she always maintained she had gotten a hernia from standing on her feet for fourteen hours a day while holding her scissors and comb above the heads of customers.

Despite her resolution to remain alive, every new day was a terror to her. By two o'clock in the afternoon she had gained a part of her battle against the morning; then she would snatch the remnant of a petticoat from the floor of the clothes closet and wipe the scum of lotion from her cheeks. If she happened to step upon an old corset cover she would pick it up and clean her shoes with it. She could not part with anything; she hoarded buttons, a piece of a chemise, a smutty chamois or powder puff, a hair switch, half of a razorstrop. They represented her life which was over.

Sometimes she took the pincushion she had had since she was in Memphis and held it in her lap while she rocked to and fro. She cringed whenever she thought of the present; what a hideous, massive heap it was, and where would she get the strength to struggle with it?

Late in the day, if she was not drained raw by her nerves, she might search for a copy of Smollett's *Humphrey Clinker* or Le Sage's *Gil Blas* and read a few pages. Since she seldom recalled where she had left off the previous day, she often reread the same chapter. Once she came upon a musty receipt, dated January 31, 1911, for the rent of the Star Lady Barbershop at 16 East 8th, and she took off her sweaty glasses and dabbed her eyes with a clout she had ripped from a worn-out window curtain. Then wandering among the junk heap of scarred saucepans, a rusted skillet, a broken meat grinder, the old Yale lock from the barbershop door, a pair of keys for the front door at 710 A East 8th, and sticky dishes that lay on the floor, atop the gas range or under the table, she suddenly pressed her hand against her heart to see whether she could feel it beating. After slumping into a chair, she staggered toward the steamer trunk where she had hidden the alarm clock, the crystal of which had fallen out. Clutching it, and pressing one thumb against the hands that were like a mangled fly, she took deep breaths and counted her pulse. When she felt quieter she threw the clock back into the trunk and locked it. Ever since she had come to New York, she regarded the clock with hatred. If she thought about it, and then reminded herself that sixty minutes had passed, she would groan, "I am one hour closer to the grave."

The only relief Lizzie had from her worries was to go back to her memories. A postcard view of Swope or Fairmount Parks gave her more hope than any lawn she now saw; nothing was green any longer except the grass in Kansas City. On occasion she recaptured a glimpse of Captain Henry Smith's jolly, bloated neck; she could see him sitting opposite her at the table on the deck of his boat, the *Chester*. Had she ever eaten anything with relish since they had had clam chowder with oyster crackers and a bottle of Budweiser? And there was gray Cromwell, wearing his moral gold-rimmed glasses, and his gray suit was as plain as his principles. When she had the ill luck to awaken from these reveries and remember that somehow or other she had to get through Monday or Wednesday, and then thought of Thursday morning, she rose and stumbled against the metal leg of the cot, bruising her ankle. As for the future, O dear, merciful Lord, let me have one, she begged, pouring alcohol on her wound. She dropped a large grievous sigh and shook her dense neck. Making a gothic arch with her hard-working fingers, she asked God for several more years; no, she was not greedy—had she ever demanded much? Just the sun and more of the summer grass. Could He not give her ten years more of autumn nights? All that she wanted was to walk quiet and slow among soft dusks; how blessed it would be to have one more decade beneath the moon, and to be able to hear the Troost Avenue streetcar growing on the tracks as it approached the 8th Street flat. If the Lord God would only take into consideration all her misfortunes and give her credit for them, perhaps she could live until she was ninety-one or ninety-three, maybe even ninety-seven—was that so excessive, especially considering all her struggles? Then she would ask for nothing else but a few scattered raindrops of hope.

Her face was bitten by anguish and the uninterrupted warfare against hunger, and the dread of it. The character of the woman was as ineradicable as the parched pomegranates, dates, nuts, beans, grapes and bread that lie whole in the mummy chambers of Memphis. Could it be that because she was so worn out she was now closer to her origins? American in almost every detail of habit, speech and dress, she was an admixture of Missouri and Babel. Could her neighbors have understood this, they might have swarmed about her. She was already a relic in a new world.

Meanwhile, I had taught for a semester at James Madison High School. But I was not asked to return because I suggested that pupils read the tales of Chekov, Tolstoi, Gorki, and the novels of George Gissing and Gogol instead of the prescribed rubbish by Zane Grey, Dickens, Thackeray and Jack London.

I was ashamed because I could do little or nothing to appease our plight; we had to live as best we could on the meager rentals from my mother's houses in Kansas City. Worse, I could not handle her pain, and I was unable to think because I could not feel. My mother's face had become dim, but I did my utmost to grasp her image. However, my sight was as diseased as that of Tobias, in whose eyes the dung of sparrows had fallen and settled. That this was the impotence of the spirit made it no less intolerable. We cannot live, sorrow or die for somebody else, for suffering is too precious to be shared.

Since I was useless, I began to sleep late; I craved to be the four-footed beast in the darkness, for the sun confused and punished me. The long shoots of evening were the tapers that gave off the light the day had denied me. I already began to doubt that my mother lived, though I dreaded that she would die, and I would lose her image. After we go down into the pit of night, when we are in our beds, we smell the fish of Oceanus, and when we awaken our palates are brackish, and the odor of Leviathan is in our mouths.

Unable to drive out of my bones that one dirge: "My mother will disappear," I fled from her. I eschewed her cruel, Gehenna mornings, and I sank deeper into the darkness. I saw that man was born to be deceived and that he is a wan image roaming an orbed plain in the Void. Sleep is death, and death is sleep because we are never alive. Strindberg said: "I dream, therefore I exist," but I dreamt, and did not live.

Each day I failed to take up her old age that fluttered like the feathers of a small wren, and gently stroke it. Why could I not be lowly and fall down before her feet? But I had always rejected my mother's countenance; in my vanity I had crowned my head with the auburn curls of Saul, and when I smiled I showed the fleece that shone so white between his profligate lips. A real physiognomy is an antique crypt, and at the age of forty my face was dominated by my mother's, as well as the thousand devils that I had come by from Saul. Though I said, I will walk all my days over the Brook Kidron until I find Saul, I was also searching for my mother. But I was plagued by the herd of swine at Gadarene; if I believed I was not evil, or dared to assume that I could be good, a demon graved in me would come up and sit on my mouth and scoff at me, and though my spirit fell out of my body whenever I noticed this, my demons grew harder in me.

I groped for understanding, knowing that the miracle of perception is involved with the miracle of love, and yet I did not know what I imagined I knew, for my acts were bad and loveless ones. Both my mother and I were the unloved ones, and the unleavened bread in the desert. This is what I said to myself, but saying it is not knowing it.

I avoided my mother's face and did not go to kiss her, and the more motionless and lethargic I became, the harder it was for me to recognize her. Many times she was in the room and I neither heard nor saw her, and so she grew fainter. When we fail to see the phantoms near us they vanish from our sight.

One night I slept and dreamt I saw a woman who was only two empty udders; I imagined I beheld her, but there was no mouth or chin or cheeks in her. As I grieved for her, water grew around me. It was neap tide, and my sleep was shoaly, and sour and dyspeptic, and I endeavored to walk in the water toward her to give her a filial kiss to restore the mouth, the cheeks and chin that were missing—but the waves held me back so that I could not reach her. Then I saw a cruse of water and a loaf of bread, and I awoke and moaned, "She is dead, and the bottle of water and the bread she has left me are for my hunger." I sat there on the bed, and the vision clung to me like the fog bank that gathers around one's eyes after a migraine. I looked about for my mother; then I hurried over to her small casket, the iron cot into which she descended every night. A skinny sheet lay awry over the pallet, but the shabby becrumbed coat was gone. I threw on a jacket and rushed out into the street, which was painted with sleet. There I saw coming toward me a woman whose back was lumped by her unforgiving hopes; she walked with unsteady feet on the ice, carrying two milk bottles under her arm. Relieved when I saw her knobby chin and the nose that fell over her deflowered mouth, I upbraided her: "O my mother, why are you so stupid? Do you wish to fall on the ice? What are you doing with those two empty udders?" Startled when I heard these words, I grasped the bottles from her and ran back to the flat. The dream would not let go of me, and I tried to shape the face I could not collect. I had resolved to kiss her hands when I saw her, but as she came through the door the devils grinned at me, and I could not forgive her—but for what I did not know. I believed I saw a forsaken and palsied heap of rags go to that accursed cot and lie down.

At forty years of age I thought that the bulls of Apis and Mnevis had expired in my loins, though Lilith, the angel of lust, visited me more often than she had. My dreams were round and wombed, but as soon as I awakened my day was a bunch of hyssop.

At this time I was thinking of marriage, but as I had not known the woman long, I was most uneasy. Would not marriage be a laudanum? I needed sensuality as others require alcohol, tobacco, gossip, loose chatter, opium or faith. Then I vaguely hoped that after I had become her husband I would no longer wander in the Hagarene forest. Were disreputable houses available and cheap, I should have relinquished all thoughts of wedlock.

When I told my mother about this woman, she promptly wrote the agent in Missouri to sell her houses so that her son might have the money to provide for a wife.

And so I was married. And at the same time I obtained a temporary appointment to teach at a university. But how long could I heed the sounding of the trumpet for the asses to come to the pragmatic donkey-prayer at daybreak? Could I be the gross Caliban, wallowing in the academic mire, while feigning to be the intransigent Ariel?

My wife and I stayed with my mother in the cold-water flat for a while. One afternoon, when my wife was absent, my mother threw open the door and ran into the room. Her shoulders were still muscular and her legs nervous and agile. Was she in some acute pain? Sitting next to her, I did not look at her or take up into my eyes the few ulcered mementos of our past—the steamer trunk, the two chairs with peeled, starved legs, those white jars of face cream and the black violet ray box. I waited to see what she would do. Removing her glasses—which she always did when she was exalted or in a desponding mood—she took off her heavy black shoes and her hat that looked like a dilapidated bird's nest. A sharp rapture seized her, and I saw her for a moment wearing nothing but her ecstasy. She was feverish, not jubilant as she had been when she stepped out of her cold bath at 710 A East 8th and rubbed her stout loins with the rough bath towel. I turned a little to contemplate the spare flesh sitting at my side, and seeing what was left of her, I bent my gaze toward myself. She was holding herself in her arms, cradling her bosom in her hands. Suddenly she dropped to the floor, pressed her lips to my feet and began to weep: "Edward, your mother's life has not been a complete mockery. Son of all my miseries and disappointments that swarmed like flies around the honey of your mother's short youth, look, I have overcome bad luck—God has not made me a beggar to my own child!"

Then she drew from the depths of her breast a sheaf of hundred-dollar bills and she placed them in my hands. I sat there regarding this kneeling woman with stupefaction, but held fast to the money. What will she do if I keep it, I asked myself, choking the green papers between my fingers. I stuffed my pockets with these grassy maggots; then I got up and moved away from her as though I hoped that distance might lessen my disgrace. Abruptly, although no one else was at home, I looked around me to see whether anybody had noticed me pocketing the money. In less than three minutes I had made a pauper of her, and how could I cure her indigence? Other thoughts smote me: "Does this most unfortunate woman expect to die? Is she insane?" Plagued by so many ailments, where had she gotten the strength to think of anything else but her own fate? For those who are sick love themselves passionately.

Standing on the one rug bitten by a generation of want, I still clung to all her drudgery in the Star Lady Barbershop. Then she took more money from her bosom and, imagining I was standing next to her, she put it in my hands which were not there, and the winged lucre flew to the floor. Crooking my back, I stooped over to pick it up. Instead of bowing to her I made a low leg to the bills scattered and crawling over the floor. All my life I have committed one of the worst of the seven cardinal sins: I had not the strength to overcome the average in myself. When we are ordinary, we do not amount to anything: our everyday life is our vermin. All that I had done for so long was to scratch the lice of my indolent sensibilities and imagine that I was showing a great deal of emotion for my mother. Now when I regarded this pile of palsied spirit and tatters before me, a shrewd, cold feeling came over me; the demon sat on my lips and smirked at me: "Will she die before she becomes a burden to you?" When I heard his leering whisper, I groaned. Where had this sin been interred? And why had it come now to make its diabolical grimace at me? Can anybody doubt that it is the malice we have towards ourselves that is our real foe? And I thought, who can behold his own worms and not shrink from himself?

Shortly after this ecstasy my mother began to decline more rapidly. Her temples burned when she lay down at night; she kept a cold compress on her head, which made her nose look rabbinic. She knew what ailed her and said in a most woeful tone, "My son, I have hardening of the arteries. Oh, my poor Edward."

The doctor told me she could live another eighteen or twenty years, and when I heard this I rejoiced and I thought of King Hezekiah, and how grateful he was when Isaiah said that God would give him fifteen more years of life. But when I informed her what the physician had said, she fell into a deeper melancholy, and I was angry with her because she was not content to have these years before her. I admonished her, "Mother, we can no longer live as many years as Enoch or Jared. Why don't you be quiet? You are so nervous, always running in the streets with that lunatic violet ray machine."

One evening I saw her staggering about in the room, jostling against the sink and the steamer trunk. She turned to me, throwing out her hands; the tears hung upon her sagging face, and I saw there all the rivers of sorrow which are of as many colors as there are precious stones in paradise. She said to me, "I am going to die, Edward. Let me sign over to you what I still have left."

I stood there, incapable of moving. Had it come, the void, the awful and irrevocable chasm between us? What should I do? Instead of taking this shrunken heap of suffering into my arms, I only shook my head. I had already stolen too much from her; I had not the strength either to lift up my guilt or to say more.

Every night after that when she lay on the cot, she continued to grease her face and arms and neck with her lotions, and before going to sleep, I came to her and knelt on the floor beside her cot and kissed her, and then I arose and went to my own bed.

With the money she had given me I purchased an old house on Cape Cod and a secondhand car, and one night my wife and I sat in the car outside the flat saying good-bye to my mother. Then I watched this shamble of loneliness, less than five feet of it, covered with a begrimed and nibbled coat, walk away from me.

For the next two years letters came from her twice a week, always beginning with "My beloved Son." Once as my eyes crawled down to the bottom of the last page, overrun with her strong, gothic script, I read: "You know, my dearest one on earth to me, what a good future we have. . . ." I took the *future* and cast it violently to the ground, and pressed my heel against it until it hissed and crept away. Had not Jehovah made enough tragic sport of her life? Now I sank beneath all her hopes and even her endearments crushed me.

On the 15th of February, 1946, I lay in my bed, going to and fro in it and unable to seal the wandering scenes that passed through my head. Again a river arose and a cruse of water and a loaf of bread grew out of it, but stare as hard as I could, there was nothing else, and when I awakened, I shrieked, "Mother, your wicked, fallen son will come to your side; you will not die alone." Shaking the sleep from me, I prodded my wife, saying, "Let us go to my mother before she dies." Her face was a stranger to me and she gave me no answer.

On the 18th of February there came another letter from my mother, but I would not open it. Had I had a hammer, I could not have broken this envelope made of black basalt. On that night in the month known as Shebat in Hebrew, which is a time of tears and lamentations, she died. She was alone, and her body lay on the cot for five days before a neighbor found her.

It is hideous and coarse to assume that we can do something for others—and it is vile not to endeavor to do it. I had not the strength to handle her tragedy, for my will has failed me every hour of each day. It is said that a wise man falls down seven times a day and rises; I have fallen and never gotten up.

My mother was born unfortunate, and she was pursued until her end by that evil genius, ill luck. The Psalmist says, "No one can keep his own soul alive"—nor anybody else's either. We despair because we are no better and are not consoled that we can be no worse. A life is a single folly, but two lives would be countless ones, for nobody profits by his mistakes.

I do not go to her grave because it would do her no good. Though everything in the earth has feeling—the granite mourns, the turf sleeps and has fitful nights, and the syenite chants as melodiously as Orpheus and Musaeus—it would be idle to say that Lizzie Dalberg, whose bones still have sentience, is what she was. She is and she is not, and that is the difference between the trance we call being and the other immense experience we name death.

Who was Lizzie Dalberg? I wish to God I knew, but it is my infamy that I do not. How often had she pleaded with heaven to lead her out of the peopleless desert of Beersheba, but to what avail? She only questioned God in anger once: "Why am I miserable, while others who are pitiless and contemptible are so fortunate?"

But she never received an answer. Not God, but gibing Pilate came to her and asked, "What is Truth?"

And I knew not why until I had heard her quiet reply: "My life."

When the image of her comes up on a sudden—just as my bad demons do—and I see again her dyed henna hair,

the eyes dwarfed by the electric lights in the Star Lady Barbershop, and the dear, broken wing of her mouth, and when
I regard her wild tatters, I know that not even Solomon in
his lilied raiment was so glorious as my mother in her rags.
*Selah.*

# The Tragedy of American Love

from *Can These Bones Live*

# The Flesh Refused

A merica for a hundred years was a vineyard. The Puritan
feared and despised all the arts as coming from the
nether, concupiscent soul; he transmuted his own needs
and appetites into meditations and chronicles that were re-
dolent of sod, vintage and flocks. His materialism was his
shrine; he knelt in devotional adoration, not to the Virgin,
Jesus or the Saints, but to the fields, the house, reverentially
white, and the orchard. From Abraham, Noah and Job he
derived the ecstasy and fervor he had for his sheep, apples,
wood and grain. The colonial farm house, rooted in and
winging upwards from the soil, bespeaks the miracles of
growth, life, birth, procreation and marriage. The Puritan's
churchly slaying of the sexual organs, like the dismember-
ment of Osiris, was a furtive and diabolical worship of
seedtime, spring and copulation.

The Puritan walked and meditated with Orion, dog-wood, the birch, and he furtively knew the nakedness of his body as Ham knew Noah.

The sensual Puritan was wiser and also cannier than the artist. He slew witches, denounced devils, adultery and fornication, but commonly had five or more wives; the naïve Pilgrim artist accepted Jehovah, Calvin and America, and denied fleshly man.

Almost the whole of American Literature has been a deep refusal of man. Early American Literature, veiled in the lilied twilight of St. Matthew and St. Mark, is a death pilgrimage, a renunciation of the carnal heart. The very pulses of Poe, Emily Dickinson and Hawthorne desolately shake as in their own Gethsemane. O Calvary, Calvary, moaned Emily Dickinson. O Eureka, Ligeia, Death, wept Poe. "Man doth not yield himself to the angels, nor unto death utterly, save only through the weakness of his feeble will," wrote Poe, quoting Joseph Glanvill.

The flight from man and nature *begins* with Edgar Poe. Ligeia, Madeline and Berenice are moon-veined Juliets, and Eleonora has "memorial eyes" and a sarcophagus brow.

Herman Melville, the most corporeal artist of the American nineteenth century, was under the pall of the New Testament. Melville read his Shakespeare as a Sermon on the Mount; his last words and Epitaph, *Billy Budd*, is a Christian hymn. Billy Budd, like Alyosha Karamazov, is Christly goodness; he is Innocence before the Adamic "mysteries of iniquity."

Hawthorne's men and women are aerial and epicene dews, like the tissueless seraphs of Simeon Solomon. There is no human pollution in any of his novels. His most evil pages distill an edenic miasma instead of rank protoplasm.

Our entire Christian literature is a sacral whiteness. Herman Melville wrote a whole chapter on WHITENESS. From Poe, Emily Dickinson and Hawthorne to the present-day painters and ghostly water colorists, we see this Parsifal

Annunciation of White Death. Witness the immaculate vulva flowers of Georgia O'Keeffe, the bleached valley of death-shells, rams' skulls, lilies, and whited roses. Or see the total exclusion of the human face, not once the stigmata or the imprint of the fingers, the eyes, the flesh in Marsden Hartley's seascapes, dead birch logs and stones. Man lies hidden and secretly veined far underneath Hartley's aching brine-washed rocks and pulsing sublunary seas. The Face remains unguessed, as in Poe's tales, walled up in the sepulcher of stones, tools and breakers, or in the bloodless wash of sedge, marge or bay of John Marin's water colors. WATER COLOR, it is so deeply American!

What is the fetish of whiteness? What does this lusting after Hygeia mean? What else but the revulsion from one's own blood and the unholy dread of the *sub rosa* Unclean Man. Thoreau, who loathed man's low habits and looked upon eating, copulation or defecating as the vile malady of mortals, wrote, "We are so degraded that we cannot speak of the necessary functions of human nature."

In almost a hundred years of American Literature we do not have one feeding, breeding, sexual male, not one suffering, bed-pining Manon Lescaut or a Shulamite. There are no ripe women here. Writes the poet William Carlos Williams in *In the American Grain*, "Emily Dickinson, starving of passion in her father's garden, is the very nearest we have ever been—starving."

We have had spectral essences, odorless, and hueless. What is *The Scarlet Letter* but a delicate aprioristic theorem of SIN. The evidence that Hester Prynne ever slept with little ether-blooded Dimmesdale is as etiolated and remote as the ontological proof of the existence of God in Aquinas's *Summa*. There is no anatomy at all in Puritan Literature. The illicit relation between Hester and Dimmesdale is a copulative dance of the Essences. Since our beginnings, we have had but one enormous Hymen Hymenee, one seminal marriage between male and female, and that is the nuptial of the leviathan who copulates upon the sweet April brit and grassy meadows of the ocean.

Aye, all essence. Edgar Poe hurried into the arms of Divine Essence, of Eleonora, Eureka, or Death, to appease his thwarted heart's pinings. The blasphemous kiss that Poets have put upon the wan cheeks of their metaphysical Beatrices or Ligeias we pardon because of the suffering denials of their lives. We moan with Poe and clasp his dear ghostly remains. But, as we descend into the underworld and pass the shade of Nathaniel Hawthorne, we move by with an oblique glance, for when he lived, he had but ghost corpuscles. Poe's diabolism was tragic, Hawthorne's, lilied. For our Last Supper of Memory we must have bread; dew, moss and sumac cannot feed our beatitudes or our grief.

We bury ghosts, Ligeia, Berenice, Eleonora, only to resurrect real cadavers, McTeague and Vandover. Refuse the bones and the worms as Hawthorne and Poe did and what is ultimately begotten is the contemporary underground biped, brain-spawn of the same flesh and bone denial. The exquisitely figurined Ligeia is sensually and humanly as nonexistent as the abstract cankered Outside Man. The ghosts, the phantoms, and the present-day economic bipeds are no-man.

Does not Tolstoi's Ivan Ilytch make his life upon this knowledge; at the abyss, before death, the provincial magistrate sheds himself as a generalized man. He renounces that conspiratorial Socratic syllogism that makes him man and mortal in consequence of an arithmetical and logical conjecture, that subtracts him from a frozen, throbless and metaphysical humanity. So long as Ivan Ilytch, the Socratic integer, despises himself and his sickness, he decomposes upon his tongue, breath and skin; the odor that steals out of his clothes and bed separates him from humanity, his family and himself. Christianity cannot help, Holy Writ is in vain—all is lost; there is no way back to the living save through the memory of his own organs. Ivan Ilytch vindi-

cates his life, just before dying, not by a rationalistic subterfuge, but through the simple cleanly act of his servant
who brings the bedpan to him and accepts this seemly
necessity of nature in his sick master. Ivan Ilytch forgives
his coarse family and children, and dies a Christian, because his peasant servant cannot make those distinctions
between a man in his social and decorous clothes and in his
honestly defecating necessities. Icons, candles, Christ, society
and superstition cannot make a man a Christian but a bedpan can!

See what all the spirit-glutted souls, the rationalists and
the ethical metaphysicians, who took to their apriori bosoms
the remote abstract Mass Man—see what the spectral human-
ity-guzzlers have done.

All, from Plato, Immanuel Kant, Hegel, Emerson, Thoreau, Hawthorne and Kropotkin, to the socialists and communists, have been adepts in the humanity cult. The broth-
erhood of man has always attracted men without ade-
quate blood-pigmentation, like Kant and Thoreau, who arrive at the love of man through the multiplication tables
and the categories. Both of these moral teachers had an
egregious distaste for man. Kant kept himself closeted all
his life in Königsberg because he would encounter fewer
specimens of the genus, man. Thoreau, so earnest and
truthful, ate a muskrat to overcome his flesh-revulsion.
Immanuel Kant devoured the categorical imperatives instead, and neither the muskrat nor the categories helped.

But the end of rationalism is not its own abstractions,
but carnal error, or blood-revenge, as Thoreau's orgiastic
and savage refusal of the woman who had proposed to him,
or Immanuel Kant's vile definition of marriage as "a treaty
of reciprocal possession by the two parties which is made
effective by the reciprocal use of their sex properties."
Immanuel Kant embraced godhead, the universe, the abstract Man, and, as he himself confessed, masturbated! While
Aristotle, Master of Schoolmen, as the story goes, crawled

on all fours, his rider, not the Golden Mean, but his mistress flourishing a whip!

Purge the flesh and you canker the spirit. Christian rationalism and nature are forever at odds. Grapes and bread do not grow upon the Categories or upon Calvary. The Cross and the Categorical Imperatives but mock their hapless bearers. Whitman unsuccessfully tried to marry Saviorism and Eros. Although Whitman sang the most carnal hymns to the pagan body, he was really a teetotaler and an ascetic. He was a St. John the Baptist of sexual love; like all friars, artistic or Christian, Whitman took the veil, for life, for frugality, for sexuality, for man. Our Americans, from Herman Melville, Whitman, John Humphrey Noyes, Henry Adams, Thorsten Veblen to Theodore Dreiser, have had the peculiar gift, native, no doubt, of annulling their deepest beliefs; like Penelope they weave their fates and then unravel them. So puzzled were Whitman's own disciples that they endeavored to prove to the American Public that the Master, who had preached the deep delights of the senses, had been himself a piously chaste male. That is an American riddle. Popes confound us because they had daughters, Walt Whitman befuddles us because he had none!

Resolve the riddle of the flesh made spirit and the ambiguities of Puritan literature dissolve. Otherwise, the tales, the novels and the poems seem to be but recondite craft. How much easier it is to know what Chekhov or Dostoevski felt or thought than it is to understand the demonology of Poe and Melville.

The Puritan failed as an artist and became an esoteric artificer; he created charnel-house dolls, an upboiling metaphysical sea, instead of a human comedy. His works are ecliptic, and his anonymity is a subterfuge art, a sacral lie. We cannot say that he was less gifted than the Europeans; for who can finally proclaim that the fires and the snows of Melville's Vesuvian brain are not to be compared with

Dostoevski's. Imaginatively, he was the European master's peer; but as a Living Voice, infinitely less. We have had the most abstruse technicians in America, but never a Voice.

The Puritan signed away his flesh for Christ's bread as irrevocably as Dr. Faustus abjured his life to Mephisto for carnal pleasure. Here is the enigma of the disembodied literature of the Puritans: these Americans would not, dared not, wed the flesh and so espoused godhead. The pursuit of the White Whale is the allegory of a disincarnate Ahab seeking after his own flesh. Although Herman Melville might create on unchristian Ahab to flaunt, "I do not baptize thee in the name of the Father, but in the name of the devil," the final text upon Melville's entablatured bones is the Sermon on the Mount. "How men lust after a piece of spirit," cried Nietzsche, "when a piece of flesh has been denied them."

Refusals beget deeper refusals. By the time we come to Henry Adams the American fable wondrously unfolds. Henry Admas was a timorous Bacchus, who revealed to the American that the Virgin of Chartres was the perfect Catholic Aphrodite. Later, however, he elevated Mary into pure juiceless intellection. Then he forswore the Virgin altogether and knelt at another shrine, the MACHINE, and so concluded his days in epicene sanctity, deriving unguessed erotical vibrations in his Gallery of Machines, from nine-foot pistons, lathes, belts and wheels. "The strain of man is bred out into baboon and monkey."

Here is the whole allegory of the Fall of Man in the American Garden of Eden. After Hester Prynne, after Ligeia and Eleonora, there is nothing left but the Iron Phallus, Adams' nine-foot pistons.

# Moby-Dick:
# A Hamitic Dream

*For Stanley Burnshaw*

Nobody can deceive a man so well as he can gull himself, and I do not blame anybody else for my own folly. My thought is to spare others, although I know that there is hardly a man on earth who will take advice unless he is certain that it is positively bad. As for myself, I am not homesick for the fusty books I worshiped as a youth; I am no victim of that most scurrile of all ruses, nostalgia. Let me guard what is sacred, and raze to the ground the stupid, indolent Thebaid of my past because I know Pindar's house will yet remain. I have changed my mind about Herman Melville, for I once loved this Cyclops whose father is Oceanus.

It is natural that we should have a wizened, intellectual literature—and who would want to empty our little Hippocrene?—but it is malignant to feign that we are the new

Attica of literature. When poeticules assert that Philip Freneau is a bard or that the pages of Charles Brockden Brown are not hellebore to the reader, he is establishing a republic of letters for solemn apes. How much noise is made for a drumbling poetaster or a Thersites of scatological fiction Let a man, as Rabelais writes, "chew ordure" in twenty novels, and for such coprology he is wreathed in tamarisk as though he were a god instead of a sweeper of privies. We venerate size and bulk and the surest way to be accounted a genius is to write the same big, ignorant book many times.

Herman Melville, who died in 1891, had been interred by the currish literati. His hapless shade is now the object of the barkings of the same Cerberuses; beagles with the graveled throats always stand at the gate of Hades and bay the moon whenever they scent carrion—dead works.

Canting, stuffed praise of deceased writers is starved malice; whenever a critic tells such falsehoods about our past he shows his hunger and envy, and instead of providing us with more opulent Parnassus, he parches the American Elysium. He carries, as Ben Jonson writes, "a commonwealth of paper in his hose."

Is it necessary to declare that there was not one erudite versifier or prose stylist in nineteenth-century America to compare with those geniuses who flourished when London was the fairest Hellas? There was no Mermaid Inn in New York where one could savor a beaker of ale with learned poets; the sepulchral Spouter Inn of New Bedford, whose proprietor is Peter Coffin, was no substitute for the coffee houses and the chocolate shops in which one might find a Will Congreve, Swift, Pope, Dryden, or Wycherley to be a whetstone for his own faculties. Dio Chrysostom said that the father of Achilles selected Phoenix to teach his son the arts of discourse. No matter how charitable we are to Hawthorne, Whitman, or to Poe, of what advantage could they be to poor, torn Herman Melville? Ruth could glean more barely in Boaz's field after it had been reaped than Melville could have culled from Poe's *Marginalia* or Whitman's *Democratic Vistas*. Boaz was far more prodigal, but kindness, the father of good thoughts, does not permeate belles-lettres in the United States.

Herman Melville was as separated from a civilized literature as the lost Atlantis was said to have been from the great peoples of the earth. Allen Tate, in his oracular poem, "The Mediterranean," has comprehended the sorrows that lie beyond the Pillars and the Sea of Darkness:

> What country shall we conquer, what fair land
> Unman our conquest and locate our blood?
> We've cracked the hemispheres with careless hand!
> No, from the Gates of Hercules we flood
>
> Westward, westward till the barbarous brine
> Whelms us to the tired land . . .

Let nobody imagine that I am unmindful of Herman Melville's scorifying deprivations; he burnt in Puritan ice, but not in woman; God shrive his shade, and may we sin less, for all flesh is error. Our best writers, Thoreau, Whitman, Melville, Hawthorne, Emily Dickinson, and Poe, produced frigid works: "admire and model thyself after the whale! Do thou, too, remain warm among ice," is the admonition of a man whose sorest affliction was that his vitals froze in all latitudes. However, I am concerned with Zeus Asklepios, the healing powers of a god-like book upon the American polity.

There was a dearth of those masculine fiery particles in the Puritan. Aristophanes averred: "By Jupiter, testicles are capital things." The nineteenth-century American was still the vassal of that Puritanic Beelzebub, Cotton Mather, the father of the Christian homosexual. What else could be the result of Thoreau's celibacy, Hawthorne's inclement identity, Whitman's ambiguous bachelordom, or Poe's and

Melville's misogyny but the contemporary Pauline invert? Not one of these unusual men could produce a seminal poem or a great confession like St. Augustine's. Born to sin because we have genital organs, we live to confess our faults, and that is scripture and literature.

Man is a tragic animal because he has a teleological impulse to prove that he is reasonable though he knows he is not. Nothing can be proved, and the need to assert that the Archangels Gabriel and Uriel exist is the valor and cosmic energy in the human race. Agamemnon reproaches Calchas for never having prophesied good fortune for him. We would have the right to blame the universe for all our faults did not such a feeble attitude bring us greater woes. One assails a poet who does not feign well. We expect an author whose life has been foolish, stupid, and full of misfortunes to be clever, sage, and quick in his books; otherwise poems betray us as much as life does.

The Word is the Logos, which is the domestic white Cock, and the phallus that impregnates the body and the soul. One of the heresiarchs claimed that the Logos was the offspring of Mercury, but the Word in New England literature never became flesh. What congealed works came from those savants! Style is the absolute limit of a man's character and bad writing shows a lack of love; its most malignant symptom is delay. Henry James postponed his periods as long as he could, and Melville deferred action until the last few pages of *Moby-Dick*. Of the hundred and thirty-one chapters, only the last three before the Epilogue are about the pursuit of Moby-Dick, and the *Pequod* is always in the calms. The whaling craft is similar to Zeno's paradoxical arrow, which, though hurled through space, is at rest in different places. There is no motion in this novel, without which there cannot be any positive affection or heat in the mind.

A good remark uttered in cumbersome words feebly put together is evil. Not one wise thought can be told without great energy. When the will languishes the demons are triumphant. Whatever one knows comes from the motions of the will. We know ourselves by our acts. Velleity is the principal reason for human perversity.

Sick books beget far more ailing ones just as potently as Abraham begat Isaac, and Isaac Jacob. Moreover, Melville's solitude was, in part, willful. As Sir Francis Bacon explains: "those that want friends to open themselves unto, are cannibals of their own hearts." We have been Ishmaels of letters since the republic was established, banished by society. Although poems are composed in sepulchral rooms, for writing is as private as dying, a healthful song is a hymn to the sun, and not, as Melville felt, "a dismal stave of psalmody." Seneca's advice is: "It is every man's duty to make himself profitable to mankind." But when the imagination of the writers is ill and distempered, the social corpus is also cankered. Melville's separation from the human race was as deranged as Bartleby's. Melville refers to the seafarers in the *Pequod* as *Isolatoes* who did not acknowledge "the common continent of men." Ishmael, who has a "damp, drizzly November" in his watery soul, is as boreal as the first Void and as much of a beggar in the winds as Lazarus.

Epictetus, who had all the fortitude of the Stoic, held quite a different view from the author of *Moby-Dick*: "Miserable man, is there any one that maintains himself? Only the universe does that." How many people, who have known the acute pangs of solitude, go abroad to tell everybody that their utmost felicity is in being absolutely alone, a rapture easily attained by simply dying? A nation that is just and strong is a commonweal of kinsmen, and a volume unimpaired by diseased organs and a morose heart is an equatorial friend. "Call me Ishmael," the opening line of the novel, is prophetic, and I doubt that anybody ever composed as true a one. But we cannot forget that in Scripture the hand of Ishmael, a wild ass of affliction, is against every man's, and every man's against his. Montesquieu wrote, "Men born for society are born to please one another."

*Moby-Dick*, a verbose, tractarian fable on whaling, is a book of monotonous and unrelenting gloom. Rozanov once said that he did not care for Jesus because He never smiled: in this respect Jesus and Melville have similar dispositions. Melville is more dour than King Saul and there is no harper in the book to assuage his implacable melancholia. Nobody can endure such absolute and unrelieved misery of the spirit and duodenum except the wailing shades by the banks of the Cocytus. What pierces us is not *Moby-Dick*, but the woe in Melville, "the wild, watery loneliness" of his life.

It has been told many times that Herman Melville had an equinoctial identity but that Hawthorne was a wintry prig from Salem. Both were hibernal stylists. Of the two, Melville, perhaps, deceived himself the more and on rare occasions to our advantage, as in the line: "the currents carry ye to those sweet Antilles where the beaches are only beat with water-lilies." However, the soft climes that had made his flesh drowsy had turned his thoughts not to Epicurus but to the anthropophagi. The Tahitian experience had not made him averse to the delights of a cannibal gourmet. Let not the Sirens, who praise Melville for the few lovely lines he composed, take you to the isles already white with the bones of a whole generation of admirers of *Moby-Dick*.

Prometheus stole the fires of Zeus to warm the human race; Melville's sole aim is to thaw those frosts within him. How astonished he was when he remarked: "the blood of a Polar whale is warmer than that of a Borneo negro in summer." Hawthorne had disclosed that human coldness is the worst of all afflictions. Giordano Bruno said that not even the snows of the Alps could cool him, but how seldom are April and May in unverdured, mizzling Melville.

"Can one warm his blue hands by holding them up to the northern lights? Would he not far rather lay him down lengthwise along the line of the equator?" asks Melville. "Would he not be moored to one of the Moluccas?" But this North American Lazarus is lodged, not in Abraham's Bosom, but at the Spouter Inn. His bed companion for the night is not a buxom tavern wench, but a cannibal, Queequeg, "a jolly good bedfellow."

The malady common to both Ishmael and Ahab is unrelieved, warping coldness. Ahab, named after the wicked king who ruled lascivious Samaria, represents the Pilgrim Lotophagi of *terra incognita*. Stendhal, mentioning the Americans, thought that "the source of sensibility is dried up in this people."

*Moby-Dick* is gigantology, a tract about a gibbous whale and fifteen or more lawless seamen, who are alone, by choice, though they are together. Ahab is Adam, Cain, Ham, and Nimrod; he is the incarnation of all turpitudes, just as Leviathan is the demiurge and the Pacific the forest of Nôdh; Cain had a beast in his forehead, and Melville writes that Ahab, though evil, has a "crucifixion in his face." In the same wayward vein he claims that the sea is a domestic household at times, and that the sailor experiences a "filial, confident, land-like feeling towards the sea"; Ishmael believes that his bed mate, Queequeg, furnishes him with ease and connubial comfort.

Melville seems to have taken his revenge against the characters in his book as a reprisal for his own solitude. These seafarers have private, mouldy hearts; at the conclusion of this heavy dirge, Ishmael is as alone as he was in the opening pages of *Moby-Dick*. Sir Thomas Browne, whom Melville read avidly, was of the mind that "there is no man alone, because every man is a microcosm."

The characters are scarcely limned at all, except gaunt, miserly Bildad "who . . . sat and never leaned, and this to save his coat tails." When Bildad is considering how small the wages of Ishmael should be, Peleg, fearing he might offer him a few pennies too much, tells him to be wary: "thy conscience may be drawing ten inches of water." Melville abhors both Bildad and Peleg—each is a "magnified species of mouse."

The unmothered, mongrel crew is made up of Nantucketers, sailors from Martha's Vineyard and the Cape, and whalemen from the lands of Asia Minor and of Hamitic Africa. Aside from Starbuck, Stubb, and Flask, the Nantucketers, exsanguious, castaway Cains, who have fished for "crabs and quohogs" on New England's coast, the other main characters, save one Indian from the Vineyard, are Persians, Africans, and Polynesians, those hot men at whose hearth Melville could warm himself.

Stubb, a Capeman, is "neither craven nor valiant." This is the rudest paraphrase of Revelation: "because thou art lukewarm, and neither cold nor hot, I will spue thee out of my mouth." Starbuck, of Nantucket, is a "long, earnest man"; Flask is "short, ruddy, and young." However, Melville cribs the Polynesian, Indian, Parsee, and the imperial African in his crusty heart. Tashtego, Indian from Gay Head, is the "inheritor of the unvitiated blood of those proud warrior hunters"; Daggoo is a gigantic Negro Ahasuerus; Fedallah, the Parsee, is a mystic. Melville moans over "black little Pip," "poor Alabama boy." Contradicting himself, he also asserts that "Starbuck, Stubb, and Flask were momentous men." We never find out why. The Carpenter is described as having a "ramifying heartlessness," and is a "stript abstract; an unfractioned integral; uncompromised as a new-born babe." Bulkington, who, as his appellation implies, should have dramatic weight, disappears from the book not long after he enters it, and for no tangible cause. Obviously Melville forgot him altogether. Flagitious Ahab is dear to Melville; he is evil, but, his author believed, washed in the blood of the lamb. Ahab nods for over half a century of pages. He is wearying because his sorrow is picturesque rather than active; like Milton's Satan, to borrow from Hazlitt, Ahab's deformity is in the depravity of his will.

Herman Melville chose to take the sea, not the fire, or the earth, as his element. "With a philosophical flourish Cato throws himself upon his sword; I quietly take to the ship." Marcus Aurelius said, "Always remember the saying of Heraclitus, that the death of earth is to become water." Heraclitus also reported, "a dry soul is the wisest." Thales said water is the original element and the end. The ancients feared drowning more than any other disaster; there would be no quiet for the deceased in those inscrutable, voracious deeps.

This is a Doomsday book about water. The sea is the foe of Odysseus, the *Odyssey* is the Orphic battle to overcome this moist substance or passion. According to Porphyry, Odysseus desired to "appease his natal daemon with a suppliant branch" of the olive tree of Minerva. Homer, as well as the Greeks, who feared the Ocean, which is the cause of Odysseus' desolation, intends to absolve Odysseus in the end so that he can be with earth-born people "who ne'er knew salt, or heard the billows roar." But Melville is the acolyte of Poseidon and not Minerva. "I am, by a flood, borne back to that wondrous period . . . Here Saturn's grey chaos rolls over me."

The Void made God miserable, and He was unquiet until the waters had receded. The Ocean is too close to Primal Nothing; neither the Cherubim nor men have composure in water, which is the corrupt kindred of nihilism. In the second book of *Esdras*, Enoch, who is said to be good, is the ruler over dry ground, and Leviathan over the drowned parts of the globe. Adamah, in Hebrew, is virgin red clay, or as Stanley Burnshaw, the poet, says: "All thought is clay / And withered song."

Go to sea, ye who seek the solace of that immense, empty Bosom, the Ocean, and ye shall lament for the teats, for the pleasant fields, for the fruitful vine. "Do you know that there is not . . . a tree in de Sade?" is an observation in the Goncourts' journals.

Water is a Babel and a confusion in *Moby-Dick;* otherwise, how can we account for Melville's allusions to "sea-pastures," "watery prairies," "Potters' Fields of all four continents," or comprehend "those fabled undulations of the Ephesian sod"? Yet the Deluge is his passion, and he only wrote *justly* when he dealt with the great flood of Noah or Deucalion or the pelagic contents of the universe. The Flood was also for him, as for all early peoples, a punitive disaster.

A plethora of water in the spirit destroys filial affection; Cyclops, who is a son of Neptune and always found on the coast, sins because he cares for nobody, neither the gods nor his parents, save himself, and Euripides considers this his most foul infamy. Whoever sees Cyclops with a wife, children, or a brother? Giants are parricides, and if they have a mother or any kin they are utterly dead to them. The Cyclopian sea-ruffians in the *Pequod* never mention their progenitors. *Moby-Dick* is an unfilial book, and the words thereof are the children in Sheol.

Theophrastus was of the mind that moisture in people was the cause of their stupidity. Tertullian, having no regard for the pagan god of the seas, accepts the ancient claim that the dolphins vomit forth in honor of Neptune. In *Moby-Dick* water is less a natural element than a biblical, allegorical substance. Of the four powers of nature, Melville selected the one that grieved his spirit the most. According to an Egyptian ideograph, water signifies deprivation; the Chinese regarded it as a negative element, and Virgil thought it a deceitful one. Homer said that Oceanus was sterile; Ceres cannot sow wheat here, nor can we find the parsley and the Orphic meadowland surrounding Calypso's cave in *Moby-Dick*. Had Melville been a Hippocrates he would have related that sea water maddens the intellect, makes men splenetic, pituitous, and costive, weakens the large, benevolent organs we have inherited from the Angels who lusted after the fair daughters of men, and gives them instead the hopeless aches of androgynes and eunuchs who are governed by Aquarius. The hermaphrodite rarely laughs, for such boisterous noise is pocketed in that bountiful Adamic sac, the testes. In Scripture it is written: "Let the waters be gathered to one place, and let dry land appear." But Melville never departed from the seas to return to the earth.

Melville imagined he had taken the paschal lamb of Christ and covered it with the coat of Leviathan. He cringed when he thought of the "universal cannibalism of the ocean, or unverdured seas"—yet most of his volumes are salt-water folios. A hydromaniac, there was very much more of liquid properties than flesh in his prose style. It was in vain that he heaved forth his pain: "Though in many of its aspects this visible world seems formed in love, the invisible spheres were formed in fright."

What is important is not brit, squid, ambergris, or the chapter on Cetology, but Ham's vice, which is the cry of all waters in man. This is the portent of water in *Moby-Dick*. "Yea, foolish mortals, Noah's flood is not yet subsided." God drowned the earth as a judgment of man, for is it not written in Psalms, "The Lord sat at the Flood"?

The human race perished in the Great Inundation, according to Talmudic Cabalists, because of the intellectual and sexual perversions of mankind. When the Body is false unto itself, the intellect is a liar. *Moby-Dick* is a Hamitic dream; water and meditation are forever married, says the author, and nocturnal visions are damp.

The making of the book took a year; Melville made no corrections, and never rewrote any moiety of it. A novel of over five hundred pages is a great, hulking hull. The Canticles of Solomon are short, the book of Ecclesiastes and the Song of Songs a few pages, and how many Hebrew scribes composed and mended these sage and amorous ballads no one will ever know. Who can know all of his errors? Is everything that falls out of the mouth a divine truth? If so, the gabbling women who chase the geese of Camelot are sibyls and canting trimmers are prophets.

In a book of half a millennium of pages, the adjectives alone are heavy enough to sink the Theban Towers, or to borrow from Swinburne: "the eyes which keep open through the perusal of six consecutive pages must never hope to find rest but in the grave." There is more sorrow in his epithets than in the characters, and moreover the adjectives are made to suffer alike on all occasions, for he had a pelting memory and repeated the same desiccated, gothic descriptions frequently.

Only the insane wish to be misologists, and, assuming that one can, at least, read with a tolerable amount of reasonableness, I find no other way of showing how shabbily written *Moby-Dick* is than by adducing the evidence, which is always the "windmills in the brain." What have we of the nature of Ahab but repetitious phrases about his head and mind, which at first may fetch the ear, but later are no more than the specious Elizabethan thunder of a very weary Zeus? The stage roar only deafens us so that all we hear is the monotonous din of surging pages that commenced to roll before the time of Adam, and which do not cease until the readers themselves are drowned in the great Deluge.

At the risk of being a burden of Tyre to the reader I quote the following: Ahab, the ocean, Moby-Dick, and even the *Pequod*, are "moody," "mad," "demonic," "mystic," "brooding," "crazy," "lunatic," "insane," and "malicious." Ahab is stricken, mad or moody on any page that he is mentioned, and this prolix refrain is likely to send a reader to Bedlam solely to hear a raving inmate declare that he is sane. The brows of Moby-Dick and Ahab are baked in the same kiln of Moloch. Melville had no understanding of heroical size in literature, and tried to achieve the epic by hurling hoaxing, hot phrases at the reader: "Give me Vesuvius' crater for an inkstand!" He attempted to convey the impression that he had large, passionate organs. "Hyperbole is the most frigid of all forms of speech," says Aristotle. Eros is said to have thunderbolts in his right hand, and a trident in his left. Cold must couple with cold, fire with heat, and darkness with night; the fat scum of vice is better than unnatural virtue.

Melville was as luckless with his metaphors, that are nearly always awry and have little connection with the thought in the sentence, as he was with his characters. Had he washed his similes in the Pool of Bethesda they would still be lame and palsied. One might say of Melville what Swinburne said of Byron: "Much of the poem is written throughout in falsetto."

His solecisms and hyperboles are mock fury: "the delta of his forehead's veins," "burnt-out crater of his brain," "Ahab's brow . . . gaunt and ribbed," "globular and ponderous heart," "my splintered heart," "the last gasp of his earthquake life," "he burst his hot heart's shell," "the wondrous cistern in the whale's huge head," "his broad milky forehead," "the whale's huge head," "his pleated head," "his pleated forehead," "his oblong, white head." Ahab and the sperm whale are malevolent monomaniacs: "The white whale . . . as the monomaniac incarnation of all those malicious agencies," "Moby-Dick, with that malicious intelligence," "monomaniac old man," "monomaniac Ahab." Ahab, the Parsee and Leviathan are mystagogues: "the mystic-marked whale" and the Parsee's "mystic watch."

I have told you all there is to know about the characters: Melville discloses in fifty phases, more or less, that Ahab is a monomaniac. This is scenic diabolism; there is more of Ahab in one line of *Hamlet* than in the entire supernatural allegory: Polonius: "to define true madness, what is't but to be nothing else but mad"; Hamlet: "I am but mad north-north-west; when the wind is southerly, I know a hawk from a handsaw." Moreover, the tragical writers do not repeatedly say how desolate and broken their heroes are.

This huffing treatise is glutted with: "the whole grim aspect of Ahab," "he was a raving lunatic," "moody, stricken Ahab," "his delirium," "the old man's delirium," "Ahab's full lunacy," "madness sat brooding on his brow," "the whale's direful wrath," "all the subtle demonism of life," "the demoniac waves."

Melville's jadish vocabulary is swollen into the Three Furies, and we flee from them as Ben Jonson in his *Poetaster* took flight from "furibund," "magnificate," "lubrical," "fatuate," "turgidous," "ventosity." For those who are reluctant to believe that such dross is not the customary ailment in this novel, the best advice I can offer is, "Read it yourself, and see."

The atrabilious Ahab is only wicked in the sluttish, supine words with which the author depicts him. Evil is energetic and must accomplish its ends that are just as essential to the Kosmos as the work that good must do.

There is no voyage, and there are no more hints of the characters themselves than were given at the beginning of the book. We see Ahab either lying in a hammock when the *Pequod* skirts the howling, wet shingle of Patagonia, or standing close to the mizzen shrouds, or upon the quarter-deck leaning on the taffrail. "But in the cautious comprehensiveness and unloitering vigilance . . . Ahab threw his brooding soul into this unfaltering hunt." Ulysses is a wise, crafty freebooter, but the *Iliad* is a regal poem of action, and the poet justly ascribes "to Ulysses, a thousand generous deeds."

Aham is no less opaque at the conclusion of the tome than he is at its inception; if, as Shakespeare says in *Lear*, "Ripeness is all," then one can say that in *Moby-Dick*,

"Ripeness is nothing." Moreover, we are drinking the waters of Lethe, for Melville did not remember whether he was describing the ocean, the *Pequod*, Ahab, or Leviathan. "The Pequod gored the dark waves in her madness," "great demon of the seas," "all the swift madness of the demoniac waves."

A good deal of bombast has come from the noddles of our intelligentsia about Melville's knowledge of the food and properties of the whale. Contrary to his usual garrulous habits there are only penurious references to these oceanic viands: "Squid . . . is a vast pulpy mass, furlongs in length . . . twisting like a nest of anacondas," "we fell in with vast meadows of brit, the minute, yellow substance, upon which the Right Whale largely feeds," "ambergris is soft, waxy, and so highly fragrant and spicy, that it is largely used in perfumery, in pastiles, precious candles, hair-powders, and pomatum." Ambergris, according to Melville is "supposed to be the cause . . . of the dyspepsia in the whale."

I should mention a few of the chapter titles and charitably refer to them as a bill of lading of a clerkly Triton sitting in a shipping office on lower Wall Street: "The Chart," "The Try-Works," "The Battering Ram," "The Affidavit," "The Quadrant," "The Monkey-Rope," "Whales in Paint," "The Line," "The Dark," "Pitch-Poling," "Fast Fish and Loose Fish."

There is not the scantiest humdrum minutia omitted: "A belaying pin is found too large to be easily inserted into its hole," "The line . . . used in the fishery was of the best hemp," "while the one tackle is peeling and hoisting a second strip from the whale, the other is slowly slackened away." Malvolio, sometimes called Leon Edel, furnishes us with notes, which are no less baneful than the brackish seawater in *Moby-Dick:* "In Sperm-whalemen with any considerable quantity of oil on board, it is a regular semiweekly duty to conduct a hose into the hold." In *Moby-Dick* Melville discloses: "But if the doctrine of Fast-Fish be pretty generally applicable, the kindred doctrine of Loose-Fish is still more widely so." Demetrius rebukes those clodpates on Mount Ida who "press home every detail as though your hearer were a fool," and Webster writes: "A fantastical scholar, like such who study to know how many knots was in Hercules' club or what colour Achilles' beard was." Milton reminds us: "What a stupidness is it, then, that we should deject ourselves to such a sluggish, underfoot philosophy."

Do you want natural history? Then let Aristotle, Pliny, Theophrastus, Dioscorides, Buffon, Darwin, or Humboldt be your masters. Melville's cetology, the science of whales, is borrowed from a hundred books and *Moby-Dick* is only the lees of other men's marine lore. Most of his knowledge came from natural historians, and, like the water wagtail, who pursues the gull until he drops the dung that is the wagtail's principal food, Melville filled himself with the droppings of many volumes on whaling.

We do not study Homer for his nautical information: besides, he knew, perhaps, as little of the sea as Melville did about whaling. One reads Montaigne, Anacreon, Diodorus, Strabo, La Bruyère for pleasure and the intellectual viaticum in wise books. But are chapters on hemp, the pots in which the "hissing masses of blubber" are scalded, and recondite nonsense about old Bible prints of Jonah, a whaling Cabala?

When I want to take a voyage, I don't go to *Moby-Dick*, any more than I read Sir John Mandeville's *Travels* —he wrote about the Holy Land and the ancient world without ever having left England. Mandeville's book is a cento of Pliny, Strabo, Marco Polo, and the refuse of sundry apocryphal Christian works. If you would travel, then go to the journals of voyages compiled by Hakluyt, or wander through the marvelous pages collected by Purchas, or take up rough Drake, or Pigafetta's Magellan as your guide.

However, so many of the borrowed facts about the habits of whales are of no unusual significance, anyway, in a novel or a work of the imagination. I am unable to enumerate the piscatory errors in Izaak Walton's *The Compleat Angler*, but I read him for his style, which is another name for perception or wisdom. The thoughts we have are only the words we use. Melville's sentences, however, are always to the windward, so that the reader is worn out by the food of the imagination; facts are the stepdaughters of the muses.

Melville writes: "The previous chapter gave account of an immense body or herd of Sperm Whales," which is gawkish advice to his auditors who, he imagines, could not even recollect a single chapter fifteen minutes after reading it. But how often we reprove others for our own faults. Hesiod thought that Zeus lay with Mnemosyne, who is Memory and the mother of muses, for nine days and nine nights without interruption; and it required that much Olympian, not whale, sperm to fecundate the intellect. Melville had never gone to Delphi to comprehend the best of admonitions: "Know thyself." A novelist, he had almost no knowledge of people. What we call knowledge of others is what we know about ourselves.

How much more fortunate is his short but renowned chapter, "The Whiteness of the Whale"? There is the same melancholia in it as in the rest of the novel. Though Moby-Dick is priapic Jupiter, the snow-white bull, white represents death. The Albatross in those "exiled waters" is a portentous wraith, and "the White Mountains of New Hampshire," are "a gigantic ghostliness" that hangs over his gray, hulled soul. "The White Sea exerts such a spectralness over the fancy." "Witness the white bear of the poles, and the white shark of the tropics . . . transcendent horrors they are." St. John the Evangelist rides on his pallid horse and the fierce-fanged tiger wears the same mortuary vesture, and Lima, a lepry city of sin, "has taken the white veil"; "all deified Nature absolutely paints like the harlot, whose allurements cover nothing but the charnel-house within." Melville concludes this white Golgotha with: "And of all these things the Albino whale was the symbol. Wonder ye then at the fiery hunt?" Of course, he is again paraphrasing Revelation: "And I looked, and behold a pale horse: and his name that sat on him was Death."

Compare this with Rabelais, who, grounded in ancient lore, reminds us that the Thracians and Greeks marked their "good, propitious and fortunate days with white stones." Gargantua wears Jovean, white slops trimmed with blue, which contain eleven hundred and five ells of phallus, bacon, tripes, roasted thrushes basted with hen-scum and wine. Paris was formerly called, Rabelais avers, Leucotia, in honor of the white thighs of the women there.

When the Archangel Raphael appears before Tobit, the latter announces that there is nothing so good and comforting as Light, which is the raiment of the Cherubim. Allen Tate writes that for Dante "Light is Beatrice; light is her *smile*." Alba, the sacred first town in Latium, was founded by Aeneas where the white sow sat down to rest. Such a legend signifies gestation, the keeping-room and the house, but who breeds porkers or reaps wheat in the Pacific?

However, it is now time for more citations.

this strange uncompromisedness in him involved a sort of unintelligence.

To insure the greatest efficiency in the dart, the harpooners of this world must start to their feet out of idleness.

[The carpenter] was singularly efficient in those

thousand nameless mechanical emergencies continually recurring in a large ship.

this omni-tooled, open-and-shut carpenter.

these spiritual throes in him heaved his being up from its base, and a chasm seemed opening in him, from which forked flames and lightnings shot up.

crazy Ahab, the scheming, unappeasedly steadfast hunger of the white whale; this Ahab . . . had gone to his hammock.

Here be it said, that this pertinacious pursuit of one particular whale, continued through day into night, and through night into day.

little Flask bobbed up and down like an empty vial.

He was like one of those unreasoning but still highly useful, *multum in parvo*, Sheffield contrivances.

this half-horrible stolidity in him, involving, too, as it appeared, an all-ramifying heartlessness;—yet was it oddly dashed at times, with an old, crutch-like, antediluvian, wheezing humorousness, not unstreaked now and then with a certain grizzled wittiness.

however promissory of life and passion in the end, it is above all things requisite that temporary interests and employments should intervene and hold them healthily suspended for the final dash.

There are some enterprises in which a careful disorderliness is the true method.

Is this the "honest manna of literature"?

But may nobody believe that I would conceal the chants of a man who had enough genius to sing on occasion, but not sufficient strength to write an epical novel. A good sentence or emotion in *Moby-Dick* will come as dear as the cost of dove's dung at the time of the famine in Samaria. Here are some of Melville's canorous lines:

I leave a white and turbid wake; pale waters, paler cheeks, where'er I sail. The envious billows sidelong swell to whelm my track; let them; but first I pass.

Yonder, by the ever-brimming goblet's rim, the warm waves blush like wine. The gold bow plumbs the blue.

But it is a mild, mild wind, and a mild looking sky; and the air smells now, as if it blew from a far-away meadow; they have been making hay somewhere under the slopes of the Andes, Starbuck, and the mowers are sleeping among the new-mown hay. Sleeping? Aye, toil we how we may, we all sleep at last on the field. Sleep? Aye, and rust amid greenness; as last year's scythes flung down, and left in the half-cut swaths . . .

let me look into a human eye; it is better than to gaze into sea or sky; better than to gaze upon God. By the green land; by the bright hearthstone! this is the magic glass . . .

There is a wisdom that is woe; but there is a woe that is madness. And there is a Catskill eagle in some souls . . .

Oh, grassy glades! oh, ever vernal endless landscapes in the soul; in ye,—though long parched by the dead drought of the earthly life,—in ye, men yet may roll, like young horses in new morning clover. . . . Would to God these blessed calms would last.

American literature is exceedingly poor in victuals and in amours. No character has been adequately fed or loved in an American novel for a hundred and twenty-five years. The sailors on the *Pequod* seem as content with biscuit and ship's beef as Cylops, a part-time vegetarian monster, is with curds and cow's milk. But the Colossus of Euripides prefers a roasted stag, a lion on the spit, or gobbets of human flesh. A heathen's collation on the *Pequod* consists of large gammons of whale blubber. These mariners have the gloomy, Phrygian throats of Bacchanal nymphs who milked a lioness and made cheese of the milk. Melville knew no subtler delicacy of the table than strawberries swimming in the milk of the sperm whale. The author thought that "brains of a small Sperm Whale are accounted a fine dish." "The casket of the skull is broken into with an axe, and the two plump, whitish lobes being withdrawn (precisely resembling two large puddings), they are then mixed with flour, and cooked into a most delectable mess." "The imagination is wounded long before the conscience" is a wise thought from Henry David Thoreau.

What wry joy does this descendant of Ham and Polyphemus, perverse in all of his appetites, take in telling the reader of those profane, Polynesian meals of human flesh: the barbecued heads that had been decapitated by cannibals in Tahiti "were placed in great wooden trenches, and garnished round like a pilau, with breadfruit and cocoanuts; and with some parsley in their mouths." Aristotle advises the poet that not everything can be divulged, or offered in plain view "lest Medea murder her children in front of the audience, or impious Atreus cook human flesh in public."

Whose gorge is not qualmish as he witnesses Stubb eating his "spermaceti supper" as "thousands on thousands of sharks" are swarming round the dead whale roped to the *Pequod?* What froward humor there is in Melville when he places before the reader "a meat pie nearly one hundred feet long" made of the innards of a whale. So much blubber gives one indigestion for "the rest of his reading days."

There is no doxy, trollop, or trull in any of Melville's volumes. He had no likerish palate; even chaste Spenser would allow the desolate tribe of males the solace of "her snowy breast was bare to greedy spoil." Moreover, who, after such an incubus, does not pine to hear the sound of her petticoats, the sweet, nourishing sight of her licentious skirts? After considering the intricate intestines of a sperm whale, as Melville advises us to do, I am as ready as Holofernes to swoon when I behold Judith's sandals.

Samuel Daniel pined for Delia, Swift wrote memorable epistles to Stella, and the singers in Israel were pierced by those maids who had eyes like the fishpools of Heshbon, but Melville lays bare the beams, the joists, the sinews of a whale. Montesquieu told his friends that the only reason he wrote was to seek favor with the Venuses at court. Herman Melville at the age of thirty, when he should have been an amorist, was as gloomy as John Donne who sat in his shroud after he had passed his fiftieth year.

None can misdoubt Melville's misogyny. The hatred of women is the pederastic nausea that comes from the mention of the womb. Robert Burton, in *The Anatomy of Melancholy*, says that a Muscovite Duke vomited when he saw a woman. Melville, Whitman, Poe, and Thoreau loathed the female, and the first three sages suffered from sodomy of the heart. No more than three generations separate us from Thoreau, Whitman, Poe, and Melville; little wonder then that we are now in the age of ice, and that one man in every ten craves to burn in the fires of Sodom and Gomorrah.

Instead of all those spermal ablutions for the pathic, in which Melville said the male should wash his heart, give me the Restoration wit of: "Two years' marriage has debauched my five senses. Everything I see, everything I hear, everything I feel, everything I smell, and everything I taste, methinks has wife in it." "Methinks my body is but the lees of my better being," declares Melville. At Sais the peplum of Isis was never lifted, and in sixteen volumes by Melville no woman is bedded, seduced, or gulled, and, by heaven, that is gross deception.

Perversity is the black angel of our century, and the hatred of the clan of females, so deep in Melville, Poe, Whitman, and Thoreau, is our Atlean inheritance which we must understand or perish. Eros is the source of masculine life and wit; what there is of gaiety in American letters is either puerile or those few parched, sly conceits in *Moby-Dick* and *Bartleby the Scrivener*.

Melville's "If ye touch at the islands, Mr. Flask, be-

ware of fornication," is a wry imitation of Paul's admonition to the Colossians: "avoid fornication, impurity,
lust, evil concupiscence." Melville's line is likely to produce a pewed smile, but far better and more jovial is
Rabelais' Bumpkin who keeps the Psalter in his codpiece.

Who wants to chase a Sperm-Whale for over hundred
pages when he can pursue a Shulamite, a Cressid, a dowdy,
or a shake-bag? Had Herman Melville never been moved
by amorous ballads? can a dolphin, a chine of blubber, or
the white hump of a whale take the place of the thighs of
Aspasia or the rump of Lais of Corinth? This is Melville's
phallic song: "Other poets have warbled . . . the soft eyes
of the antelope . . . less celestial, I celebrate a tail [of
Leviathan]."

Melville composed amorous canticles to an oceanic
brute, and the sea was his hymeneal bed. Leviathan is a
"luxurious Ottoman," with "all the solaces and endearments of the harem"; the Sperm Whale has a "beautiful
and chaste-looking mouth . . . glossy as bridal satins." The
pelagic brutes are "unprincipled young rakes"; Leviathan
is a "Lothario, like pious Solomon among his thousand
concubines."

What else are "the submarine bridal chambers of
Leviathan," and all those spermal remedies that he said
Paracelsus advised the ill to take to allay their wrath, than
epithalamiums? Though Melville could not reject the old
Hebrew law of retribution, he had little of that masculine
fire in him; Empedokles believed that "in its warmer part
the womb brings forth males."

Ahab's solipsism comes from the pride of Narcissus,
and there is no hemlock so pernicious as the arts of self-
love. Ahab represents moisture, and in the Psalms it is "the
proud water." "Blind is the man who does not hate self-
love," said the author of the *Pensées*. What reason has
Narcissus to regard a woman when he finds so much satisfaction in contemplating his own face?

Woman is still the imperial booty of the races, and men will sack towns, capture cities to furnish their courtesans with money to purchase cosmetics and soap, or rape the Sabine virgins when they cannot obtain wives otherwise. Plato knew that nothing was so acute as the pleasures of the body, without which men will hanker for a whale, a dog, a cat, and go stark mad to be like "that lecher that carneled with a statue." Origen horrified the Christian Fathers by castrating himself although they were intellectual wethers themselves. Men suffer either because they have testes or because they have none.

Rather than dissect the corpse of one woman, which Balzac advises the novice in amours to do, before he selects a wife, Melville offers the American the anatomy of Leviathan. Here is the cause of Melville's woe, and ours. He wrote a book for men, or, at least, hermaphrodites and spados. I would just as lief reread *Moby-Dick* as live in a volume or a world without any females in it.

Woman is a perfidious creature in *Moby-Dick*, and he cannot refer to Judith or Cleopatra without giving the impression that it was not Holofernes nor Antony who was betrayed but Herman Melville. In an allusion that has no reasonable connection with the sentence or the chapter he speaks of the gory head of Holofernes hanging from the girdle of Judith. "Towards noon whales were raised . . . they turned and fled . . . a disordered flight, as of Cleopatra's barges from Actium." When Melville writes of Jupiter abducting Europa, his sole interest is in the "lovely, leering eyes" of Zeus; of Europa he says nothing. "By Jupiter, I must not fear a woman," say Beaumont and Fletcher in *The Philaster*.

Melville believed Sir Thomas Browne who wrote that woman is "the rib and the crooked piece of Man," and that "man is the whole world, and the breath of God," which, if true, indicates that there is something amiss in the Lord's respiration. The mariners of the *Pequod*, like

Adam, must have been "born without a navel," for none appears to have a mother; all are either unwived or unsocial, despite the few reluctant references to those "faraway domestic memories" that afflict Ahab, a "houseless, familyless, old man."

After the blubber pots and the love scenes of these corrugated mammoth Don Juans of the sea, what virile male reader does not yearn for the witty bouts between a smell-smock and a flirt, or a sweet bosom that would set Ilium on fire? Whatever Sir John Brute is aching for it is not the Ephesian dugs of a whale, the matrix of a porpoise, or the oceanic marriage bed of Leviathan. Wycherley's Dorilant has enough wit to penetrate the most amiable feminine heart: "A mistress should be like a little country retreat near the town; not to dwell in constantly, but only for a night, and away, to taste the town the better when a man returns."

The Roman virgin sat on the image of the phallus; in Egypt at the time of Philadelphus Ptolomey there was a festival in which the matrons carried Priapus who was a hundred and twenty-five cubits in length, and that is as long as a seminal book should be. Now that we are prepared to hawk this divine god, Priapus, let us announce that what we are willing to sell, barter, or even give away is, *For Women Only*.

What nature makes us we are; contend with this absolute force at the risk of your sanity. A virile male craves his opposite, and that is nature and habit which are the parents of morals. The wise Rabbin said that the contemporaries of Noah were defiant sinners, and drove the Shekinah away from the world.

At the risk of sowing dragon's teeth, and acquiring another legion of foes I have never seen, I must impugn *Moby-Dick* as inhuman literature. What kind of a moral novel is this? Alas, the word moral has been the shibboleth of the philister. That gentle genius, Herbert Read, mislikes this word, and prefers justice in the place of it, but what will prevent the academic presbyters of literature from preempting this word, too?

Who worships vice, arrogance, or a brute of the salty deep? Since the beasts and demons are within man, what need is there to pursue them? Nobody should resolve to be vile: "See! Moby-Dick seeks thee not. It is thou, thou that madly seekest him!" What is bad will fall out of the soul anyway. Who looks everywhere for trouble? In Proverbs it is stated: "A prudent man seeth evil, and hideth himself." Jesus goes into the wilderness to withstand temptation, but the Gospels are gray, plain truths. Moreover, who wants to be worse than he already is? And who would not care to obey Ben Jonson's maxim, "He that for love of goodness hateth ill."

Goodness did not tempt Melville sorely. Pascal says that "Milton is well aware that Nature is corrupt and that men are hostile to morality." Melville, a Pauline invert, remarks: "Bethink thee of that saying of St. Paul in Corinthians, about corruption and incorruption; how that we are sown in dishonor, but raised in glory."

We only recognize men's virtues when they benefit us. Moreover, morals which do not come from a concupiscent nature are a cold wind upon the frail, reedy spirit. He who is in agony because he is not hot hankers for the fabled Apples of Sodom.

Melville was unable to understand St. Paul because he himself was the prey of corrosive acedy. The work of the moth and rust had deprived him of energy, without which morality is a basilisk. "For the flesh lusteth against the Spirit, and the Spirit against the flesh." No one can avoid this battle, whether he be a hedonist or have strong ascetic inclinations, lest he be a viper to his brother and detest everybody for no other reason than his reluctance to overcome his faults. One who has tepid or cold privities can never pardon anybody, especially those whom he has harmed. Worse, he regards the human race as his foe, though in his secret soul he knows the real adversary is himself.

It is told that Paul fought with the beasts at Ephesus; but with what sort of clandestine lust was Herman Melville concerned in *Moby-Dick?* What turpitude does he wish to drown in the great Deluge?

Says Seneca: "A man may dispute, cite great authorities, talk learnedly, huff it out, and yet be rotten at heart."

We are not dealing with Melville's torn, empirical life, but with his imagination, which is the truest experience. Men reveal themselves most when they dream, and Moby-Dick is the Titanic sodomite serpent that crept into his dark, blighted heart, never to quit that lair in which the most abominable passions lurk, as we see in his last, homosexual, work, *Billy Budd*.

Though he has been somewhat touched by that dreariest of screeds, the perfectibility of man—"immaculate manliness" is what Melville calls it—one can look in vain for a piacular sentence in *Moby-Dick*. But what savant does not talk as though his heart were not decayed? St. Paul and Pascal spoke simply, never failing to understand that they suffered because they were obsessed by foul imaginings, a truth that Herman Melville never understood. So much of our lives is given over to the consideration of our imperfections that there is no time to improve our imaginary virtues. The truth is we only perfect our vices, and man is a worse creature when he dies than he was when he was born: "and Jesus said, Why callest thou me good? None is good." Men cocker their vices and whatever they do that is good is the consequence of vanity, and thoughtlessness: he is born stupid and dies depraved. Christ sent his lambs to go among the wolves, and Moby-Dick is no lamb.

Ahab does not seek glory but scrapes the bottom of Tartarus and all obscure depths for infamy. The Puritan is a clandestine lecher, and dreams are beasts that come in the night; *Moby-Dick* is the vision of the noctambulist and a furtive, dark trance. Ishmael, Ahab, Daggoo, Queequeg, Pip, Fedallah, Tashtego, the detritus of Tartary and Asia Minor, are symbols of nocturnal orgies. Moby-Dick is a primordial animal, and his watery home is the Pacific, which is an Asiatic ocean, for the first peoples came to the new world over this vasty stream. Leviathan is one of the Minotaurs, Sphinxes, and Centaurs, which Plutarch thought were the products of the monstrous, incestuous, and ungovernable lusts of man.

Melville abhorred nature, and thought that God was not the peer of the demiurge, who, as one of the ante-Nicene Fathers held, was the cause of corruption and death. The Gnostics also referred to Sophia as the Spirit and the Demiurge as the Devil. The suffering atheists, or self-gnawing agnostics, who composed the Book of Job, had the same conception.

The author of the Zohar said that before Noah there were only three just men in the earth, Methuselah, Enoch, and Jared, and who can forget that Noah is the father of the first sodomite, Ham? Moreover, who has not the most acute compassion for Herman Melville's ontological pain? Had not the prophet Jeremiah also cried out in anguish: "O Lord, Thou hast deceived us," and does not Jesus in a rueful, gnostical mood lament: "Your Father is a murderer from the beginning"? What concerns us is that Melville was a perverted Christian, and that the tawdry writing in *Moby-Dick* is to some extent willful self-hatred.

Herman Melville had committed sodomy, as it is meant in the Old Testament; in his mind he had had connection with a beast of the deep. Take woman from man and he will yearn for an angel, a porpoise, a whale. This starveling became a hunter for profane and nether flesh, dolphins, sharks, leviathan, and man, whatever could ease those clinkered, lava lusts. Unable to be consumed in the flames of Troy for Helen, he was cindered in the fires of Sodom and Gomorrah. Read his last work, *Billy Budd,* a piece of inverted mariolatry, for it is the virgin boy, Budd, the name of a maiden, who is his Mary.

The only real marriage in the book is between Quee-queg and Ishmael. "He pressed his forehead against mine, clasped me round the waist, and said that henceforth we were married." "No place like a bed for confidential dis-closures," and this is as close to the bed of Venus as he ever comes.

Melville's Christ is "soft, curled, hermaphroditical," "negative" and "feminine." Give us a pagan Christ, in part Apis and Mnevis! Why does Jesus wear a loincloth? The women at Pompeii substituted the cross for the image of the phallus they had worn around their necks. The cruci-fix hangs against the fertile paps of the Catholic virgin, and what natural woman carries the image of a man close to her carnal bosom without sensual pangs? We must cast out such diabolical conceptions of goodness, as the Lord him-self "opens the kingdoms of heaven to eunuchs," and "it remains, that they who have wives so be as if they have not" or there will be a universal Sodom and Gomorrah.

Melville is an Ophite and his supernatural whale, "the starry Cetus," is a species of Dagon, the fish-like deity of the Philistines. The whale, though a mammal, was a great fish and a serpent to the ancient fabulists, and Christ is a moist star—Jesus is Pisces.

Leviathan in the Zohar is feminine. The Leviathan, the oldest foe of man, is called Rahab by Isaiah and the Psalm-ist—the Dragon and the serpent. "Thou hast broken Rahab in pieces" and "Art thou it that hath cut Rahab and wounded the dragon?" both come from Isaiah and refer to a feminine creature, and is not Rahab also the whore of Jericho? Elohim, too, is often feminine in the Cabala and in the Gnostic theology. Proclus in the *Timaeus* believed that "Nature is suspended from the back of the vivifying goddess." The female part of God was known as the

Shekinah to the cabalistical thinkers. Clement of Alexandria writes that the symbol of the Bacchic orgies is a consecrated reptile and also that the name Hevia, or Eve, signifies a female serpent.

But for Melville, a superstitious scientist, or a Talmudic one, the pelagic Demiurge is masculine. His mammoth, in part, is one of the "monsters of Rahab" of the olden Rabbin; Leviathan is Tiamat of the Gilgamesh epic, the dragon of Isaiah, the Psalmist, Job, and Enoch. *Moby-Dick* is a hybrid of Scripture and zoology, and this brute of the sea is the product of the "half-foetal suggestions of supernatural agencies." Thomas Traherne wrote that "to call things preternatural Natural is Monstrous."

Osiris, the personification of the generative organs of man to the Egyptians, was second in importance to Isis, the begetter. She is the Ancient One just as God is known as the Ancient of Days in the Book of Daniel. It is Isis, the goddess, and not the aboriginal hermaphrodite, masculine in front, but feminine in the hinder parts, who is searching all the waters of the Nile for the genitals of her consort. Did she find them, or are we men with only a tithe of a prepuce?

However, it is the spermal deity Melville worships, not the Generatrix, as is apparent in one of Melville's extraordinary raptures: "In thoughts of the visions of the night, I saw long rows of angels in paradise, each with his hands in a jar of spermaceti." Of the sperm Melville writes: "I washed my hands and my heart [in] it."

In spite of the fact that the novel is a doxology of a wicked beast of the seas, Melville believed in punishment, for the *Pequod* is a "whited sepulchre" on the outside, but full of "dead men's bones within." Furthermore, in the Cabala it is explained that the human race perished, save Noah and his family, by drowning. But why was homosexual Ham spared, and does not Melville follow the same parable since all die by water save Ishmael, who is really

Ham? And the universal Hamite is grum, aqueous, and froward.

*Moby-Dick* is Christian zoolatry, a Puritanical bestiary, and in some respects, not dissimilar from the Egyptian *Book of the Dead*. Philo Judeaus had rebuked the Egyptians for their idolatry of crocodiles, dogs, the ibis, and cats. In ancient Cairo superannuated cats were fed in charity hospitals. One cat in a house is a sign of loneliness, two of barrenness, and three of sodomy. *Moby-Dick* is the bestial Bible of modern Ham.

The darks races awakened his concupiscence: is not Ham the Father of Africa? Melville called his seafarers mermen. Only dark or olive flesh stirred in him the ashes of Borsippa, Ur, and Canaan. Ham is also the father of Canaan who is the primal forebear of the Canaanites who were destroyed because of their terrible wantonness. The "imperial" Negro Daggoo was his phallic idol, and the name was obviously derived from Dagon, a god with the tail of a fish. There were Tashtego, black Pip whom he fondles, and Fedallah the Parsee who is the only one before whom Ahab stands in awe. Water is vice, retribution, and Ham; the spermal whale is Priapus who has deprived Ahab of his phallical leg. As Fedallah is drowning, Ahab, for no overt cause, moans for the "unforgiven ghosts of Gomorrah." The words in the soul rise to the lips on a sudden, because no lust can sink them. Ay, it is a dry, dry book in which a man can drown all his sins.

These are seafearing Nimrods; Nimrod is the hunter whose iniquity is his pride, and the *Pequod* is a Babel, as Melville shows in the chapter "Midnight, Forecastle"; it is the Tower of Hubris on the watery plains of Shinar.

Since we are as bad as our dreams, and our books are no better, it was inevitable that Melville should have had Cyclops' anthropophagous palate, and that after *Moby-Dick* he should have written *Pierre*, a novel about incest. Those meager sentences that are supposed to be cetology in *Moby-Dick* are very close to quack erudition because there is a failure in sensibility and a drought of the organs of the body. We can only write well about our sins because it is too difficult to recall a virtuous act or even whether it was the result of good or evil motives.

There is now a pederastic hagiography composed of people who prefer the bad to the good, who like excrements instead of pond-apples, sumach, dogwood, or hyacinths, and who choose men rather than women to be their paramours. Intellectual sodomy, which comes from the refusal to be simple about plain matters, is as gross and abundant today as sexual perversion and they are nowise different from one another. This kind of pathic in literature has wan, epicene affections. A misologist, he takes ophidian pleasure in the misuse of words, and his sacerdotal gibberish sounds more like the cries of animals than the holy Logos or the alphabet of the god Thoth. Is there a genius in Christendom whose holy credo is not: "In the beginning was the Word"? Specious rebels, they are the advocates of the rabble arts.

The martyrology of the sodomite consists of St. Ordure, St. Incest, and St. Matricide. The inverted Christion eremite nowadays has a matricidal heart, and is either totally separated from his parents, or utterly detests them. How feeble is the image of the father in nineteenth-century American literature; had Poe any parents at all? What do we know of Melville's male progenitor, or Whitman's, and was the great savant, Thoreau, born of stocks and stones? The misogamist spawns the homosexual, and *Moby-Dick* is the worship of the male sperm. Phallic idolatry is the concern of women, and no literature can be bawdy, human, and sage unless men love women; no nation can survive, not Hellas nor Jerusalem, when the stews for males are substituted for the hetaira and the olive-complexioned damsels who were the solace of the harper and his son, the amorist Solomon.

# "I Was Naked; and I Hid"

L ook at the New England Rebekahs, Sarahs, Isaacs, Samuels, Abigails—Hebrew savors and names—who dwelt in Ipswich, Salem, Falmouth, Truro, as in Shechem and Ai. The Hebrew used the grape, pomegranate and Lebanon cypress, for bed, table, tabernacle and Shittim Ark; while the Puritan added up his land, tillage and sweet-shingled houses into a yoke and fast for toil, Sabbath and prayer. Hebrew and Puritan multiplied: Abraham in Canaan cherished the fruit of the womb and blessed the breasts; he lay with his beloved Sarah unto her ninetieth year, when she conceived; while Pilgrim Abraham, Isaac or Samuel stealthily crept from his bed as from vice.

Abraham, Jacob, Joseph always journeyed toward the bridal East, the Jordan, Euphrates, Goshen. Joseph the Dreamer was embalmed in a coffin—so ends miraculous

Genesis from the Void to Egypt. The Puritan Patriarch, however, made a New Genesis beyond Asia and Europe, in the West, turning creation, memory, fable and man, hindwards.

From the Old Testament the Hebraical Puritan took a garbled Jahweh, added to it an inclement, Atlantic Christ and a Devil, and of these made witchcraft New England— the allegory of Adam, Eve, the Serpent and Cotton Mather. Satan's Bible, Cotton Mather's *Wonders of the Invisible World*, was the fountainhead of Puritan diabolism: *The Scarlet Letter, The Mosses, Moby-Dick,* Poe's *Tales* and the poetry of Emily Dickinson—the little Puritan devils, and the vestal witch of American Literature.

All of the Puritan fantasies were unholy, libidinous quests for the WONDERS of the INVISIBLE WORLD, the wicked spermaceti, the sexual *Scarlet Letter*. Hid within the carnal-hued Letter was the concupiscent WONDER of the Privy Teat, escutcheon of Cotton Mather's witch.

For two centuries American Literature was the unresolved Riddle of the Disgrace. Poets and scribes in America were telling Satan's beads as vassals of Cotton Mather. Almost two hundred years after the Witch Trials, Nathaniel Hawthorne was denouncing the Sin of Salem in a Pilgrim scripture, *The Scarlet Letter;* Poe was steeping himself in a saturnalia of murder rites.

Herman Melville chose as the name of his tragedian the most iniquitous King Ahab from Chronicles; then he took as a second Hero an Animal, an infernal whale; clothed in the Paschal garment of the Lamb, he turned it into pure, spermal Demon.

Each one took his impious revenge against Mather's Shade, and wrote his Devil's Orison, save Emily Dickinson; fearful of the sign of the Teat, she hid in immaculate Lamb's Clothes.

Hawthorne nibbled at hell's bread, sowed evil seed, created aerial goblins and sexual scented dews in *The*

*Mosses.* Melville shaped an antichrist Ahab, who roamed blasphemous, upboiling seas in pursuit of a Mephisto-Lamb, Moby-Dick. Ahab spat into the sacramental silver calabash, uttering in final profanation a mock Lord's Prayer in Latin:

*Ego non baptiso te in nomine patris, sed in nomine diaboli.*

Melville broiled in ejaculatory blasphemies; of Ezekiel's Vision and Cotton Mather's Shade, he composed spermaceti Angels; of a Satanic brute, Moby-Dick, he made a leering monstrance, transubstantiating creamy foams and breakers of brit and squid, Leviathan's Mead, into a wine and wafer supper.

Yet none could speak: Hawthorne could scarce mention carnal embrace; Poe had uttered in vain, "And Sorrow shall be no more, and Eros all"; Melville made vasty, inverted oaths.

What cunning equivalents these demonic Puritan artists used to announce the body! Melville created out of a Dream an epithalamium to the Seed: "In thoughts of the vision of the night I saw long rows of angels in Paradise, each with his hands in a jar of spermaceti." He celebrated the naked living sperm; a nocturnal symbol, it was a wedding song of Moby-Dick rather than the sun-leavened acclamation of the flesh. Of sea grass, drear wave-plaited oceans, he wove a nuptial bed for copulating whales. Upon his brain was painted naked, voluptuous woman; what he chanted was the milky, musky breasts of leviathan, the sexual embraces of porpoises.

Other poets have knelt before the magic of the eyes and the tresses of sweet-thighed girls: Heine sang of *Nordsee* maids; Dostoevski ached for the Foot of woman; Melville, in rapt, torn paeans, warbled the festal founts of the teats and the anus of the whale! He caroled the "delicate side fins," "the palms and the flukes," "the chaste-looking mouth," "glossy as bridal satin," and the exquisite hid leaf of ear, of Leviathan!

Melville pined for the "tinkling cow-bells in Uz," for the wells, the orchards, the flocks of Canaan, but pursued white blubber, squid, brit, ambergris. Melville gazed, as Charles Olson has said, in fervid faith and hope upon Mahomet's Crescent, the Eastern Star over Bethlehem; and roamed, as Ahab did, a finny, Topheth Pacific in a womanless whaling ship.

His life, like outcast Ishmael's, was as sundered as the crew of the *Pequod* in *Moby-Dick*: here were two opposing human climates, sealed up in an accursed, salty hull until perdition. There were sanguinary Quaker whalers, Nantucketers, lonely Starbuck and an Atlantic atheist crew, "whelped" "by the sharkish sea" with "small touch of human mothers in them." There were Asian primal Fedellah, Afric "Ahasuerus Daggoo, imperial Negro," Polynesian Queequeg, and tropical Tashtego. These were Atlantic and Genesis men, wandering together over a boreal, brackish sea, chasing a "dumb vast sea brute" compounded of an unyeasty Jahweh, Dionysus, and the Philistine idol Dagon, to satiate the metaphysical hunger of a Puritan Devil, Ahab, "with a crucifixion in his face."

Melville ached for the Jordan, the Euphrates, those "gorgeous skirts of Asiatic land older than Abraham"; in *Moby-Dick* he was Adamic Ahab, "staggering beneath the piled centuries since Paradise"; and in *Mardi* he was witness of man's Full Cycle: "I was overwhelmed in Gomorrah . . . I was at the subsiding of the Deluge . . . with the Israelites I fainted in the Wilderness. . . ."

Creation was hallowed to him: how earth, Adam, Eve, the Garden were formed; yet void and water, the Lord's First Day, were his Primal chaos—his beginning and end.

Ahab roved "sea pastures," "watery prairies," coursing through sod and swaths of ambergris, looking for Land, a jot of Nineveh or Babylon. Poe had sent out the Raven; Melville waited in vain for a returning Noah's dove with a green leaf.

Whatever Melville blessed, he refused, cursed. He had commemorated the suppers of Xerxes, Ahasuerus, Montezuma and Powhattan, but his own viands had been mouldy crusts of ocean. Ahab, like Odysseus, weeping for Ithaca and Penelope, cried out for a bed, a hammock, a saddle, a sentry-box, a hearth, a pulpit, a coach—a dry, snug hearse.

He worshiped an inscrutable creator, the Lord and his Son, but shaped out of an heathenish animal, a fish, flesh and fowl idol, Dagon. He adored the pure, albic vesture of gentle Christ, the fleece of White which he heaped upon the hated hump of Leviathan.

In Melville land and light are forever foresworn. Ahab, "darkness leaping out of light," prowls murdering seas of sharks and swordfish: the Night—"horrors of the half-known life." All the bodings, those stepmother intuitions, foretold in the archangelical shrieks of birds hovering above the *Pequod*, go unheard.

The malediction is consummated. But before the doom, a choric lament rises up: Ahab mourns for the marriage-pillow, for green land, for the "magic glass" of the human eye; Pip pores in revery over the lilies. While the *Pequod*, the Atlantic World, goes down, and the musky spermaceti Angels are forever lost, Stubb, bemoaning a crusty ocean mattress-grave, cries out: "Cherries! cherries! cherries!"

The dirge is done and only Ishmael remains. A psalm and genesis of sperm, flesh and copulation, decrying celibacy, had been imagined; a Doomsday Book had been conceived.

What does *Moby-Dick* portend? Is there not something drearily amiss? Here is a human, cosmological Atlantic Tragedy, without one female figure. *Moby-Dick*, like Melville's watery planet, is a sundered shadow: earths and fruits are only intimated or dreamed: Ahab, Starbuck and Ishmael are ecliptic heads and torsos—woman is unguessed, uncreated. Melville made a Cosmos of evil and Satan, but without an Eve, and so composed an apocalyptic revelation without serpent wisdom.

Thoreau, "bachelor of nature," indeed! wrote of war, economy, ruminative sitting, waiting and eremitic patience, altogether excluding women, and erected in *Walden* the Western Fable of Ennui.

Poe's demonic tales never emit erotical lusts; in Emily Dickinson, the appetites, sensual throbs, were always attributes of dew, the bee, a wagon.

The books of the Puritan visionaries are the Lamb's testament; they lack the joyful knowledge that is the comedy of guile, habit, pleasure, the grape and wit of the house, the table and the bed. In the whole of Christian pilgrim literature, including the erotical saviorism of Walt Whitman, there is scarcely a laugh or a sigh, the gambol of a Puck or a faun.

Without woman, the Tree of Good and Evil cannot be tasted. Before the First Deception, Adam is Primordial Clod. The truthseekers, Jehovah and Abraham, are impotent before the froward artfulness of woman. When Sarah is told that she will sport with Abraham and conceive at ninety, her raillery at such ridiculous visionary idealism, "After I am waxed old shall I have pleasure?" is of the blood and bread of nature, custom and art.

The magnetical lodestar is man's—the cunning belongs to Sarah, Rachel and Rebekah; Sarah laughs at the Lord's guileless truth, because it contradicts experience: with a piece of goat's skin Rebekah can dupe Patriarch Isaac.

The Dreamers in the Bible, Jehovah, Abraham, Isaac, Jacob, Joseph, are male innocents! Jacob may wrestle with an Angel for Foreknowledge, but after seven years' toil in the fields of Laban for his beloved, he does not know till morning that he has slept with "weak-eyed Leah" instead of radiantly formed Rachel. Joseph, interpreter of Pharaoh's dreams, and shrewd overseer of Egypt's kine and granaries, is a gawk before Potiphar's wife.

Visions and ideals are intermixed with the pang and mirth of warming sensual lies, deceit, habit, the gossipy leaven of art, Rabelais' "cup of dissimulation."

Abstract truth is a peril: the MAN-Jehovah will destroy the Cities of the Plain for an abstraction, morals, law, righteousness; and by fire and death cleanse the sinning, slothful bones; but Woman, like Lot's wife, will look back to Sodom and Gomorrah, though she be turned into a pillar of salt.

Man, apart from woman, makes a carnage of his destiny; torn, he chases a dumb leviathan till death; he sups on a trencher of quagmire, or upon Gethsemane's grief, as Thoreau and Dickinson did. There is no such withering of man's fruits in the Psalms of the Lover, David, or in the polygamous wisdom of Solomon, or in that deep draught of grape-brewed vanity, Ecclesiastes.

Had Jesus married the illuminated prostitute, Magdalene, he would have forsaken the Acts, the overthrowing of the tables of the pigeon and money-venders, and the Bleeding Cross and given man as inheritance an imperishable generation of gentle little children or Galilean verse.

But there is no Magdalene, not even a Mary or Martha, in the Puritan Testament; woman does not exist in these literary masterpieces, in *Moby-Dick*, or in *Walden*. There has never been a *Mater Dolorosa* in America, Our Lady of Succor;—those sorrowful inclined surfaces of the Primitives, upon which man saw the pity for his own pain, have never existed here. Christ, as healing "feminine" image, has always taken the place of the Virgin Mary.

For Melville Christ is the Spouse, "the soft, curled, hermaphroditical" Son. In Shaker theology Jesus is male and female; for celibate Rappites, He is Adam and Eve. Paul is the teacher of the bacchic Perfectionists at Oneida, and the master of the Fruitlanders is Pythagoras. For Emily Dickinson, Christ is the Bridegroom!

Melville had come to deny woman as a planetary creature. In the brief pagan heyday in *Omoo, Typee, Mardi*, he believed he had moulded nude female cannibals in hue and shape; however, he had limned insubstantial and aerated phantoms of sensuality, Fayaway and Yillah.

After the ritual sloth and sex of Polynesi, Melville had essayed a North American *Niebelungenlied*, with the sea-dragon Moby-Dick, and Ahab, as half Christian seer and half warlock.

In *Pierre* it was incest; but Isabel, the beloved of her brother Pierre, is an air-substanced, leafy, bowered Yillah —only more Atlantic and fjord-like in speech and temper. Whatever Isabel was, as inward form in her creator's bosom, she walks upon the imaged page as Shaker sister who loves her brother in Christ! "There is no sex in our immaculateness!"—"thy nobleness unsexes me!" declares Isabel. The real "Aphroditean devotees" are Pierre and his boyhood friend. For Melville those perfervid, ideal courtesies between Paolo and Francesca, Dante and Beatrice, were more palpable between men.

No lady ever had windmills in her brains: Dulcinea del Toboso could powder porks, but never comprehend the imperial courtesies of Don Quixote's heart.

Herman Melville had turned to man for angelhood, Lamb and Christ. Of the inclement New England wife he had said: "Juxtaposition marries men"; of the troth between men: "Warm friends . . . are the Trades."

In that womanless Atlantic hull, the *Pequod*, wrathful and fissured men are always celestially courteous in their speech with one another. Pip, the Cap and Bell Fool to Ahab, as Charles Olson has identified him, is, in spirit and breeding of the heart, no less than the Fool is to Lear. Stubb's cry to his mates in dire peril is a tender exhortation: "Pull babes, pull sucklings." Queequeg, the Polynesian cannibal, makes a ceremonial of his affection for Ishmael—Queequeg "pressed his forehead against mine, clasped me round the waist, and said that henceforth we were married; meaning . . . that we were bosom friends."

In *Benito Cereno*, slave, villain and friend show one another "courtesies even to the point of religion." Babo, mutinous Negro leader, is magisterial in his attendance upon Benito Cereno, although he is ready to cut his throat. He conceals his wily stratagems behind the most refined obeisances! A lapse of breeding in Benito Cereno is the cause of inward suffering to the good captain Delano.

What was Melville's quest? His insatiate hunger for absolutes, for the Platonic Forms of gentleness, mercy and understanding, was taking him whither?

In his pilgrimage for the "heart's virgin experience," Melville, in his last year, had conceived in *Billy Budd* pure Male manhood, but had drawn a vestal maiden in the likeness of one of Fra Angelico's seraphs.

Billy Budd, the sailor, in complexion, charm and modesty, is a girl: his name, Budd, lovely April's darling. He is one of Shakespeare's angelical beauties of the Comedies, in rustic attire or page's suit. But Budd's damsel features, unlike Shakespeare's boy's garments, unmask rather than disguise him. His "fair cheek" is like "Ruddy-tipped daisies," his ear, small, the "arch of the foot," and "curve in the mouth and nostril," shapely. Moreover, Billy Budd, as so many rural maids, cannot read or write: he is as illiterate as Heine's peasant wife or Goethe's Frederica, the cook.

Is Budd maid, cherub or Christ? His clothes are washed and mended by the crew with the love and piety bestowed upon the tender vestments of a girl or the sacral dress of the Virgin Mary.

Was the *Pequod* a Sodom on the seas? Did Melville,

in heart's rage and obscure lust, burn, as is hinted, in the Fires of Gomorrah?

*Moby-Dick*, *Pierre* and *Billy Budd*, are legends of St. Paul's "mysteries of iniquity"—Evil washed in the Blood of the Lamb. Cloven Ahab, we know, is antichrist; incestuous Pierre is "a visible token" of the "invisible angelhoods"; assassin Budd is mantled in the "fleece of the Lamb of God" when he is hanged; the spar from which his pinioned figure is suspended becomes a holy relic to the sailors who keep "a chip of it" as " a piece of the cross."

Pierre, Isabel and Budd are as chaste as Shakespeare's Miranda and Perdita, those female abstractions of purity. Shakespeare, however, had had his loafy, mealy Falstaff, his Mistress Overdone and Doll Tearsheet: in hell's heat he had unclothed Regan and Goneril; his ladies, Rosalind, Kate Hotspur and Cressida, can be full, ripe bawds. The closest Melville had come to free, ribald speech is the one line in *Moby-Dick*, Quaker Captain Bildad's warning: "If ye touch at the islands, Mr. Flask, beware of fornication."

In *White Jacket* he had recited all the vices in a man-of-war, thieving, skulking, flogging and drinking; however, he had only mentioned that Cherub Man carries within him the profligacy of Ham.

Shakespeare had expired in his fifties in his Last Prayer, *The Tempest;* but Melville partook of the "penitent bread of the Supper" when he was thirty-one.

Melville had read the Poet deeply, but Backwards—in his moan, grief and prayers—"St. Shakespeare" "full of Sermons-on-the-Mount, and gentle, aye, almost as Jesus."

How quickly were the voices of Melville, Poe, Dickinson and Whitman entombed. Before the American satyr had grown his bacchic horns, he was wedded to the Holy Ghost and the Worms: Poe and Melville had fawned upon the devil, and Whitman had wrapped himself in maggots; but each one, long before he had spoken his abysses, was chanting dissolution, Poe's "Eureka,' Melville's muteness, Whitman's Flower of Death, "Calamus."

In America Mephistopheles was translated into a Gothic gargoyle, to murder forever the vision of Helen. The renaissance, the legend of a mocking, European Mephistopheles and a carnal Faustus, dismally lapsed into a long Puritan *Walpurgisnacht* in which Faustus, Helen and Mephisto reappeared as medieval devils, hags, Ahab, the wicked whale.

To damn sensuality, laughter and irony, Cotton Mather had turned woman into a witch; Poe took the infernal witch, begot by Mather, and buried her alive; Melville exorcised her! Lady Dickinson hid in Christ's Bosom.

The rage of Ahab for the milky spermal substance of Primal Evil, which he pursues to murder, is the same fury that is in Cotton Mather to destroy sexual iniquity—to find the devil's excrescence, the sign of the teat!

The witch, the whale, the sperm, the teat! While Ahab chases Moby-Dick upon blasphemous Sea Hells, he proclaims that it is he who is being pursued unto damnation by the Devil!

# II  On Writers Faire, Foul, and Full of Variation

## Bawds in the Beauty Parlor on Mount Ida

from *Truth is More Sacred:*
A critical exchange between
Edward Dahlberg and Sir Herbert Read

# On James Joyce

Dear Herbert:

It is my fear that in this century of woe and panic literature may pass away, and that after the terrible hecatombs to come, it will be harder to find good books than the body of Osiris. These letters to you are poor oblations to the Muses, for like the Athenian women sacrificing at the tomb of Tereus, I offer you gravel instead of barley groats.

Your *Annals of Innocence and Experience* are lovely bucolics, and your sylvan notes are quiet, whereas I am rough and feral, and am likely to bite the tradesmen of letters. Dryden owned that he could censure bad works more easily than he could praise good ones; no matter, I prefer a virile negation to a comfortable, flaccid yea.

I abhor venal authors as well as the poet who is solely concerned with his dithyrambs and iambics, and who gives all his thoughts to words, without thinking about justice, affection and hope. His verses are the stibium pot of the harlot, or the hair-dye of the Colchian Medea. Though the external work be as white as the marble sepulchre, it is corrupt within. Socrates prayed to Pan asking that the inward and the outward man be one. Poetry today has been sacked by pleasure and novelty just as Troy was by Helen. In the English *Spectator* it is asked: "Who is the better for beholding the most beautiful Venus?" I regard James Joyce, André Gide, Cocteau, Rimbaud, Verlaine, Eliot, Pound, as the bawds in the beauty parlor on Mount Ida. They worship the manes of Oscar Wilde. However, it is my purpose to give a caveat to the raw apprentices of beauty.

There are many reasons for our task; there is a good deal of the eavesdropping criticism of Polonius on present-day literature; Polonius will never praise an audacious book by an obscure poet, except behind the arras, nor will he attack a renowned bad poet. If one assails a famous malefactor of the beauty-arts he not only incurs his venom, but raises up a sodality of foes. There is also the bodkin of the poltroon, Silence: he won't bury a volume in open battle or in the whoring book-review columns, but shuffles the book into limbo by not mentioning it. The tyranny of Silence has brought about a censorship of books. "The discouragement of all learning, the stop of Truth" we attribute to countries where dictators proscribe what intellectual victuals are pernicious to the entrails of the State. When Pope wrote the *Dunciad*, those whose books he stabbed to death answered him, and some with valor. Dr. Johnson says that to attack a stupid book is a benefaction to the nation; if the writer goes unpunished, he will harm the race of bards, and murder a whole century. But these are pusillanimous times, and most authors are more concerned with selling wind to noddles than in going to Golgotha which is suffering for mediation and truth.

We live in the heyday of the liar; there is scarce a man who utters the word, honest, who is not a skulker, or one who sighs for candor who is not Iago. The only way to return to wisdom, to Plato, Aristotle, Solon, Erasmus, Linnaeus, is to expunge from the lexicon the words honest, genius, art, and beauty.

Many readers go to critics with a simple heart, hoping to find out what authors are not quacks, or which books will enliven their identity; they quit acquiring a few hard terms, such as brachylogies, eikonologies, solecisms. Though their conceits are more stuffed than they were before, they are still committed to read the same squab grammarians and poetasters.

I cannot tell anyone how to write well, and aside from asserting that the god Thoth invented vowels and semi-vowels, I have no grammatical knowledge. Philo Judaeus spoke of those who grew gray in grammar, and Clement of Alexandria had no patience with those who chattered like turtle-doves about punctuation and syntax. The grammarians are always boys. If the language of the author does not smell of the mountains, the forest ash, or the rude hearth, the poem is wicked. There is no good verse that does not make the reader stronger in intellect, and which does not give him legs and arms he did not have before. The *Iliads* enlarges the mind, and strengthens the will no less than the river Skamander, or Mount Taurus. A truthful book is in the best of health. When Sokrates was making ready to take the hemlock, he asked his friend Crito to sacrifice a cock to Aesculapius, the god who gave him the vigor to discourse on wisdom in the agora. For Hermes, god of speech and messenger of death, guides the poet, and he, whose words are laden with some moiety of the Kosmos, also breathes forth a brave destiny and death.

A book is a battle of the soul, and not a war of words. The art of logomachy is a useless one, and those who indulge in it are a mischievous brood. They know what is sometimes pleasant, but seldom important. Suppose we inform our readers that Anaxagoras of Clazomenae was the first Greek to publish a book, that Lasus invented the dithyramb, Stesichorus of Himera, the hymns, and that Alcman the Spartan furnished us with the choral, and Anacreon the amorous song; will this do any more than to give us airs and lard our pride. True knowledge purges the intellect better than hyssop. Nobody can write an immaculate book, save an empty person, just as no one is ever virtuous, except unexpectedly; for the right idea rises up from the soul as suddenly as Hermes when he brings lamentations to men. Only a coxcomb is positive that his next book will be a masterpiece: "A shallow mind thinks his writings divine; a man of sense imagines he writes tolerably well," says La Bruyère.

Everything is a surprise to man; if he writes badly he is astounded, or, well, amazed; when he says something virtuous, he is delirious. He must be on guard every instant of his life not to be an evil person, and then not to invent verses which engender more witlings and dunderheads than there are already in the world.

What our age lacks most of all is sense and health. There can be no just words well arranged without vigor. "I swear upon my virility," testifies François Villon. That a great deal of modern verse is senseless, and belongs in the spital-house, only an enervated fool will deny. Few are strong enough to eschew a diseased book. Plato tells of a certain Leontius who knew that there were some corpses on the outside of the wall, which he wanted very much to see although he knew he would be disgusted if he looked at them. Unable to resist his impulse, he ran up to the cadavers, saying to his eyes, "Take your fill, ye wretches, of the fair sight."

The longing to be mad or ignorant is the delirium of the multitude, and it is as strong in men as the craving in swine for dirt, or in mullets for turbid water. To spend one's life in the sty without books is the misery in Erebus. Next to a friend who provides the heart with the honey in Hymettus, no less than a steadfast wife, is a wise poet who is the only cure there is for having to be in this world. Literature empowers the spirit; the *Iliads* is bread and patience no less than Noah. We wander everywhere in our souls to gather ourselves up for death and a good epitaph, and there is little rest save in a book which is like that unwrought stone which relieved Orestes of his madness when he sat on it.

Send me to the home for Ishmaels, or to Bedlam, where Christopher Smart composed "Rejoice in the Lamb," and I am not ill, or insane, or niggard, but deprive me of the *Iliads*, or *The Compleat Angler*, or Blake's *Jerusalem*, and I am the ululant brute in the wilderness.

A sage is the strength of the people, and wise words are the gudgeons and the loaves of the nation, but they are more than the raiment and the meat for the flesh. A poet, who is not simply belly and pudendum, wants to instruct others; he himself is a suppliant, begging alms of the Kosmos, who is our Father, our Bread, and our Health. Who can be impervious to such precepts as Anarchasis offers us: "My covering is a cloak; my supper, milk and cheese."

Literature is about what is innocent and first. It is a doxology of heroes and localities; the *Iliads* is the catalogue of maritime towns and ships, Messe's towers for doves, and

Tryon near Alphaeus's flood. For Ptolemy, virgin America on his map was Albion. Hermes, who gives us intimations of death, wears white raiment. When the commonalty is vigorous, the people remember their sacred origins. Homer tells us that Protesilaus was the first Greek to leap from his trireme and land at Troy. Pausanias admits that he saw the lump of mud which Prometheus used to mould original man. Protogenia, according to the Hellenes, was the primal woman. This interest in what you, Herbert, call the Annals of Innocence, is the energy of the polity. What man did at first makes for a literature of giants. Our search for beginnings exhales energies and oracles. Memory, or Mnemosyne, is chaste. Many of the poets know very little about the fathers who settled their homeland; some deserted their country, like Henry James, T. S. Eliot, and Ezra Pound.

The lotus-eaters are bestial because what they fear most is knowledge; they cower before the vast archives of ancient wisdom, and shun the graves of Apis and the headstone of Poseidon; their minds are too timorous to invent a colossus. The piety of Homer for the earliest fables is shown by his use of obsolete words. He preferred the old names for Chaeronea and Lebadea, and called the Nile by its archaic appellation, the River Egypt. His whole life was such a legend that it was told that his father was the river Meles. We are either Pigmies by the river Strymon who are overcome by cranes, or we are Titans. Man creates legends to avoid having a mean fate; Linnaeus adopted a nomenclature for his plants and insects derived from mythical Greek characters.

The spirit stinks when it is feeble, and it is no different with amorous exercises, for Aphrodite is surnamed Praxis which means action. Mnemosyne dilates the soul, for the spirit is either filled by memory or is unclean. Forgetting is one of the marvelous pleasures of man, and it equals his delight in being gross. Homer never wrote personal memoirs, like the novels of Flaubert, Proust,

Lawrence, James, Joyce. This is an occupation for the lagging ear, and for the garrulous mind, and not for a potent intellect.

Man is either epic, or hates the sublime; he invents chimerae, harpies, eponymous giants, or he is scatophagous. Baudelaire said that the pothouse men of letters dote on excrements, which is the gallic salt of the novel. The *Ulysses* of James Joyce is the story of the scatological sybarites of the business world; it is a twenty-four hours' journey through ordure; a street-urchin's odyssey of a doddering phallus. James Joyce did in his novel what every business man craves to do, to be an epicure in the toilet. Has not the bourgeoisie relinquished every vision for the water-closet? Swift had far more learning than Joyce, which was not considerable, but he had passion and character. Still, *Gulliver's Travels* barely escapes being a tract on the Lilliputian revulsions that attack men without powerful minds and beliefs. Were it not for the legendary horse-people, the Houyhnhnms, *Gulliver's Travels* would have failed, and I think Dr. Johnson thought it did, for he pays much heed to Swift's life but gives only a laconic page to the *Travels*.

Joyce's *Ulysses* is the novel of epic cowardice; I do not blame him for divulging all the vices of men but for reducing them to unheroic dimensions. We must call wrath, dirt, lust, drunkenness—Agamemnon, Thersites, Ajax, Nestor, or sink the giants into little everyday characters. If the bad smells and ugly habits of men are the principal obsessions of the author, he has to translate them into Yahoos or Brobdingnags. Books are as ill as their authors, and often more so. Swift was sorely pained because men defecated and had evil odors. Both Pope and Swift, who were not scholars, showed an unusual interest in the vile. It is worth observing how far genius can go without great learning.

No poet can cocker his faults on the public pages of a book; he has to make them look a little like Cato or that

Roman Curius who preferred his garden of turnips to gold. Poets are a profligate lot, and many a reader has been enervated and ravished by a book. Pope, born feeble, lived to be weaker; he had the body of a dwarf, but the fierce lusts of a burly Ajax. Richard Savage disappeared for weeks to drink and carouse with trulls in secret places outside London. Though Pope and Savage practiced the vices of Faustina, their verses show the visage of Marcus Aurelius. It is not my purpose to judge the lives of the poets, for they are vain all day long and more amorous than a quail or partridge.

Pallas Athene signifies wisdom and war, and the olive which is sacred to that goddess represents peace but not ignominious submission. Wisdom has to be fought for with the same valor that the Greeks defended Thermopylae, and the javelin, the pike, the spear of Pelian ash are study, fortitude, and chagrin. The image of Minerva which Diomede and Ulysses carried away from Troy was made of the bones of Pelops, but a savage art is better than an effeminate one. The slovens of the muses are like that Greek who was so lazy that he had never dropped his hand as far as his navel. They are the enemies of Minerva and Aphrodite, both of whom are goddesses of action.

Joyce adopts the ancient hero, Ulysses, as the title of his novel, though his men of Dublin are not demigods but everyday gnomes with watery volitions. All that comes out of a man's mouth is not wise or reasonable; were it so we would be Aristotle all day long. But words, when not governed, are a symptom of velleity in the author. Dedalus, his principal thinker, is the architect in Greek myth, but who can imagine that this shadow of torpor was constructed by Daedalus. It cannot be claimed either that a ledgerbook of legendary names can add to our understanding. Aphrodite, Artemis, Nereus, Isis are the inward elements of our passions; we mould them in our blood as the ashes of Prytaneum were kneaded in the holy waters of the Alpheus.

No one can exercise his faculties by reading a simple list of the appellations of the gods, nor is it original to turn two diverse words into one, giving it double organs. Who cares to exhaust his brain searching for a verb which has wandered away from the substantive, or look for a noun that has been abducted by Pluto, or was never born? What reason is there for trying to make an adjective behave like a male verb? These eunuchal adjectives sigh forth their concupiscence but are unable to perform their duties as verbs to the sentence. There is a labial failure in *Ulysses* similar to the confusion of tongues of the people in the plains of Shinar; the noises in the belly and the rasping and hawking of the throat take the place of the alphabet. Besides, his words are lubricious, and a book ought not to send men to the brothel, especially in my country, where there is much vice, but so hard to acquire if one is poor or modest. The houses of Venus are either in the hands of Plutus or hidden in Tartarus. There are few prostitutes for the commons. What we need in America are more chaste books and more whorehouses. The poor you will always have with you, says Christ, and prostitution is always necessary, declared Tolstoy.

My dear Herbert, I regard this epistle as plain book husbandry; first of all reading is a purificatory rite, and as your own muse pacifies my nature let me then hear from you the songs of your native England. Coleridge, as you so well know, having written with such compassion of his miseries, was a great but wretched nature, and it was Charles Lamb who told him that if he would read *The Compleat Angler* he would be quieter.

# My Tutelary Muses and Woodland Seers

from *Alms for Oblivion*

# My Friends Stieglitz, Anderson, and Dreiser

I have not known twelve good men—plain, honest Galilean fishermen of the soul—but I have been the familiar of twelve talented ones. Alfred Stieglitz, to whom seven or eight volumes of fine writing were dedicated, had genius, but he was not a good man. We are so double in our values that it is necessary to say this. An artist should have some kind of single personality and there ought to be a oneness about a book or a deed; but faces, writing, and acts are no longer very reliable.

Stieglitz had the most gifted countenance I have seen and it was always an artistic pleasure to look at his eyes, brown as those of the cow-goddess Io; he had a good brow (we know that Plato in Greek means wide forehead) and his square chin was like an example out of Euclid. Schopenhauer believed that the face always divulged the nature of the man, though he also realized that it required a sooth-sayer's ability not to misjudge it. The aged Priam of ruined Troy satiated his heart as he contemplated Achilles. When he knelt in supplication he knew that he was kissing man-slaughtering hands; as he gazed at the ravening lion of Greece we are not sure what he saw. After Stieglitz removed his glasses one expected to find in those deep orbs the compassion of Isaiah's pools of Heshbon. I think he suffered from what has been called man's most malignant affliction, coldness. Genius can be cold too, and often is, but there is a dragon, a sphynx that is half-virgin and half-beast, in frigid art. I say all this not to appear complex or to make more human riddles than there already are. But Alfred Stieglitz baffled me, and I am sure that he did not understand himself very well; I believe that people who are as unreliable as he was are not at the essentials of them simple as Christ or Jeremiah. A prophet learned his trade and he went about his business of being a seer—you always knew you were with him; you can be a friend of a man or a book when you understand the relationship between you and the person or the book.

I have observed writing people a great deal; I recall how perplexed I was the first time Sherwood Anderson came to see Stieglitz. Then past middle age and sick, Stieglitz used to lie on an austere barracks cot in a whited alcove that opened out to An American Place at 509 Madison Avenue, where exhibits of Marsden Hartley, Dove, O'Keeffe, and Marin were given. He had been told some years before to go home and die, or wait for death, but he was very impatient and had turned this little monastery-alcove into an open sepulchre. Lots of people, like Dreiser and Ford Madox Ford, said he was senile and obviously mad. He was as repetitious as older men can be, and as the young are. There was only one mark of dotage that I ever observed in him: he played with his handkerchief just as fatuously as decrepit Lear might have done, or as Dreiser himself did. Sherwood Anderson was much kinder to Dreiser than Dreiser was to Stieglitz, and one remembers with the most agreeable feelings Anderson's tribute to old Dreiser playing with his handkerchief in *Horses and Men*. Stieglitz used to lie on the spartan army cot with his hand on his bad heart as though he looked into his grave all day long, like Donne.

Had I not seen Stieglitz's photograph of Anderson, the Ohio populist and sex rebel, with the midland bangs of hair, I don't think I would have paid much attention to the man sitting on a stool in the alcove and speaking in a drawl. He was wearing purple socks, a shiny brown store suit, store teeth, and his throat had a loose sick hang on it. Stieglitz never bothered to introduce me to him. He was a crank about such matters and thought that people ought to make things happen themselves. He had established 291 for his disciples of the arts, but sometimes he acted as though he wanted to keep them apart. He was full of these crotchety intuitions about the deportment of everybody.

I found Anderson in the first meeting a far from piercing human being; even Dreiser was less commonplace looking than this human platitude that had warmed many fine books and women. One never knows where genius is; in the hands, the trembling fingers. In Ezekiel the Angel has a dove in one cheek and in the other a predatory eagle. Sherwood Anderson had, as I later saw, hot brown eyes, and what was most revealing in Stieglitz were his wrists. Many looked at the crazy clumps of hair that grew out of his ears like satyr's horns, but this was artistic show, his gaudy affront to the philistines. He had doll-like wrists that were as fluent and feminine as Lawrence's. Stieglitz was an astonishing little doll of the arts, but one fondles a doll rather than loves it, and everyone that came to see Stieglitz wooed and caressed his moods, which were as unstable as water. Except for John Marin, the watercolorist, I don't think he cared for anyone. Marin was the only artist he never maligned; he hated Hartley, whom he had helped for thirty years, and he showed Hartley, a remarkable painter, to have the heart of a *flâneur* in that photograph he made of him. Marsden Hartley was an uglified dandy of the arts; he was the superlative male bitch artist of his day, and perhaps the best painter America has ever produced. A species of cyclops, one could neither love nor like him; Hartley had a titanic, swollen head, almost no mouth, and a voracious, orgiastic nose. Baffling enough, he had a satanic intellect that was always writhing on the cross.

Stieglitz was a little D. H. Lawrence talking like Buddha. He spoke as D. H. Lawrence wrote: he kept on talking until he said something good, just as Lawrence continued to write until he blundered into an amazing intuition. Stieglitz and Lawrence were intuitive, automatic people; if you listened to Stieglitz long enough you would hear a gnomic remark, and it might take you as long as to read the first two hundred dull pages of a Lawrence novel, but both ordeals were worth the patience. Many called him a bore because he said the same things so many times, but this was the charge brought against Socrates by quibblers and enemies. I like a man to have a little of the easy, relaxed bore about him; it is a comfort to the soul and gives peace to the bowels to hear a good man say good things often. One of my main objections to Alfred Stieglitz was this: his conduct was not boring enough. He was, as I have said, a waterseer, like Proteus, the Nile prophet with whom Menelaus had to grapple and who kept changing from a river whale to a shaggy water camel, and Polonius is the same sort of person; the pocketbook sage, to avoid raising Hamlet's choler, is willing to admit that the cloud looks like a lion or a waterhog. It is not how clever a man is that endears him to us, but how stable is his nature. Goethe once said of Byron that he was not a poet but a nature, and this is what I imagine Dostoevski was. Whatever he did or what book he wrote his acts appear to me to be a part of a whole, virtuous man.

Stieglitz was a chameleon in his affections. Sometimes he would attack a friend because he himself felt old, rancid, and already coffined. On one occasion he railed at Hartley because the latter had been sitting on a wooden stool in the burial alcove for hours. "He won't move!" exclaimed Stieglitz, almost beside himself; but Marsden Hartley was not only motionless, he was also deaf. When Stieglitz was not thinking about art, he was obsessed with death, and Hartley considered the one almost as fatal as the other; art was always mixed with death. When a woman praised Hartley's show at the Walker gallery the artist replied: "My paintings ought to be good; I'm just about ready to be cremated." In this moody, irascible family of geniuses, one could not be sure of anyone. There was William Carlos Williams who came to the Place, and who wrote a very fine essay in a very bad book called *America and Alfred Stieglitz*. The late Paul Rosenfeld, another acolyte, who had helped O'Keeffe and Anderson, was flightly, feminine. I remember Waldo Frank, a bombastic cherub, rushing into the arms of Stieglitz who stepped back with congealed composure, causing me to rebuke him afterwards. I told Stieglitz I thought that art and literature were for human love. Though Waldo Frank had unusual sensibilities, he had hardly any sense of judgment, and Stieglitz, the greatest art peacock in America, had scant use for the great Frank who was such an art hen about his books.

Frank was one of the initial criers for the brave Randolph Bourne, the discerning friend of the poet Hart Crane, and the first to appreciate Anderson's *Winesburg, Ohio*. Anderson and Frank had been good friends. Frank told Anderson that the world's greatest writers were Joyce,

Anderson, and Waldo Frank, and then when Anderson made one of his sententious midwestern replies, "Waldo, if you don't cut out that I am great stuff, I won't see you any more," Waldo wept. After some assuring words from Anderson they went out for a walk and Frank burst forth with "Sherwood, Europe is waiting for us."

Two things destroyed Frank as a writer: the grossest vanity and the adjective. I think he might have written a remarkable book had he not been so greedy to be known by everybody (for he always had the neck of a crane for fame); and had he not always used an adjective for a verb, which makes for a feminine sentence. There ought to be a strong man in a sentence, to make it active rather than passive; we are astonished by Homer because he writes as Achilles casts the spear of Pelion ash. Every verb should have that epical and martial force.

Stieglitz had said many times that he did not like the word "artist"—that if a man painted or wrote it was his own fault. He often fell into the most destructive nihilism about literature and painting, saying that he hated art and that he intended to burn all his photographs, for great as his faults were he could perceive them most plainly—in others. Once when he was wallowing in the role of Timon, hating everybody, Williams became very choleric and told him to go home and die, that his sniveling melancholia was murdering everyone at the Place. Williams was right, but hardly the man to rebuke him, being himself a ravine and cold-water man. Williams was a provincial pill-satchel man of Rutherford, New Jersey. He was a doctor perhaps because he looked all his life for human staples, for direct potato-and-apple people, with simple arithmetic morals and plain salt and pepper in their acts. Art people today have not honest bread, pear, and chicory or grass in their vices, deeds, and souls, and Williams, the genius of *In the American Grain*, had as much loose water in his nature as there was in Stieglitz.

When Stieglitz was in good fettle as a seer, and sure of his animal intuitions, he would call out as I stepped into the alcove, "Just when you opened the door, Sherwood's *Many Marriages* fell off the top shelf. I said 'that is a neglected book and that's Dahlberg, a neglected man, coming in.' " After Stieglitz had talked till dusk he said, "We've had a rare talk today; you must come soon again." Although I had seldom been successful in interrupting him, what he said was the truth; the best conversation between two persons is a monologue, the art that Alfred Stieglitz knew best.

Stieglitz had a passion for white. An American Place was a white sepulchre—his East River penthouse reminded me of the albic tunic Melville said the Leviathan, Moby-Dick, wore. Georgia O'Keeffe, his wife, had the same mania for Hygeia, the old, sanitary goddess who ruled so many of her paintings in the Stieglitz-O'Keeffe apartment. Against the white apartment walls were the bleached cow skull, the tombed lilies, and the frigid vulva flowers.

One night at the East River penthouse Stieglitz was in his prophetic season, and he said to me with the greatest gravity and in the Hebrew meter of Genesis, "In my entire life I have entered twelve women; I am seventy-five, and still very potent." He spoke like the law-giver writing how Abraham went in unto Hagar, and this was said with such patriarchic purity that I thought of Enos and Methuselah who lived when there were no feeble men on the earth, for otherwise Methuselah's long years must have been a curse rather than a blessing, particularly the last eight hundred and thirty years or so. The Psalmist tells us that after seventy all is sorrow and affliction and impotency. Of course, I don't know any more about Methuselah than I did about Alfred Stieglitz, who may have been lying; but then all good storytellers, like Stieglitz, Anderson, and Ford Madox Ford, were marvelous liars.

Once when Stieglitz was raving wildly about Georgia

O'Keeffe's paintings, he showed me his photographs of her hands—large hands, with fierce knuckles and punishing fingers which somehow resembled the face of Savonarola, and I told him so. He nodded with rare enthusiasm and took out more camerawork he had done on her hands. Stieglitz, no less than Aristotle and Turgeniev, had to be whipped by women; he was unusually fond of women, up till the last, for one chit who went to see him after he was eighty said he had wonderful, prehensile hands. Virginia Woolf would have called this fingering lewdness. All of these people of An American Place were sex geniuses, but lacked the stuff out of which are made the sorrowful windmill visions and Sancho-Panza laughs and the great erotical sports of the *Sonnets*.

I mistook Ford the first time for one of the pigs Circe had fed with acorns and mast. He had a large, loafy face, and he used to shamble fatly down Eighth Street, slowly fetching air. He had two rooms at number 10 Fifth Avenue, a brownstone across from the old Brevoort Hotel, and gave Thursday afternoon tea and talk. Ford was insanely kind and his gray eyes were warm oracles. Ford lied about everything; he said that he never looked up one quotation for his *March of Literature*. His belly, loosely suspendered, so that his obese trousers were always below his navel, shook when he cited some early English writer, Izaak Walton, or White, who had written that birds "copulate on the wing," or contended that all of Shakespeare's plays were potboilers except *Timon of Athens*. Who would have imagined that there was a darkling vein of Timon in such portly, good-natured blood? One day he told me, with the utmost affected confidence, that he believed most of the Americans were impotent. Yet I never knew anybody who thought American writing was so puissant and important as he did. His kindness was a wind that was always blowing his head about in one direction or another. He simply could not do enough for our talented authors.

He also lied about his southern manor to which he invited everybody he liked—and he had the fattest affections for people—but there was no manor. Then, when he first met Stieglitz, Ford said he was crazy! Sherwood Anderson, whose autobiographical books are plain, honest perjury, said that he was very fond of Ford, although he was a preposterous liar.

Both Ford and Anderson were sex visionaries and they understood people because they touched them. Touch is our misery, our disgrace and our knowledge. In John it is said that the truthseeker is without pity, but that the sensual man sorrows for others. This profound observation explains Sherwood Anderson, who did not have a great head, but whose flesh was always growing and ripening for others. I think that Anderson was the man Whitman adumbrated for us in his astounding manifesto on physiology, *Leaves of Grass*. Nobody in this country has ever been so close to Isaiah's "All flesh is grass" as Anderson, for his skin was as nervous and touchy as grass is in the sun, and he had to cohabit with every woman in his books, whether she was Helen or the hag Hecuba, because he was entirely sympathetic. He told me that one day Edgar Lee Masters' fiancee came to him weeping, "Edgar won't marry me," and that he had put his arms around her and said, "Don't cry, darling, I'll wed you," and he did.

His aching skin took the place of what we others call mind, but which is more important than the human brain, because it is infinitely more loving. One does not have to be afraid of a meadow, which won't hurt you; what is to be dreaded is the mind without feeling, for it is a most malignant faculty. Anderson had a large respect for Dreiser, thinking of him as someone big with child, who, when he conceived, brought forth a monster, the USA Titan, that has assaulted Zeus and the heavens for lightning and atomic bombs. God take away our powers and give us instead the grass in Sherwood Anderson.

Anderson told me on Christmas at Marion, Virginia, but without malice, "This is the way Teddy writes: 'It was a dark, inky, mizzling, misty night; in fact, it was a terrible rainy night.' " He said that Dreiser had to swear whenever he was amorous, which tells us a lot about Molly Bloom's four-letter words in *Ulysses* and the obscenities in *Lady Chatterley's Lover*.

Anderson cowered before money, fearing it might destroy what was fecund in him. When he was in New Orleans, the publisher Horace Liveright asked him to write a novel, offering him a hundred and twenty-five dollars a week while he was working at it. Anderson, who had run away from an Ohio wife and a paint factory because money had become a sign of impotency to him, agreed. He told me with his midland guitar twang, "I had forgotten how to spend money like that, and soon the $125 checks began to overlap, and I grew cold and unable whenever I looked at those bank certificates." When Liveright came to see him, he asked, "What's the matter, Sherwood, you look so gloomy; has somebody offered you $150 a week for the book?" "No," replied Anderson, "that's not it; but, Horace, you've got to stop sending me all that money, those checks are killing me, I can't write." Liveright then sent Anderson a modest weekly sum and Anderson wrote the one book, *Dark Laughter*, out of which he made money—lucre that was the source of wife and house trouble for Anderson. One of his wives wanted him to build a fancy house, and he did, somewhere near Marion, Virginia, paying the workmen such good wages that the people in the town were bitter in their complaints: they said that before he had come there was none of that northern city dollar discontent in Marion. To begin with, Anderson had gone to Marion to be humble and to get away from money, which separates people. There is a very fine example of this dollar-fear in *Poor White*. Hugh McVey, who has become a rich Ohio inventor, is afraid of his nuptial night and runs away from his bride. He had been a desolate railroad depot telegrapher, and then had grown wealthy by inventing a grass-seeding device. He, who taught the farmers how to plant in the shortest time, was afraid to seed his own bride.

Sherwood Anderson never got over his money-fear, any more than his friend Dreiser did. Dreiser is the greatest dollar genius of the American novel. The best interpretation of any of his books is the Mount Kisco mansion he had, which resembled a Log Cabin syrup can. He had a luxurious writing table made out of an airplane wing, and in his heyday he went to parties with a pair of autocratic Russian hounds. Everybody in a Dreiser novel wants dollars; Sister Carrie sacrifices Hurstwood for money, and the carriagemaker gives up Jennie Gerhardt because should he marry her, he would have only ten thousand a year. Cowperwood, who is really Yerkes the capitalist, in *The Financier* and *The Titan,* is only creative when his brain is boiling and scheming for new fortunes.

Dreiser was an extraordinary business novelist who dismissed Stieglitz as a crank because hair grew out of his ears. He had vehement barbershop morals, and, regarding my long hair with a merchant's suspicion, advised a haircut. He was much more reflective than his books. Teaching me how to read Shakespeare, he said that all the plays were man-eating parables, and that life rather than the poet had written the tragedies. He was always rewriting Ecclesiastes —rather badly—and he had unusual emotions about the Sermon on the Mount. One night he got very testy with me when I would not agree that the song "Annie Rooney" was as good as a Beethoven symphony. When he became somewhat ill-natured, I reminded him of Matthew's Sermon, and, laughing, he said, "Ho, let's go and see some girls." His women were girls that looked like boys—at least those that I saw—and I wondered about these breastless, skinny college hoydens. Our women in beribboned curls and skirts to their knees dress up like little children to whet the appetite of the men.

One afternoon on a Central Park bench Dreiser told me that he was getting his convictions into order. He said that he had seen a fair-haired boy in the park and had come to appreciate the Greek's preference for men. This astonished and troubled me, and I wondered why this large masculine figure, seldom wrapped in a winter overcoat, had come so to think. Although his face was something like a dry gourd, he had a smile that must have enfeebled the will of many women, so these were not the words of a hungry man.

Masculine will has greatly dwindled and we are producing feminine verse and literature. Billy Budd is really a Greek boy like the late Hart Crane. It is the mother that dominates American literature. Dreiser, who was in temperament an anarchist, may have become a communist because his mother was an Indiana Mennonite, a member of a religious communistic sect that had its origins in Martin Luther's Germany. We have a Mother Literature, and the male parent in our verse and novel is very weak. Melville's father is far in the rear, ineffectual, as we see in *Pierre*, and in Whitman it is the Quaker mother with whose image he was connected. Poe and all the men in the tales are wan. And who fathered desolate, seagoing Ahab, moaning for a bed, the marriage pillow, a dry family hearse? We are making a homeless culture, for there is no one to father the household. There is no hearth in Thoreau, Poe, or Melville, or celibate Whitman, and we never see people at table in their books. There is no bread in a hempen basket, a flagon of claret, or a chine of beef in Marsden Hartley, O'Keeffe, Marin, Dove, or a remarkable Stieglitz photograph.

Dreiser, Stieglitz, Hartley were fatherless men, without the essential masculine force to love people. Dreiser had a hard, craggy apathy toward people, and Stieglitz's passion was as refrigerated as O'Keeffe's paintings. Stieglitz was exceedingly generous, but not tender, and he was entirely sympathetic with the economic problems of a painter. Still, he rather detested the artist. Very vain himself, he loathed anybody who laureled his own canvas or book. He was as nihilistic and outrageous as Lear; he had the opportunity to reveal to me that when his mother was cremated he had no feelings about it at all. Maybe he was attempting to astonish me, but I have learned that whatever a man tells you about himself is true, even though it is a lie. Stieglitz had the exquisite feminine sensibility to resist, but he had not the will to resist enough which makes great male art. Like Socrates, he questioned everything, asking the most random gallery visitor what he meant when he used the word justice or love; but unlike the sage at Athens, he said that justice and love did not exist, and when a man says that he eats his own prayers and strivings.

He did not set aside human ends, although in fits of melancholia he often destroyed them. Whenever a young, raw, apprentice painter told him he wanted to become an artist, Stieglitz asked the enthusiast in the iciest tone, "Are you ready to starve?" and if the youth faltered in his reply, he sent him away. When Marsden Hartley was an obscure Maine artist he asked Stieglitz to show his work, declaring that he could live on four dollars a week. That was enough for Stieglitz, who exhibited Hartleys in his various galleries for thirty years.

That whole generation of artseekers was not so sick as we are. Dreiser had none of that being-busy malady; he had time for his writing kindred, and he never put you off by telling you that he was either beginning a novel or finishing one. He had none of that wordsickness in his soul, and any adjective he might lose one day he was certain to recover the next. Stieglitz ran open shop at the Place for conversation; fat, gracious Ford was as hospitable as Zeus, and would beg you to come for tea and to bring along some early or late book you had written so he could find out whether you were a quack or not.

Whenever I pass the 10 Fifth Avenue brownstone my steps fumble a little and I think of Ford's eyes, the dove-gray eyes of the Shulamite, as Lawrence described them. They were amorous eyes, soft and almost wet, because they were always feeling something. All these droll, perceiving natures died at about the same time—first Ford, then Anderson and Hartley and Dove, and then Dreiser.

Somehow or other the whole literature and painting movement is the fable of Alfred Stieglitz, the little figure in black pancake hat and gypsy cape. Almost everybody at one time or another was in Stieglitz's gallery, and he was the crazy art-autocrat of them all. He was not only the angel that foolishly rushed in where others feared to tread; he had no fear afterwards of being mocked, either. He brought Cézanne over when New Yorkers jeered at that master's work; he was one of the first of D. H. Lawrence's readers, buying his wonderful small volume on our literature by the dozen when criticasters like Van Wyck Brooks and Edmund Wilson said it was a hoax. I mean Lawrence's *Studies in Classical American Literature*. When Stieglitz cared for a book he bought two or three dozen of them to hand out to friends or prospective followers.

Stieglitz was a doting-mad camera man, and he refused ten thousand dollars for Steichen's photograph of J. P. Morgan, which he offered to the Metropolitan for nothing, provided they would hang it alongside Rembrandt. They wouldn't and he called them great boors of philistia. Stieglitz was a quacksalver as well as a sage; doubtless there is a charlatan in every savant. He was the first to demand outlandish and immoral prices for American art. That he did not make a penny out of the sale of a painting does not make his error the leaner. When a woman hesitated to buy a Dove, an O'Keeffe, or a Hartley he would urge her to go home and think it over for a year or two. He would say: "It may be that you and art are not quite compatible with one another; for instance, if there is the least amount of marital strife in your household, a Hartley could easily disturb the sexual relations between you and your husband. However, there is no connubial sedative as good as a Marin. Come back one year from today when the sun is in Aries."

Those who have known the sorrows of penury will eulogize Stieglitz for what he did; but there is no reason why a painter or a writer should be paid more than a porter or a charwoman; that he is given less than either is a part of our occidental idiocy and waste. No matter; it is just as ridiculous to ask $5,000 for a Marin as it would be to demand that much money for a sonnet. He was full of the most trifling paradoxes. He declared that he hated America and then named his gallery An American Place. He would remark that this is the cruelest land in the world for the artist, but maintain that a Marin seawash was American. He insisted on a kind of biblical USA geography in art.

Alfred Stieglitz was the most exquisite of all heart-wounders. The people he hurt most came to kiss his hand as he lay on the alcove cot or to press the fragile tortoise-shell wrists, and to bless him for making them whole. Everybody fondled him because people were already or-phans in the big-cold-street nation. Stieglitz was a father and mother doll for the literature and painting orphans who had no playthings besides their books and canvases, and no one to love. Alfred Stieglitz, who died in 1946, danced before Art in a white stole, like David at the Ark.

# Lawrentian Analects

It has become common to regard D. H. Lawrence's work as the tiger with the flaming colors of Joseph's Coat, but to cast the man in the ditch. When I was in diggings in London, sleeping until mid-afternoon so that I could sustain myself by one meal a day at a pub or from the tuppenny meat-wagons, he sent me five pounds. He wrote me didactic, bullying letters which were accompanied by the two gudgeons and the barley loaves. I had not met the celebrated man, or given him any hint of those blighted London days. But hunger is an angel, and though I regret many other torments in my life, I do not cast out indigence, my dearest teacher. We are eunuchs because we believe in money which can beget nothing. The epitaph of Thomas Churchyard is "Poetry and Poverty this tomb doth inclose."

I saw D. H. Lawrence for the first time at Sylvia Beach's bookshop in Paris; he had already written a preface for my first novel *Bottom Dogs*, receiving a pelting guerdon for his valiant work. I watched this lissome man talking to Sylvia Beach, because, for me, he embodied the wild, rioting muses. He had a goatish jaw with beard, russet, earthed hair, and a potato nose. He looked like a Mayan idol, with beans for eyes and squash seeds for teeth—to use his own phrase, he was a crucified faun.

Some days later when we walked across the Boulevard Raspail I realized that the man was dying in his clothes. I had to help this spirited forty-two-year-old nature, for he was that rather than a writer, to his room at the Hotel Grand Versailles.

He was the most moral man of his age, and he never ceased advising me to be the bony Spartan. He urged me not to let publishers cozen me of my lentils, and I never have because they never gave me any. He also counseled me not to be unlucky and always write with a great bitterness. I have heeded his advice as best I could, for I have been a bitter stylist, and I have always been luckless. For all his fame, which he thought a disgrace, he replied to my letters at once. Being a genius he was alone, needing even my callow epistles without sun, wheat, grapes, and rain. He quoted La Bruyère who said that all our miseries come from not being able to be alone.

It was I who left off writing to him because I was ashamed of the empty, Cana words I sent to him. Of his person I can say what Lord Bolingbroke asserted of Bacon, "He was so great a man that I do not recollect whether he had any faults or not." Idol-breaking is seeing what we did not perceive in our purblind youth; unchanging yea-saying is stagnant water, for those who do not continually reject their former ikons and idols are always boys. Though I have altered my thoughts regarding his gifts, let it be my portion when I retire to Erebus to have as companions the disembodied dust of Hesiod, Homer, Musaeus, Apollo, and D. H. Lawrence. "Eat and carouse with Bacchus," Lawrence says, "or munch dry bread with Jesus, but don't sit down without one of the gods."

from "Lawrentian Analects," a book review of *Studies in Classic American Literature* by D. H. Lawrence: published in *Poetry: A Magazine of Verse* (March, 1954: volume 83)

# III Quomodo Sola Sedet
# Civitas

from *Cipango's Hinder Door*

# Walt Whitman

Sing the Alpha forest gods,
  Sorrel, purslane, and the uncured sassafras;
We forsook the soft, doved waters of Venus and Daphne,
And the oaks of Ilium
To quarry our Ghost in the marsh.
Concord was unsown violets and bog-cress,
At Nona the waters smelled of the fox.
Sorrow was our father and hope,
Penury sang in our pockets.
We sowed affliction in rank marl,
And called this Adam's ground.
Then came the cities of Cush and Ham,
And the granaries of shrewd Pul.

The midwest was a Mesopotamian corral for Laban;
Omaha, a stable for the cattle of Asshur,
Roanoke and St. Joseph were as Erech and Calah;
The Missouri was laden with the boats of Tarshish.
Togmarah sold mules and horses to Kansas City,
The mart for the melons and the leeks
That shone as emeralds in Paradise.
Venus came from the bins of Joplin,
Fragrant with rye, oats and papaw.

There was a man named Walt Whitman,
Prophetic goat and Buddha of the states,
An evangelist of the rank gullet,
And the pagan works of Phallus.
An Old Testament Balaam was he,
And as lickerous as the Angels
Who parted the thighs of the daughters of men.
He strode the cities of Shinar,
As though they were the oaks at Mamre.
At Sodom he sat at the gates as Lot.
Strewing his affections as palms and boughs.
Gaza and Akkad comforted his navel.

Every aged man was father Adam;
He went soft upon the ground
Lest he trample Abel's blood.
Among the thorns he grieved anew for Manasseh.
Did the Pharisee he kissed moult the canting hands?
Nimrod has giant laughing shoulders
Which hide the sinews of Cain.

We cannot bear each other,
For we are immense territory
And our malignant folly was to mew us up in cities,
And take away our ocean past.
For the sign of Cain is solitude
And he that goes in the earth apart
Grieves as the worm.

We are still mostly landless,
And a water people,
For we are not yet earth-born children,
And our Abraham, Isaac and Jacob
Are New Mexico, Arizona and Texas,
Residual sand and flood clay,
And the red that came out of it,
Iroquois and Algonquin,
Which means the blood, we slew.
Now the long wastes of flats,
And the terrible inland oceans
Are like our fierce black and gray burial cities.
The country is still more than half whale,
For we go to water quicker than to fire or to blood,
And we are a kinless people
Still suffering for the flood sins.
Whitman, our Adam, has died in our loins.

# Something Is Rotten in the
# State of Denmark

### from *The Flea of Sodom*

# The Flea of Sodom

*"O my friends there is no friend."*
**ARISTOTLE**

Let us admit, going over the Atlantic was a tragic mistake, and that he who drinks the vile, oceanic froth of Cerberus loses his memory and goes mad. Hercules took his cows no farther than Cadiz, beyond which men haunt the pitchy fens of the cormorant and the unclean ibis. How soon Cadmus forgot the Phoenician shores girt with shells whence Helen's robes got their Tyrian purple, and sowed dragon's teeth from which the gory Theban buckler, spear and iron javelin were wrought. The barbaric Lydians offered an iron dish to the oracles at Delphos. It is better to be slain by a bow of cornel wood or face a warrior in a helmet made of the rind torn from the cork-tree than perish by metal. The weapons by which man dies reveal whether he lived with the roe and the hind close by the founts of Helicon, or in Boreal, gloomy towns.

Homer's geography is purest metaphysics; Cimmerians occupy fetid, purblind Bosphorus near Hades; Tartarus almost touches the Pillars more perfidious than the Sirens. Goddess Hera went no farther than Europa's Oceanus. Menelaus took his elysium on the Iberian ox-hide. Odysseus trod upon the marge of sea at the Gates and retired. The lotus his companions ate yields spicy, Afric sleep, not Atlantic's horrid Lethe. Do not pass the Pillars, hankering after new places. Shun hyperborean lands; impious Prometheus was banished to the blizzards of Caucasus. Unknown countries are sorcerer's regions of baleful ore. The fleecy Ram of Colchis, Jason's cargo of copper, iron and coal is Caesar's Furnace. The Erinyes are fiercer where snows sepulchre the violet and the heavy-lidded daisies. Zeus's docks are in soft Libyan climes; the Bethlehem manger is not far from Apollo's Ethiopic stables. Jerusalem, Sidon, Crete, Egypt, Demeter's basket, is the Kosmos. Orion's rain, blowing against the reedy Naiads, is mired in the iron. What Scythian horde sacked the cities, leaving titan rubble over the grass and rivers that nourished Jacob's herds? Did Hannibal strew dust upon the malignant, herbless plains? Forsake the metal cities, brewing Chimera's noisome gas, lest you disappear. Let Saturn rule for Rhea to give the infant son again to the teats of goats to beget a race of fragrant Jovian babes.

Nobody can be born when the gods are not recollected. Cybele is a clinker, and Adam cannot moult his shame. Leave these cities, steel-gulleted Coelus and Iapetus, that fury the veins, and let Euphrates and the Bhagavad-Gita be your holy zephyr and truth. The dog parent, Atlantic, is the sea of oblivion; unhallowed people, return to the tender fig where the Muses sing.

Elijah's mantle has vanished, the asses of Kish have decayed, and men are wild, hairy Esaus. Man is doomed because he detests the parable. He hates a maxim or a legendary, Mosaic face upon which is inscribed the Nile and the hills of Judea. Man has cast away the proverb as Onan spills his seed into the earth. He will demolish the planet until he has the pastures of Carmel and the sheep of Gilead again. The Myth cannot ripen where the olive does not grow. Men abhor the gods, the houses are Satan's bile, the ground, infernal asphalt of Gorgon Medusa. The harpies have bedunged the streets and victuals because the Oracles have been forsaken for Progress which is sloth. This Atlantic nonentity, muttering Babel's homogeneous words, hatches his slovenly cities anywhere. All his inventions are for his piggish apathy. He travels in machines to remote places to shake his bowels. Bothering little with manual arts his hands are so testy that he commits crimes to handle a tool! Cyclops dungs more privily than he who lives in a house on the highway for the companionship of tin automobiles. He furtively diets on prurient newspaper pictures of female legs until he has the priapic fit, and loses his seed in Onan's cinema pit. Machinery, lathes, pistons, vibrating cars and subways constantly chafe his genital organs, and, O gods, Onan cannot fornicate!

Man is more spiteful without the pruning-hook and Boaz's granary floor; he is not as repentant as Ahab going quietly on a mule to Samaria. He is very perverse, and it is the froward tongue that is the vine of Sodom. Is there a David who weeps when he has humbled a Saul? The tents of Kedar and Job's flock at Uz yield a sweeter savor than the rubber tire, and Zeus's bullocks make them less malevolent than the automobile.

Perversity is the vice of Gomorrah. The pederast denies gnomes and visions—Jacob's Ladder at Peniel, old sayings the mountains and the deities have dropped into man's mouth—just as the nobody does. The quest for Babel is to be a mediocrity. Can a parable come out of a double-breasted suit? Make an apothegm, a parable, a goodly barley loaf, O nonentity, and save your soul. The race must have myths or perish. For the Fable is the Bread, the Spirit and the Redemption.

The Cana waterpots are empty, and there is no wine in my portion. Though my nature is as obscure as Jesus's, who spoke on the sudden, letting fate utter the words, reason is my Gethsemane. I do not want to be rational. I tell my Reason to go as soft before my soul as Hezekiah did, and say, O my head, come down and sit in the dust of Babylon. I hunger to be mythic and to crop the Prophet's footprints!

Man is malicious because he cannot be quiet. The cunning of the mind is used for going to some other place. Unable to sit, I could bite off my flesh because I have eaten of the Tree of Reason. Man was cast out of Eden into Reason. After he has partaken of the Tree of Good and Evil he meditates upon Time which is death. He is miserable because his days do not decay rapidly enough. How unimportant is Time in Seth and Enos, grassy knolls of flesh that ruminated for more than nine hundred years.

The greatest profligacy comes from tedium. The garage proletariat will blow up the earth to make his existence less monotonous. Were I quiet, God would not have put the dynamite of Sodom and Gomorrah in my veins. My boredom is viler than Domitian's who caught flies with a bodkin. It is obvious I have no gregarious pleasures. That is why I toady to everybody. If a ninny wipes his nose on my sleeve Helen is reborn! I am also a solitary and loathe everyone, though I realize that as many owls and cormorants are in the wastes of spirit as in company. My feelings are as cunning, on the quick of my soul, as the stung Iscariot waif,—passing crowds I exclaim, like the disciple, "What a stench!", but let one oaf drop a smile on my vest, and I make Jesus's reply, "How white the teeth are!" When I have dirty crucifixes in my face, and everybody runs away from me, I could ravish a chit or commit a

criminal violence simply to touch human flesh. I am more
ashamed of my wild ass's solitude than anything else. I
have wept as Hagar did for water, "Give me to drink of
a mouth," and I have begged for the leeks, the melons and
the loaves of Pharaoh, "Give me the bread of hand." I
pine for a face, a lyre, a David's Harp to play upon the
Saul in my brooding soul.

Besides sitting, the Triton's kelp is a pastoral simple. It
is not the affliction of the Holy Ghost, resting at the foot
of the mountain by the Galilean lake, but Poseidon's gull,
wheeling in the air above him, that pierces me to prayer.
Give me briny Oceanus, not Matthew's Salt; the dolphin,
sacred Hesiodic fish, was a symbol of the ancient city.
Under Egypt's furrows lie scallop shells and stones once
fingered by foamy nymphs. Was not Ammon's temple by
the sea? Tides and surfwinds are prophecies to pebbles and
men. Agamemnon enjoined the Greeks to wipe off their
pollution in the brine. Take heed of him who abominates
the trident; he is unclean and will send you to Erebus.

Do not think I am trying to make a Golgotha out of
a pismire destiny. I admit I have a fleabite of a fate. God's
apothecary herbs have not fallen upon my spirit. Do you
believe I care to announce I am Job or Lear to be abhorred,
or that I want to wash people's feet to get a wry look.
I can be meek, and give my cloak away, under the proper
circumstances. I acknowledge I cannot bear a jibe. Cato
tore out his entrails rather than expose them to Caesar.
Be content, mockers, ruin enkindles my deity; and underneath my little rock of Peter sings the worm. Suppose
I imagine I am Messiah, and I also think I am Judas, I just
betray myself. The evening I went with the soldiers and the
servants of Caiaphas, carrying lanterns and torches through
the rueful olive groves and over the brook Kidron, and
cried, "Master, Master!" I betrayed Jesus for a kiss! for
the Galilean glances he had given the eleven and denied
me. O what lore was in the world then. "Judas, betrayest

thou the son of man with a kiss?" Yea, Master. If I am not Christ, it is a disagreeable mistake. Will people say, "Is not this the son of Joseph the carpenter, and Mary?" Nobody will say anything.

There is one reply to lips that question the existence of Abraham, and fleer at the chronicles of Shem, Japhet and Ham, "Why do ye tempt me, ye hypocrites?" Any other answer is rational rather than allegorical.

One goes to Messiah or to Medusa, the ratiocinative mind, that turns the entrails to stone. I think the dialecticians had trouble with their evacuations. Is it a low query to ask how Diogenes voided? or to say that Socrates, Antisthenes, Crates and Zeno had a hard stool. In Boreal lands, remote from the oracular springs, the intestines are a sherd, —take heed, then, O rational people! I crow at each awakening to the morning star, Lucifer, or put a cicada in my vest. Unless I cry out Attica, Abdera, Joppa, just to tremble, I am depraved. What is truth? asks my bowels, and who made beauty and shaped Venus, says my lust.

---

Pilate sent out a hundred and fifty invitations for an informal anchovy and cracker evening. Everyone suspected a ruse except eight persons who were sent away with a sample ketchup bottle. Andromache was with Bedlam or Ajax Proletcult and Thais was still absent. I thought of the wenches that fled with curly, spearminted boys and plainclothesmen to Joplin and Wichita. Farmers came in from Armourdale to ease their lust. When my mother drank April bock and ate oysters rich as those bedded near Abydos, I heard the oxen of Jacob and the neighing of Abraham's horses in livery stables off Admiral Boulevard. I was doting mad on indian summer evenings, and a gingham dress made me faint for Aphrodite's buxom apples. The hilly streets roofed with the elm and maple I misconceived a Padua. Loafing in the weeds I watched the Missouri making a sluggish furrow a Glaucus would despise; drink not this potion of stupid river mud.

Has the amorous apple been eaten? The season of Venus is short; before the August peach is bruised the planet is empty in the throat. I sue Boötes for the humble kidney pie, bean and lentil; but the race of factory titans are hurling steel thunderbolts at Jupiter himself. Were not the infidel Cyclopes that built the first towers the same rebel Giants who conceived Babel? No wonder that Mnemosyne, my faculties, is raving on asphalt! Thais reappeared, walking up and down Sappho Boulevard in bedroom curls. When Pilate turned out the art and marxian mendicants, it was said everywhere the ideal bourgeois archetype had been debauched. He had been devoured just as Saturn ate his sons, which made somebody ask, "Who is Saturn? and who is the son?" It was also asserted that underneath Agenda's double-breasted suit the Mandrake Root was hidden, and the reason for the separation was Pilate's priapisms. Suddenly everyone returned. People were constantly leaving the city to create excitement or to be more legendary. Bedlam remarked that a land without female, rondured knolls and the pomegranate produces empty dugs and tepid testicles. The mediterranean sponge and Biscayan cork had appeased those who look at the zoo crocodile and elephant for erotical satisfactions. Do not mock, low dogs, for how far is the amphitheater from the Rock of Peter?

Pilate Agenda announced a cuckold buffet-supper. Andromache and Golem, who had been photographing Georgia crackers, came back with a Negro sharecropper whom they exhibited to Scranton and Pittsburgh steel workers. A Barcelona workmen's basement was rented to honor the Chinese people and to get money for the relief of the Koreans in the flood areas. Tickets were issued, with Agenda Russian caviar advertised on the back of each stub.

Those that could not afford to purchase tickets counterfeited them on a private printing press. There was some difficulty copying the caviar; some drew sardines, the dolphin, the mackerel. Everybody was delirious again about the lascivious canaries, and the anchovies were the olive and palm branches strewn at the Gates of Jerusalem.

When Pilate announced that he wanted to sow infants in Andromache's womb, she replied, "I laugh at copulation," and left. Alone, Pilate's rooms were gorged with sick memorials of alien lineage. At night he put spices on the table next his bed for the image of his dead mother. Slavish infidels do not know it is our Mother who art in Heaven that is our daily bread! Without an earthy compost of kindred a baleful Genius devours the Deity in the mortal breast.

Andromache's reply aroused very droll enquiries. Some wondered whether the bourgeois importer was not luckier with Spanish cork than with Venus. Suitors came to the Agenda apartment under the impression that Pilate was not epic enough to relax Andromache's knees, giving her the opiate darkness the *Iliad* heroes afford their enemies with the entrail-drinking spears.

Everything became rapturously bizarre; the cuckold buffet-supper was given. The canneries and coal diggers playwright, Ephraim Bedlam, came with his own celery, dried dates and prunes; Ajax Proletcult, just released from the Tombs for a milk-price march on Albany and for picketing the Siamese consulate, was dropping cigarettes on the oriental rugs. A woman, with hair the color of rotten carrots, once famous for her meltingpot novels, and now accumulating poverty for a book, was shouting *merde* at each guest that arrived. The radical dregs from the automat entered, followed by the lesbic dowds with false maiden cheeks buttressed by a mastiff jaw, more horrid than Scylla below her bodice. When Golem, wearing a walleted back, dropped upon Pilate's breast, crying out, "Barcelona has fallen!" Pilate handed him some consolatory Agenda Brothers' blotters. I then uttered softly, "Gentle Sir Golem, Lute and dulcimer spirit of dying Europa," at which he joined two coffee merchants who wore fat hydrangeas that gave off a sleepy scent of money. The coffee dealers embraced Pilate, not because they had read Plekhanov or Engels, but because bald men are nourished by thick, oily hair. Pilate, kissing each on the cheek, wept, "My Abraham, Isaac and Jacob is the warm American sheepcote of nonentities." Andromache, wild field flowers and petunias sprouting from her sandals, greeted each defunct, illegal spouse at the door with "I would go barefoot to Jerusalem for Pilate!"

Pilate and Golem were on the floor playing steeplechase. Andromache joined me, confiding that Pilate was going to give away several five-hundred bills to his friends as a business novelty. Could I bridle the ninny on my tongue? Any attention makes me such a milksop I cannot refuse a slut or a cookie, though I am queasy. When Pilate stroked my coat-lapel I reeled. Strangers, surrounding us, asked for my name, address and visiting hours. Golem brought tea and hickory cheese, sitting so close his knees nibbled mine. After Pilate stuffed my pocket with a pair of socks and Andromache called to him, "Remember, Judas is our brother," I fainted and was carried to a sofa. Golem gave me a wry look and returned to steeplechase. Man, coveting knowledge, fame, gain, crows out avowals as he sacks his neighbor's brain and goods, leaving the looted person so forsaken that he will eat tree bark, the soil and tackle of boats for another Antony knave to make foul booty of his soul. One will take to his heart an Heliogabalus or a Nero rather than be deserted.

Ephraim Bedlam was declaiming an aeschylian coal miner's tragedy in which the strophe was "Bituminous!" and the antistrophe was "Anthracite!" As he was reciting "O Pellagra, company towns, diphtheria creeks, and burial funds!" the drugstore and food counter stalinists arrived with mealy briefcases, marxists books and a roulette wheel. They collected the cans of Columbia River salmon, olives and caviar tins and then sold them from tables for the support of the locked-out millworkers in Fall River and a streetcar strike in Toledo. Volumes of Lenin and pamphlets on the Molly Maguires and the Chicago Haymarket hangings were raffled off on the roulette wheel for the "liberation of our black brothers." The steeplechase was taken away from Pilate and Golem, and played for the benefit of an unemployed organizer at San Quentin prison. Several cartons of Biscayan sponge and cork were found and set aside for the Andrew Jackson Liberty College for proletarians. When Pilate Agenda objected, a longshoreman denounced him as a chauvinist. During the quarrel chairs and tables were carried down the stairs and loaded into taxis while everybody shouted, "Down with War and Fascism!"

Andromache and Thais took a room to entertain persons whose names had been compiled from the Agenda Brothers' list of merchants. But no one appeared except marxists and the people of Gomorrah. Pilate came to force Andromache to return, but when Colette poured him a burgundy from a bottle with an Agenda label he grinned and left.

Pilate maintained the 5th Avenue Spanish loyalist office by shipping oil out of General Franco's port. There was a quandary about seething the kid in the milk of its mother. However, everyone was more preoccupied with Pilate's erotical eclipse. These rumors obviously came from the impotent or the sapphos from the psychoanalytic and dance cellars, always ready to cut off the genitals of the gods as Alcibiades had done, just to make everybody uneasy about his powers. Then Pilate, who was collecting tin foil from Hershey chocolate bars for the Abraham Lincoln brigade in Madrid, was expelled from the communist party. The mother of the Passaic mills trade union movement, and the grandmother of American communism had made a sex-complaint against him. The rank and file at once denounced him as a petty bourgeois harlot and an enemy of the working class.

People were more testy because of false prices. Beggars and stale whores had money, but the covetous tribe of Plutus had made everyone so poor that olive oil was as costly as dove's dung in the famine of Samaria. How rancorous was Prophet Elisha in miserable, pelting Beth-el when the base children called him baldpate. Christ, bred up in dirty Galilee, was irascible with Iscariot who rebuked him for using the 300 pence worth of the spikenard for his feet. When Saul went up to the Mount of God, Zion was a timbrel, the hallowed loaf and a flagon of wine. Lycurgus' table of cheese, meal, the grape and the fig is a noble commonweal. One blue clymene from Agamemnon's tomb can pluck up the sweetest pith of the soul.

When the Dog Star, Ennui, was parching the leafy veins, I saw a child hold out his tender, eden fingers to a street-urchin, and the child had put his hand on the hole of an asp. I heard shouting of summer evening flesh in the streets and the noise of music which I abhorred. For I sing in decayed places and have flayed my head for psalms and judgments that none will hear but the moles and the bats when the windows and lintels are rubbish.

---

Walking in the evening air I mused, "All is basely mingled, the people, the goods and the genders, for the tender vine of remembrance is broken. Where is the street for the baker and the shops of spices? Who weighs the egg and the sweet cakes, and what idol stands guard over the flesh on the table?" And I said, "O defiled flock, take a harp, and chant to the ancient relics, lest understanding perish." Then I labored for the miracle of seeing and knowing, and thought I heard murmuring Euphrates, and perceived the first-born leaves of Eden whose savor of apple, elm and hazel-nut garnished the lips of Jehovah. But it was nothing, and my spirit was a mute tomb. Inside the 6th Avenue cafeteria were Andromache, Thais, Golem, Bedlam, Proletcult sitting at a table with the tittering art-hags of Tartarus and Pilate Agenda. Going away, I turned back, hungering as Lot's wife did for the lascivious hearths of Sodom. Would I take Cain's guilt, Ham's shame and Rahab's vileness to warm myself in the sheepfold of adhesive mediocrity? Perhaps I would go to Los Angeles, which is the orchard of Gomorrah, and not the fig of Israel. I knew I had slain my blood, for Abel was crying out of my veins. What should I do? "Sit," whispered my heart, entreating, "Will ye go away?" to which my soul and flesh replied, "Lord, to whom shall we go?"

# The Rational Tree

*"While Israel sits beneath his fig."*
CHRISTOPHER SMART'S SONG TO DAVID

In Israel the measure was holy and in Attica the idols stood guard over the markets. Bread was placed in the Lord's Scale and the cost was sacred. Gideon's meal for the Angel at the wine-press was a kid and unleavened cakes of an ephah of flour. How much barley Ruth gleaned in Boaz's field, and how the lentils, millet, fitches and beans were apportioned for Ezekiel's bread of affliction, is told.

Absalom's Vanity is the weight in shekels of his polled locks. The delight Jesus took in the spikenard ointment for his feet is reckoned to the pence by Judas Iscariot. The Lord weighs the waters by measure, sings the Psalmist. Plotinus, in a Hebrew meter, says that God renders everything by balance and weight. The seer took the age, the culture, and the people, and asked, What is the weight of its spirit? just as Osiris judged the shades by the weight of the heart. Job puts his Integrity, Archilochus his Iambic, and Shakespeare his Sonnet, in the Balance.

Statues of Zeus, Hera, Demeter, Dionysus stood in the midst of the markets as the guardians of bread, wine, prices. Bacchus kept vigil over fruits, spices, sheep. The poet Socrates said Bacchus invented the penny loaf. Hesiod's bones were buried in the market place, and Bacchus was the tutelary god of Thebes: "Good is the bread in seven-gated Thebes." Bacchus taught the Greeks not to drink wine unmixed with water. The fable of the infant Dionysus nursed by the Hyades, nymphs of the rain, is such a maxim. The flight of Bacchus to the sea is a similar homily.

The ancient city was as savory as its bread. Demeter and Bacchus established the hallowed loaf. The poets said, "Fat and deep-bosomed Ceres," and Jacob's blessing for his son Gad was, "Out of Asher his bread shall be fat." In the *Fasti*, Ovid tells how loaves were strung across the backs of the asses in the Festival of Vesta. Millennial goodness was where the bread and the damsels were as plump as Demeter, the kidneys of wheat as large as the kidneys of Arcadian oxen, and the figs and pomegranates sold and measured by men that fear Orcus. The Jewish Sanhedrin, room of Justice, was half of a round threshing floor. The grain-goddess Demeter gave laws, and the Angel stood before King David on the wheat the Jebusite had winnowed.

The streets and gates belonged to a people in sane health. Apollo purified the streets in Hellas, and in Jerusalem there were separate gates for sheep and asses and camels, each under the authority of a priestly porter. Nehemiah tried to restore Zion by repairing the gates for herds and the dung! No animal's carcass was buried in the city, and no debauched corpse was laid in David's Sepulchre. King Jehoiakim was given no other rites than the dead ass that was drawn and cast outside of Jerusalem.

Wisdom is wherever the mule, the goat and the fig

have flourished for a thousand years. Arcadia was known for its breed of asses. The ass was a companion of prophets and kings in ruminative lands. Solomon rode on David's mule to be anointed at Gihon. Moses walked beside the ass with the Rod of God in his hand. Jesus, for once a mirthful Silenus or Quixote addressing Madonna Toboso, announced, "Fear not, daughter of Zion: behold, thy King cometh, sitting on an ass's colt!" Go to the fig, and to the she-ass for prophets and kings. Abhorred Pluto wheedled Persephone with pomegranate seeds, and Joshua's spies returned from Jericho to the Israelites in the wilderness with grapes and summery fruits. Good towns grow up by Bacchus's yews on warm-nymphed seas twined in Poseidon's kelpy trident; Ilium, Joppa, Abdera are the cribs for pensive races until they are Caesar's; then the parable perishes like a Roman Egypt whose figs give suck to the asps in Cleopatra's basket.

What demon drives modern Ishmael to lands sown with cockles by windy constellations and fierce, protean seasons, or fetters him to earth farmed with the potherbs and the nettles Aristophanes thought were the first vegetation in the world. Why is a nation today reckoned doughty because its towns are founded on briars, thistles and scorpions? The lewd witch in the *Satyricon* tries to revivify the youth by smearing a mixture of oil, ground pepper and bruised nettle seeds on an emblem of Priapus.

Golgotha's nails punish the spirit no more than a hamlet or city that has nothing left of the holy footprints of Elijah but the crop of gravel Virgil cast down the three throats of Cerberus. The face is hindered and the navel sickened in abominable places. It was a soul in its nauseous moan that chided the twelve disciples for exclaiming, "What a stench!" when passing dog carrion, by replying, "How white the teeth are!" Had not Jesus, who doted on the albic stole and the frankincense, been reared in Galilee whose twenty foul towns Solomon had guilefully presented to Hiram of Tyre?

Men devour their lives in a gross locality where there is not a David's Lyre in a face to play upon a brooding Saul. "Take a Psalm, and bring hither the timbrel." Ishmael in his wild ass's solitude will bite off his flesh for a soft look. The mendicants run after the low loaves and fishes, but Ishmael hungers for man. Five tender persons speaking to one another for a lustrum can make a book of proverbs. Did not twelve fishermen and a carpenter's son, who ate and talked and pensively crossed the brook Kidron together, produce a legend? Lonely artists create pariah wisdom; Matthew's Salt is not in his Text. Culture is conversation; a noble people are remarkable talkers. Underneath the wholesome tongue is the Tree of Life.

The fool and the troglodytic Onan feign a weariness with friendship and speech, but a man of feeling kneels in his heart at the mention of such Jovian companions as Solomon and Chaucer. When the Dog Star, Ennui, parches the energies of the soul, and man no longer trembles, Diogenes' remark, that all he wished was a peck of lupines and to care for nobody, is a pious maxim.


Evil and spoiling are in the imagination of families and races. The descendants of Lot's daughters were harlots, and the cunning children of Ammon and the predatory Moabites were of the same defiled stock. Ham, the pederast, was the forebear of Cush, who begat Nimrod that built wicked Babel. Phut, who put the helmet and the shield on the soldiers of Israel, derived from Ham; while good Job of Uz came from the house of modest Shem.


Was not Onan, that spilled his seed like Vulcan, the brazier, the brother of Er who made linens and whom the

Lord slew? Names and crafts in the Hebrew Testament were a memorial of a people that were quiet Jacobs, lowly artisans, or booty-seeking Esaus. Jeremiah makes a list of profane occupations. Horse-traders came from Togarmah, and venders of brazen vessels and slave-merchants were from Javan and Meshech. Sacred work was thinking, herding, keeping the olive tree and the oil.

The sons of Asaph prophesied with harps and cymbals; but the potter dwelt among rude plants and hedges. When Nebuchadnezzar sacked Jerusalem he took the smiths and the makers of gold pots and shovels with him and left behind the meek vinedressers and husbandmen. What need has man to go beyond the sheepcote, the threshing-floor, and the augur's timbrel? A mortar and a pestle are enough for a culture!

---

Vine, cattle, fruit, and sea gods are far better than none. Aeneas showed the most polite learning in not leaving burning Ilium without taking with him the image of the household goddess, Pallas Athene.

Who would not prefer to burn poplar to Zeus than tremble at nothing? Who would not rather sow a hundred songs and proverbs in his breast than be Nabal the Churl with three thousand sheep and a thousand goats?

"Have you not heard our soul is immortal?" Plato's Glaucon is asked. "No, really, I have not," he replies. Stoical Brutus was no less shaken than Saul in the Witch's cave at Endor, when the figure appearing at his tent spoke, "I am your Evil Genius, Brutus, you shall see me at Philippi." Socrates consulted the gods, and Democritus kept himself alive a few days longer by smelling honey loaves so that his death would not interrupt the Festival of Ceres.

Nations without stable forms and deities are brutish.

A populace, mad for novel raiment and bizarre amusements, breaks antique idols and proverbs, and canonizes trash. "Whom Jupiter desires to destroy, he first drives mad." People that are not Janus-faced remember little, because they are always changing their customs and calling it Progress which is a sly word for Mammon.

Epic men, observes Plato in the *Phaedo*, pass the springs of Lethe that they may drink from the lake of Memory. But the insolent Centaurs feed and gender upon the Macadam Meadows in the remote regions of Lethe, far from Eden's Cherubim and Zeus and Aphrodite's Oceanic Kypros.

# Bellerophon

A man ought to study his genius, since one's Muse is
his destiny. The vices of the intellect are perilous, and
what a ruin of a nature there is in a gift improperly used,
for the mind is the lair of the lurking pard's tooth. Let a
man go quiet and low before any knowledge he has lest
he make a gorgon out of it; each poet must regard his
Muse as a begetter of some obscure nether turpitude. The
poet often prepares a pot of honey but conceives gall, and
he never knows whether he has perceived the Pleiad Maids
or devils by the tombs. Many times the poet has said to his
soul, "O my love, I fed the sheep and the little lambs, but
when I went to look for them in their pens they were
torn and bleeding."

No one is on guard enough against his nature, for
each man is dear to himself, and thoroughly unprepared

for his vices. It is sin to believe in one's character. Man is continually astonished at the moral weather of his identity. Who knows what mineraled sins are in his visage? The truths believed to be mild, April aphorisms were rough, impenitent Winter lusts. The knowledge labored for, to destroy the hard tree roots and primitive ravines of identity, was brutal Mountain apathy. Knowledge is always dying in man, and this dead knowledge is the arrogant Solymi and the extinct Centauric crags in the human bosom. Take heed, wily, Protean dust, the Angel you saw by the river Sihor is the lion, goat, and the dragon.

Return who dares to his own truths. Consider wisdom, it is like the apples and the pomegranates once trembled for, and when recollected is no less a plague than disgrace. Who can look back at any period of his life without cowering before his bestial intellect? What a pitiless, artful, ravening beast is the mind, and O the loathsome wounds it inflicts upon the soul! There is so much choler, spleen, vanity, hardness, ungovernable coldness in the intelligence one would surmise that man made it his heart's fable to be caitiff—savage, natureless, petty, inert—never to shake for others in trouble,—and yet—there is nothing else but this constant moral convulsion to break into pieces the Cyclopic iron Mountains of the intellectual faculties.

Men differ from each other not in knowledge but in the pitying touch; for MORTAL TOUCH is the parent of all literature, and the brain void of affections is a terrible deity. Intellectual agony is cold, wild logic, and is as the raging of stones in slain hills. The owl and the eagle lying in wait for the lamb is logical poetry. The owl has fierce beast nostrils that are in horrible tumult, smelling unto dying, the ungraspable Almond and the dear Orchard fruits, and though it spoils the flock with its deep tooth, it will perish to take unto its bosom, and to crib there, the soft, bleating Lamb it kills. The mind, in which the valley and the apples have failed, is depraved, but its negations, provided the Lamb yet lives, gladden the lilies. No knowledge rightly understood can deprive us of the mirth of flowers.

What is the mind that it should bray, or go proud and alone? Genius is a sacred Animal that trembles more than others and requires an Archangel to prevent him from wearing out his heart for human sorrow. Return to the fig-trees beneath the walls of Ilium to chant to the timorous, dove-winged mind. Go low, Bellerophon, come down, O learned Dust, Wisdom is our PRAYER.

# Thoreau vs. Contemporary America

from *Can These Bones Live*

# Thoreau and Walden

We cannot perceive what we canonize. The citizen secures himself against genius by icon worship. By the touch of Circe's wand, the divine troublemakers are translated into porcine stone embroidery. Think how Thoreau and *Walden* have been shunned. *Walden*, the purest parable ever written in America, remains shut. However, *Walden*, which takes its inspiration from the Vedas, is the secular bible of our ethics. What it hints of—*how* to resist evil, society, patriotism, poverty and war—we dare no more neglect. How to resist? Therein lie all the morals and all the terror of this world.

There is an uncanny shrewdness in those well-governmented Americans who have looked at Thoreau as a kind of cranky male sibyl, a crabbed and catarrhal water sprite of our woodland culture. Little wonder that his "Civil

Disobedience" lies dormant and half forgotten as a curio in libertarian and anarchist anthologies. Imagine were it otherwise: what state would dare render sincere homage to its greatest malefactor, Henry David Thoreau? What society of men so beautifully groomed in submission could countenance "Civil Disobedience": "How does it become a man to behave toward this American government today? I answer, that he cannot without disgust be associated with it. I cannot for an instant recognize that political organization as my government which is the *slave's* government also."

How unconsciously astute is the Massachusetts Commonwealth to garment Thoreau, an anarchist and militant defender of Captain John Brown, in marble robes while mortally detesting John Brown, and in our own lifetime executing those simple pure apostles of free men, the shoemaker and the fish peddler, Sacco and Vanzetti. His Journals overflow with such anathemas as: "My thoughts are murder to the State; I endeavor in vain to observe nature; my thoughts involuntarily go plotting against the State. I trust that all just men will conspire." And his curses fillip the stars whenever the dust of his native place is upon his tongue: "As for Massachusetts, that huge she-Briareus, Argus and Colchian Dragon conjoined, set to watch the Heifer of the Constitution and the Golden Fleece, we would not warrant our respect for her, like some compositions to preserve its qualities through all weathers."

The State is adept in the mysteries of evasion and interment. Henry David Thoreau is honored; but his books lie buried like the fresh barley seeds stored by Joseph in granaries and scattered in Pharaohs' tombs. Administrative Philistia needs no economic astrologer to help it read "Civil Disobedience" or *Walden*. Society is clairvoyant, knows how to govern, when to load its musket, when to erect an obelisk—and when to canonize. The antiquarian is the State's best servant and art's most formidable foe. Sequester the writer, make him an "early American" of a Golden Age of Letters, and you refuse him. You disclaim him by a spurious exaltation of his period.

Writes Hans Ryner: "We say that the age of Pericles was magnificent. Yet Pericles was the object of all sorts of accusations. Phidias was prosecuted; Anaxagoras was exiled; Socrates drank the hemlock." The artist in any age is a divine accident. In what time and place was Herman Melville's genius born: whence came this Job? this creator of the Cabala of Whaling Science? Where is the American signature furrowed in Henry Thoreau's Himalayan brow? "The social condition of genius," wrote Thoreau, "is the same in all ages. Aeschylus was undoubtedly alone and without sympathy in his simple reverence for the mystery of the universe." No other American but Bourne has taken such a deep and accurate measure of the secular despotisms of government as Thoreau. None has had his ethics —a social conscience with a moral auditory nerve which responded to the finest shadings of injustice. Writing with the intense Christian fervor of a Leo Tolstoi, Thoreau says in "Civil Disobedience," "Is there not a sort of blood shed when the conscience is wounded?"

Thoreau was an opposer: he was against society, slaves, institutions, church and politics; and the sum of his giant negations is a more illuminating text for a way toward understanding the subtler courtesies and gentler urges of men than those weedy and unkempt affirmations in Whitman's *Democratic Vistas*. The "canting peal" of Sunday morning service was as raucous to his ethical senses as the sound of an air-biting drayman's whip was to the ears of Schopenhauer. "I am too high-born to be propertied," he said. Announcing his total disallegiance to organized government, he wrote: "Know all men by these presents, that I, Henry Thoreau, do not wish to be regarded as a member of any Incorporated Society which

I have not joined." To him the body politic was "covered with scoriae and volcanic cinders, such as Milton imagined."

Should we mistake this anger for misanthropy, we wholly misconceive Thoreau, for his virtues were heady enough; it was nature in him that was so diluted. He might do all within his abilities to ameliorate man's condition, his poverty and judgment and humble life in this world, but he could not stop loathing his low mortal habits. But he had ample goodness and urgently wanted on occasions to be easily familiar with the rhythm of habit, usage and ordinariness. We must curse the heavens for Thoreau's limits, for they were beyond correction.

Thoreau could say that the "utterer of oaths must have honeyed lips," sadly surmising that his own were so niggardly clothed. He could write, "There is no remedy for love but more love," without being able to love anyone. In one line—"I am not above being used, ay, abused, sometimes,"—he makes us his subjects; for he who can so trust life lives forever after. We see this long-nosed and thewy New Englander with flinty eyes walking through Concord village, hoping that the meanest man, "Sam" the jailer, will call after him: "Thoreau, are you going up the street pretty soon? Well, just take a couple of these handbills along and drop one in at Hoar's piazza and one at Holbrook's, and I'll do as much for you another time." "There is some advantage in being the humblest, cheapest, least dignified man in the village, so that the very stable boys shall damn you."

Thoreau belonged, if he belongs anywhere, with the Christian anarchists of the world, with the Nazarenes, the Mennonites, the Dukhobors, with Tolstoi, although he lacked the Christian, tragic impulse that made Melville, Keats, Shakespeare and Tolstoi sit in Job's sackcloth and enact in their own lives the eternal Passion Play at the tomb of man's misery. *Walden* is the nearest he ever came to the drama of man. It was the drama of Fortitude succored by Logic, without any hidden trap doors of the heart. *Walden*, because it is so untouched by miscreeds, casts a dry light upon the Bible socialists of the Forties and Fifties, the era of the American communitarians: the Oneidans led by John Humphrey Noyes, Yankee apostle of pietism, socialism and complex marriages; the Rappites, shrewd colonizers and communistic economists, and "God-propped"; the Owenites of New Harmony, the Brook Farmers, the Shakers. Here we had, perhaps, the prefiguration of a Democratic America, the individual emancipated from State hegemony, or living apart, Statefree. "If a State is governed by the principles of reason, riches and honors are the subjects of shame; if the State is not governed by the principles of reason, riches and honors are the subjects of shame." So wrote Confucius and so believed Thoreau. Thoreau was concerned only with the Orphic politics of the soul, the only politics for man—no politics. Character must sculpt its own background and Fate, and emit its own historical aureole.

This seer, whose body is fog, fen and vapor, was as subtle as the modern *diaboliques* of the flesh, as an Emile Verhaeren or a D. H. Lawrence. Thoreau feared conscience as much as evil; too much conscience bleeds the soul to death, and too much morality cankers the whole man. Thoreau eschewed all doctrine and all saviorism. Whitman's humanitarian bathos, his democratic rodomontade —"I will not exclude you until the sun excludes you,"— was wholly alien to that quieter individual.

A visionary democrat, Thoreau was not too democratic, not too common, nor too clean. Thoreau was not the Common Man, although he reverenced what is innocent and humble in man and in himself. He wrote that Emerson was not "comprehensive" enough to trundle a wheelbarrow. He, of course, could build a fence, caulk a boat, hoe potatoes, although he made no occult humbug of the homespun agrarian life. When the triviality and dust of Concord galled him and he had to refresh his olfactories, he retired to Walden, picked the "hairy huckleberry" at Truro, fished, trekked through Maine, or lived with the Indians; and when he grew weary of all these changes he returned to Concord. Henry Thoreau had a sane imagination; he saw how great was the fall from man to farmer. Thoreau would have had no patience or sympathy with an Occidental cult of industry: in *Walden* he writes with a sententious tartness: "Why should they eat their sixty acres, when man is condemned to eat only his peck of earth?" Here again he was close to Tolstoi who said: "The exaltation of work is as monstrous as would be the exaltation of eating to the rank of a virtue."

He never wrote any fig and nut homiletics on the unmitigated beatitudes of the life of the American Farmer, or, like Hector St. John Crèvecoeur, turned America into an exotic Bible land of wild bees, maize, snakes and Indians. Thoreau never saw any vestal fires rise out of manure composts. He was so singularly without doctrine that he could write an essay, "Life Without Principle," and no conscientious reader could conceivably garble his meanings. He went wherever life sent him and made no credo of his private experience. He recorded it beautifully, and, if we have eyes, we can profitably read it and then pursue our own private follies, tinctured by his.

*Walden* itself is not a Manual of Conduct, but a mood, a Chanticleerian ode. Thoreau lived and sang it and, when he grew tired, he entirely forsook it. "I lived there two years and two months. And at present I am a sojourner in civilized life again." Elsewhere he writes in the same simple, unswollen vein: "I am naturally no hermit, but might possibly sit out the sturdiest frequenter of the barroom, if my business called me thither."

He was too alert, and, with what irony we must confess it, too *dry* for the general pitfalls of men and the herd cures that each generation prescribes for itself. In this spirit he wrote about literature, democracy and America, jotting down rare observations, and offering no nostrums, "those quack vials of a mixture dipped from Acheron and the Dead Sea." Thoreau tells us that he liked a "tawny grammar"; relished a phrase that had the fiber and woody odor of sturdy hickory. But he never ruralized English or speciously Americanized it. He could write preternaturally exquisite passages on New England soil, grass, berry, Indian relic, swamp, tarn or tare, without making a fetish of locale. "I wish," said Thoreau, "to get the Concord, the Massachusetts, the American, out of my head and be sane a part of every day."

When we read Thoreau we no longer misconceive democratic literature. Thoreau's prose has the astral fragrance of dawn, an early "morning prescience" rather than the hue and emanation of apotheosized place. He is a Vulcan hammering out of lichen, maple, alder, sumac and berry, the purest essences of truth. His "Musketaquid" flows through those remote mountainous regions of the inward man.

There is Thoreau's New England—the soil, fertilized with the arrow and flint and immaculate bone of Indian and American Farmer—that he revered. There, fronting the Atlantic, are the severe weather shingles, skeletal remains of puritan bigotry and beauty, transfigured by sun and apricot blossoms into human flesh. There! Albert Pinkham Ryder's charred fumes of waves illuminated by mineraled moonlight.

Thoreau is the parable which will never be experienced until America has transmuted the logic of *Walden* into the lore of the heart. Keats has said, "Shakespeare led a life of Allegory: his works are comments on it." There is no other way of seeing *Walden*, ourselves, America, at this fevered moment.

One Oriental has suggested that if you take out the

names and places in *Walden* it reads like a Chinese masterpiece; and it is true that we think of Henry David Thoreau as an Eastern sage; for the thought, vines, leaves and herbs of *Walden* are laved in the summery winds of the Vedas. Thoreau himself said, "The pure Walden water is mingled with the sacred water of the Ganges." From the Brahmans Thoreau learned patience, how to sit and wait, and, so needfully, how to be bored! Thoreau writes: "Hippocrates even left directions how we should cut our nails." At the nethermost core of history, and at the underside of war and poverty, lies tedium. It is the grand malaise of the Western world. Europe today has a "crisis" every few weeks. It is the national flagellation which the dictators give to the wretched and the starving instead of bread. When Thoreau said that "the mass of men lead lives of quiet desperation" he read the funerary lines of Western man. How true it is that every little man, newspaper reader, shipping clerk, "rank and file" socialist and communist, cannot abide more notes, conferences and diplomatic parleys, not because he is so wicked and hypocritical, but because he needs a spurious, historical event, the pungent excitement of troop and fleet movement—another sexual dramatic "crisis" in the world—in his empty, slavish life— to save democracy and defend Soviet Russia! Is this exaggerated? A close reading of men's beliefs discloses that they do not emanate from the stars and heavens, from planetary ideas, but from the frenzied and agitated blood vessels. The exquisite poesy of carnage is at the root of the intellectual, the revolutionist, the student, the war correspondent, the fascist and the laborer. Look not at their principles but at the "nature" of them. Noble partisanship today has an undercrust of beast.

Since it is the mind that is the vessel of all good and evil in the world, why is it that we so distrust its strength in opposing the violence at large today? Thought is always prior to deed, war, history. Baudelaire said: "Every mind is a weapon loaded to the muzzle with will." However, never before have the seers of the world been so despised. And never before did Americans so need *Walden*. Is *Walden*, it is demanded, a system of economics, a doctrine, an organized panacea for social ills? It is none of these. *Walden* is a vision; it is the "Bhagavad-Gita" of the moods and seasons of Conscience; it is a poet's rather than a lawgiver's prayer. Conscience is various, brooding and chameleon, and is not a law any more than are the works of Shakespeare or Keats. Teach men to understand one single line out of *Measure for Measure* or the "Odes" and you teach them all they need and can ever know of the fervor of beauty which is the poetic ecstasy of justice. *Walden* is such a fervor and such an ecstasy. Know it, and none will raise his hand against another, none will be poor and none go to war.

"Justice," "beauty," "moral fervor," "ideals,"—are these not taboo words out of the unclean and stupid mouths of the unproselytized Gentile, the bourgeoisie? We live today in an age of foolproof certitudes. We ask, has Thoreau a theory, has this thinker an economic metaphysic? We have constructed out of economic theories an Atropos-like dogma, an iron fate, that is as certain to slay our minds and bodies as will the evils it is to correct. Man must eat, but must man eat man to have his loaf of bread? Can a bread and butter culture sustain society? Can idealism be held, historically, in abeyance, while men murder for food—for ideals? Is there not a grim and baleful contradiction here; for there is more than one kind of feeding for mankind. "Woe be to the generation," wrote Henry David Thoreau, "that lets any higher faculty in its midst go unemployed!" Let us take care that the bread men get may not be the offal from Circe's sty. For man cannot *afford*, as he is doing, to neglect the chivalry of ethics in his pursuit of economic salvation. His *hunger* in the end will be so great, his denial so desperate, that he will break out in more bloody fury than before to reclaim his spirit; for spirit is so good and so evil and so chemic that, if you starve it, man will *eat* the whole world to have it back again!

But how can we overcome evil in the world, or can we? We have drifted far, far from the simple Christian logic of humanity: "Thou shalt not kill." We believe we are wiser, but we are only craftier. We know how to meet our enemy on his own terms: tank for tank, bomb for bomb. That is all. Thoreau with his face toward the East wrote: "The Brahmans never proposed courageously to assault evil, but patiently to starve it out." Men who see, see slow. The Buddha sits with his knees ruminatively folded under himself and waits; and the Occidental never learns the true vision of this posture. The wise Buddha waits upon history so that it can unfold itself in its own time; waits upon evil which must live its own life and die its own death. The Buddha patiently teaches and lets life do the rest.

Is this fatalism? We are fatalists only when we cease telling the truth, but, so long as we communicate the truth, we move ourselves, life, history, men. There is no other way. This is the simple epitome of the wisdom of nonresistance to evil. It is what Confucius, Thoreau and Tolstoi taught. It is the incredible, the visionary way, and it announces treason and betrayal more boldly than fire-arms or airplanes. Tolstoi, who deeply saw the virtue of comprehending simple things simply, answered the sophists who garbled his words: "All this apparently complicated proposition about non-resistance to evil and the objection to it reduces to this, that, instead of understanding it, as it is written, 'Do not resist evil or violence with evil or violence,' they understand (I even think, intentionally) that it says, ' Do not resist evil, that is, be indulgent to evil, be indifferent to it': whereas to resist evil is given as a rule how to struggle in the most successful manner against evil. It says, 'You are in the habit of struggling against evil by means of violence, or of retribution. This is a bad, a wicked, means.' "

We had in Thoreau's own time the Hopedale commune, the gentle Oneidans, the Harmonites, all of whom warmed over their socialisms with the Sermon on the Mount. We have as an immortal lesson in truth the way of the Christian Dukhobors of the Caucasus who refused to submit to military service and who burnt their weapons lest they be tempted to resist injury with violence. So powerful was the spirit of these meek Dukhobors that the Cossacks who guarded and whipped them had to be sent away because in the end they refused to do either. These are among the rare conquests of humanity.

The reason that we forget our true spirits so readily is that there is no frailer phantom, spun of such seraph-breathed tissue, than faith. Men require dogmas to support their eternally expiring beliefs. Great lives are moral allegories and so soon became deniable myths because we cannot believe that such good men could have existed in such an evil world. So we doubt the existence of Christ, the authorship of *Hamlet*, the profound human heart logic of Tolstoi, the miracle and wonder of *Walden*. But *Walden* does exist and for us. It is a revelation of the inward unity of the man that the beginning of *Walden* is on poverty and the conclusion on war. Show man that life at its apex is a supreme allegory and he will memorize *Walden* to the last syllable of its pulse. But persuade and hint. *Walden* cannot be rushed into men's hearts. "The light," says Thoreau on the final page of *Walden*, "which puts out our eyes is darkness to us. Only that day dawns to us to which we are awake."

# IV Letters: 1939-1964

## To: Sherwood Anderson

December 12, 1939
New York City

Dear Sherwood Anderson:

It was most inept of me to have failed to call you sooner. I was very eager to see you and to talk to you. I suffer a good deal from speechlessness, as who does not in the Iron Cage, the City. Since I met you on the street, I have reread *Poor White;* it is a lovely, winged book, and I dare say I don't know of any writer living upon these wasted plains of Sodom whose mood, cadence, pollened, fruity prose, is as close to me as yours. But no more; if I continue, you will think me a hypocrite, a liar, and a most cunning fellow. But I speak of you so in my book [*Sing*

*O Barren*] which will be done now next summer. But to return for a moment: I think you are potently right in believing that it is the machine that has deprived every one of us of talk, sexual communication, the human companionable touch. And as for myself, I'm a medievalist, a horse and buggy American, a barbarian, anything, that can bring me back to the communal song of labor, sky, star, field, love. . . . .

## To: Mrs. Sherwood Anderson

July 27, 1941
Santa Fe, New Mexico

Dear Eleanor Anderson,

My full thanks and poignant sorrow for your sad, warm note. I am profoundly pleased, of course, if the words, so deeply meant, and written in the temple of the heart, I wrote into my book [*Sing O Barren*] for you, were some insignificant solace to you. Little it could be! How I cared for poor, dear, good Sherwood as a writer, ranking him in my book as the first since Walt Whitman, you must know, and how I am rifled of his sun-leavened grassy, sweet temperament and person, I can but ineffectually tell you here. My spirit has been a poor thing since his death; there are, today, so few left, and none to take his place. I am, really, Eleanor Anderson, more of an orphan in this racked, torn world than I dare to put it.

Do let me hear whether you have read the book, it is only important humanly to me, I mean, not egoistically, and whether what I said about Sherwood in celestial eulogy and as criticism is for you right or not. More important, let me know when you will be in New York, for I shall surely want to see you then. I am here working on a novel and will return to the East in Fall.

I hope you have a little mended your own life, and taken back unto yourself the earth, not as savoury as it was when fine, full-flowing Sherwood walked upon it, but this, lest woe be multiplied by woe, you must do.

## To: Sir Herbert Read

March 5, 1954
Santa Monica, California

Dear Herbert:

Your letter is the ore of Ophir, and I shall never cease thanking you for it. I would have replied instantly, but I have been tormented by an acute gastric disorder. Besides, we have just moved into a rough and humble flat of the sort you see in Chelsea. At least this does not smell of money and Philistia.

Now I must tell you that I am concerned about you; do not damage your health. Mimnermus, who was tired and bored, said one ought to live to be no more than sixty, but Solon, much wiser, thought eighty was the right number of years for a savant. I pray you will have ripe faculties longer. But you must seek a quieter life. Don't go to India next to give an award to three ceramic artists, or fly, like Nimrod, to Chile to present a nosegay to a muralist. I earnestly wish you would give over all these swollen efforts for painters. There may have been a few who were worth it; but everywhere you go today there are modern art committees, tumid funds for illiterate abstractionists and paint cannibals, and hardly a soul reads Porphyry or Augustine or *Piers Plowman*. As I have said so often there is no road from modern art to the *Dialogues* of Plato or to Erasmus. Bosch is great because what he imagines in color can be translated into justice. Of course, he is marvellous for other reasons, too. But since we cannot avoid the age, and we see that men are raving because they do not know which way the wind blows or where the equinoctial regions are, or whether a savage living by the waters of the Magdalena is not more human than an auto citizen of the occident. Art must be a teacher or infamous; maybe in some other time a hyacinth will breathe as much deep uses as the coca-tree of the Moluccas, but not in a day when to kill the soul is the most greedy pleasure of men. You know I do not like the prate about what is good in one time, believing that what is of most value to heaven and earth in one century has the same weight in another. You can move from garlic and cummin seed sold at an honest price to Euripides, but when leeks are scarce, and vegetables sold at capricious costs, you are not likely at all to produce Eudoxus or the great apostate Julian. We need the word more than beauty; the beauty artist is really not concerned with the geometry of the spirit; for him aesthetics is the stibium pot. It may be that *What Is Art* is a prophecy rather than a correct appraisal of Rimbaud, Mallarmé, Baudelaire. But what was so wrong about these men? The barest few have escaped. Do not imagine that I read all of Baudelaire with cold eyes, or that I have not been affected by him. He taught me to use adjectives cleverly, to exaggerate the possibilities of wit, to simper a little at male whoring in syntax, and to be a misogynist. There is almost no sympathy in Baudelaire. Yet I do not exclude him—his savagely dismal life with a Negress as a sole consort is his defiance and cross. Someone told me of a Jewish poet from Poland who went about in rags to remind everyone of what the world had done to him.

But I rejoice in the emeralds, the ebony, the chalcedony of Eden, but unless they are angels or the rivers of paradise, goodness or compassion, we are back in the cultus of the beauty parlor of literature. I marvel at the obelisks, and it may be the rosy-faced Sphinx is Rhodope the courtesan, but the hieroglyphs of the granite are great moral injunctions.

You may be right that my disgust with sex is Hebraic; still I do not set aside the Nile at flood, or reject the exuberance of the tiger or the flights of the frigate bird. Enthusiasm is a remarkable thing; there should be no shame at twenty or thirty, but eroticism at fifty is quite another matter. Poor Lawrence was an intellectual onanist, and so was de Maupassant, and one went insane and the other was worn out before he could comprehend his talents. I do not believe, my dear Herbert, that Lawrence ever understood this. Like Poe whose waste he fathomed, he himself is much more trash than genius. You imagine he was not influenced by Stein. May I ask you, when did you last read *Mornings in Mexico?* Pardon me, but he was. I had unusual feeling for Lawrence, and do, but take a look at his acolytes. Do you imagine genius rightly understood could have such a large influence? What baited so many women, and nearly all zanies, lewd, cult skirts? He seems to have attracted not Ariadne by whose thread we somehow manage to come out of the labyrinth but Schopenhauer's volitional and short-legged bipeds. He hated will in women, and I never saw one Lawrence female who had not a brutish tongue and the arms and hands of the man-hating feminist.

I cannot tell you how grateful I am, dear Herbert, for your words on *The Sorrows of Priapus* and on the verse. Your suggestions are good, and I thank you very much for your critical markings. I shall in all cases follow them. You know I am not ashamed to tell you how indebted I am to you, and one of the reasons I wanted to dedicate something else of mine to you was to make another public avowal of the benefits I have had at your hands. Without your help could I have survived? I have great doubts. A

*283*

man can shake hills and rivers and ravines, and this is the battle of the soul, but without one nod of approbation from a trembling and gifted mortal, the earth will fall upon his head and break his intuitive life. . . . .

We are very discouraged; poor R'lene [Mrs. Edward Dahlberg] is tired, and she wants to quit the country; I write and cudgel my head and walk in Tartarus. America is very likely to be a fascist land in a lustrum; you know I have been mortally punished by the Communists; they have killed my books, mired my table and my lot, and yet I cannot observe these investigations without being very troubled. If the Communists grow stronger in the country, Soviet power will vanquish all lands and values. There is little doubt that despite all the Marxian gibberish the Russians live more sanely than the American who is a lunatic. Should there be a war every American will be expected to regard the Russian as a monster. How I am to expel from my heart all the joys and didactic sorrows I have derived from Gogol, Tolstoi, and even from Andreyev who was a little icon of mine when I was twenty?

The intellect is always the target of the dictator, and every man of mind, Marxist or anti-Communist, will be in a labor camp should this country go to war with the Soviets. It is a mirthless jest to think that people regard me as a reactionary or a statist. They don't read me, they simply assail me, kick my bones and head. What am I to do? . . . .

How much longer do you remain in America? I shall feel like a waif when you are gone. Is not a writer the most miserable beggar in the universe? Look, I am on my way toward my fifty-fourth birthday; we haven't a penny, and each time I write a book or even a piece I acquire fifty unknown enemies.

Guard your health, Herbert; there is no day in which you are not on my mind. I pray for every good soul in the earth, and it may be that five spirits can redeem the wounded ground. Maybe the tears of one heart can heal a corrupt holm oak. . . . . I pray for you and Benedict, your hearth in York which warms you and your precious family, for every good fireside is Christ and Lazarus. . . . .


## To: David Ignatow

July 12, 1954
Santa Monica, California

Dear David Ignatow:

Please forgive me for not writing to you earlier. The reasons are egotistical and boorish. I have been ailing and writing. Then there was your book of verse [*Poems 1948*]. I glanced at the worst poem in the book, "For Edward Dahlberg—Sincerely," the usual Laodicean salutation of the American, neither hot nor cold, gravel.

I appreciate your own warm letter about *The Flea of Sodom*. Your epistles have been very good. Now to the poems: your probity I honor; it is as hard to get to a man of honesty today as it is to find one's way out of the labyrinth by Ariadne's thread. You are as true as Hamlet, and you grasp your perplexity with a plainness seasoned with gall and hyssop. Often you drop into the rudest of facts to hide your suffering, and you succeed as a man rather than as a poet though you are one. I have no poetic creed; I abhor the alphabet buffoons, and scarce look to you to be one of the capons of the Muses. Thank the dear ground, you are also masculine, and no male vulva of the arts.

But your identity is far deeper than your statement of it. There is lower sea-water in you than you have yet fathomed; it is not that you are at all content to be a poet in shoaly water. The limits you have made; the whirlpool you have created. For reasons best known to yourself you have so far shunned the parables that are the equivalents of your inward losses. I suspect you have cast more bread upon the seas than you or I know or these poems can tell. Do not imagine that I set aside the book; do not respect it. I like the man a great deal, would even dare to say more, were it not that I, too, have been trimmed by Polonius every day, maimed by him, until I fear the risk. Curious it is that we who seek the hot Canicular days in the souls of men, ourselves appear cold and rocky, and feign that we are barren because we cannot expose the whole inside.

I could here cite what I like, and what I do not, suggesting that here you are hackneyed, which you know, because that is what you resolved to be; your shibboleth is to be ordinary; it is your way of hiding away, sepulchering what is tender and most vulnerable. Yet, despite your valor, for your colloquialisms are brave (and even so, do they reach me? They do, despite your own unwillingness to do so, to be a mendicant in words and images, and to give me pauper's gruel) you starved us both, perversely. Still, you are no Balaam whipping the Ass that perceives the Angel. You could be plain, and make a fable of it, gather up out of your diverse identity the myth that can heal you and me.

I could say this is a first book, and it would be the cheap remark of the writing mandarin. Or that it is far better than I had done in my own wandering beginnings, and that would be overweening and insulting. What I feel is that you could be of great use to a people if you want to do it. How much energy have you for rolling the stone of Sisyphus? A great deal, no doubt, as a city drab of wages. I would, if I might not be harming another soul, beg you for fire, the fennel stalk of Prometheus, and more feral meditation. I could say to you: See, we live among devils, for they tempt us because we sorrow, knowing that each time they can bait us, and eat our flesh for the asking. To go on, I would tell you, because we are bestial Ishmaels, living, separated, in the wildest places, we need the human song, small or big, I care not, but let it be grass and meadow and the pitch of mountains and pines, and not the self-loving pederasty that passes for poetry.

One can tell nothing about what another person may do inside? Of the cairn of failure is the living bread? This you know, and have said in so many different ways in your book. We stink when the will lags or simpers.

Obviously, it takes obsidian fortitude to write as you have done; for what is lacking in the States Whitman celebrated is character, without which you have Eliot, Pound . . . . and that malign brood of punctuation urnings. Almost all of the writing cormorants will dismiss you, and you— hating ambition as you do, and it is an insanity, but loving the shoes of a child, or the fingers that glow in the presence of sun upon a tree, and having the Kosmos in your head and in your arms and sleeves—can go on being a small Lazarus who awakens us when he comes out of his own grave. But will you leave the mould and the scum of your burial nature? I wish I knew that, or better that you would tell me, with that volition we find in hills or ravines or coves, for it is the will that sings, no matter what the inward thistles be. If you have that, for nothing else can save us, I look, then, for a brother.

As a statement of fact, there is hardly a word I would annul; maybe, now and then, in your recantation, when you imagine because you are unaffected, and because all dead matter in you is rising, Patagonian shingle, that you can take the world to your heart, or put it in your pocket.

So much, what have I said? This letter, too, is a failure, and may be dead coals for your eyes. You may think I am being a little furtive, too refined; but not so, I repeat, and call me boob or churl, if the words kindle derision or sorrow, if you have in you bald Teneriffe, and I care less for what seems fertile than I do for scoriae, I look then for the laval ashes. I, too, at this moment cast the cinders into the river and walk to its source.

I would write you more, but I feel I have done badly. I fear so to appear to you no more than a Parnassian critic in the vomitories of our little magazines, *Poetry*, and *Sewanee*, and *Hudson Pews*. But then give me an ounce of civet to sweeten my imagination. But one last word to your own person; I am no asp to drain your failures; no serpent to slyly betray your chagrins. I do not play the Iago with you. Continue to be plain, but as uninvaded as you pretend you are, there is still, even for so redoubtable a nature as yours, your kindred among the mosses, in the wild bogs, and, forgive me, in some loamy furrows we title books written by sad little gnomes called Spenser and Christopher Smart. You know the others; maybe, you will go to them not for show or to prank up your homilies, but to be simpler to the fisherman who talked about the wheat and the tares, the loaves and the stones. You have, too, no doubt a chassidic past, coming as you do from those East Side Jewish streets which to you are like the apocalypse of Baruch, or could be, if you cared to make them so.

Well, I will never stop; something hidden in you, maybe it is the Old Testament Jew still wandering in your soul, and crying for house, wife and hearth; looking for Joppa that was said to exist before the Deluge. You are somewhere in those waters, and maybe legend can heal your fact and make the poet in you the old son of Tigris and Euphrates. You are the homeless one, and your star is negation, and who will say that wise men sought not this as well as Venus or the Pleiades?

## To: Donald Paquette

November 5, 1955
Santa Monica, California

Dear Donald:

I pray that you are now working, and that you are not ill. You must gather up your nature, and labor for your feelings. You owe it to yourself, and to your wife, for you cannot sit, diseased by inertia, and lapse into sick nihilism, and be of any worth to your marriage or to the Kosmos. It is no good prating about scruples if you throw away your head, heart, and vitals, and still imagine you are a good, moral nature. This is depraved, and even venal, and you must weigh your conduct each day, asking yourself, What have I done this day that is savory, and that adds to my inward identity that is a credit to myself and to my wife? Otherwise, you do not fail, energetically having written, say, a poor poem, or some shabby lines, which we all do, to slough our guilt before God, the earth, and His vines, because you have cast away your living waters. We are not born to do nothing; this is a sin; and no matter what you may think of yourself, or how ethical you deem yourself, so long as you do not accept Adam's portion, to work among the thistles and briars for your redemption, everything that falls out of your mouth is cant, cunning self-deception, and the fox that spoils our vineyards. Please, for your sake, heed me, so that another lustrum may not pass, for which you may have to shed those tears over waste, willess days and hours, easy, lazy broodings never brought to any fruition. Knowledge that is not translated into Pauline Acts is a ditch and a falsehood.

Now, my dear Donald, I want to ask you and your charitable wife for a kindness in behalf of two suffering natures in this earth. There is a talented heart, Richard Newman by name, whom I met in Paris, and his wife, . . . . who are in fell need of money. This summer they picked fruit on Long Island, New York, to get those few pence for the barley loaves and the pair of gudgeons. Now there is no work, and neither of them, in truth, has the strength for manual labor. He has a government pension, and the two of them could live in Denmark on that could they gather together some money for passage. I am writing to others in New York for help. You would deeply ease my soul could the two of you come to their rescue.

You know I don't make maudlin remarks about writers, and when I tell he has that wheat in his nature, which more suffering, as a result of want, may be choked by the tares, believe me, please, I speak clearly. The two of you could make [your check] out to Richard Newman, send it to them yourselves, if you wish, or to me, and I will mail it to them. . . . .

Meanwhile, let me know how you are; what you are doing to heal the many sorrows and bafflements in your soul. I try to advise you as best I can; but it is hard. Man is either a rock or a marsh; he is all will for the wrong purposes, or he has none at all, and sinks in that water which he cannot shape into those glyphs we imagine is our wisdom.

## To: Isabella Gardner

September 27, 1957
Palma de Mallorca, Spain

Dear Isabella:

I am troubled about you and fear that my reply to your good epistle was not what might heal your despondency. Perhaps, I babbled too much about my own book, which is foolish. I cannot, as you know, offer you canons for good writing. There are no laws; there is only the energy of the soul and the mind. What with the help of Plato, Chapman's *Iliad*, and the *Georgics* and *Bucolics* by Virgil, who can say what may not be the bourne of your identity? I believe we are producing throughout the world a cold and morose literature which is wilder and more of a bog than some quagmire in Scotland.

Why does one write? It is a very hard question to answer; yet there are some simple replies which the blood offers. One, for affection. When I served my apprenticeship, as though one ever did anything else throughout life, I imagined that after writing books, and divulging my own trembling pulses, I should have many friends. The opposite was the truth. When I wrote badly, and received the cheap applause of the press, I had those herd acquaintances, which one had better eschew in this earth as well as in Tartarus. When I wrote better, it seemed as each good book, if I do not seem arrogant to you, were a dagger in the head of those who could not write. Little by little I found myself more and more cloistered. Now, most, if not all of my friendships, are of an epistolary sort. I fear to see people lest it should be a querulous encounter. Everywhere there is such a distrust of the head, not worth very much, true, because there is so little love. If I cannot write or compose in some way or another the hymn to Demeter or the cry of the tender Shulamite, I reckon my life as all dross and no Helen.

This is a note and an entreaty; please read those books which I suggested, and do not be too impatient. I cannot tell you how they will affect you; but is it possible for Homer, Horace, Lucian, and Virgil not to dilate the spirit? You must find the source for yourself, not directly in private experience; it is curious that though one has felt acutely, and that all, as Keats says, presses down upon one's identity, the approach to his woe and travail is through ritual and myth. One has to tread lightly upon one's veins or blast them into a great darkness. Art is not straight and plain; were it so, then all that is chaff on the palate could easily be translated into a Golgotha or into the Cana marriage wine. Quicksilver is most useful in an ass's skin, for everything must in some way be covered if the naked truth is to be found and deeply felt.

This is a reverie.

# To: Isabella Gardner

May 10, 1958
Palma de Mallorca, Spain

I thank you very much for your two letters, and for the very kind remarks you have for *The Sorrows of Priapus* and for the Sir Herbert Read piece. I just returned a few hours ago from northern Spain, and was poignantly moved by some of the cathedrals, the baroque portals, and many of the bleeding, suffering Christs. In the occident there is no substitute for a Man of Sorrows, for the pangs of the entrails, and the ten thousand wounds that life is, and so there is surfeit, the automobiles, that immense mortuary cartel, AMERICA. I fear to go back to the cement towns, to those demented and peopleless hamlets, to the synthetic houses with the starved, blank windows, the inhospitable doors, the barren rooms which so symbolize the sterile and unseminal marriages. I suppose, then, we shall never talk, but life is the master, not I, though I strive against all mountains, sierras, and deserts to accomplish my fate.

In Salamanca there was a bust of Unamuno, and Anthony Kerrigan said there was an astonishing resemblance between us. I hope so. No one really transcends a truthful voice. I have other inward necessities now, that is all.

I keep your letters, Isabella, but do not know where the one about your poem is. Moreover, it does not matter; what is deeply good is that I misunderstood your epistle, and that you are not *sure*. Please know that my only aim is to save you those years of waste I had in finding out what form is. Does that mean I know; no, I am always learning, finding out, and casting my old feeling into Daniel's Furnace.

Despite the malevolent burial of my book [*The Sorrows of Priapus*] the volume has done better than *The Flea of Sodom.* I received my first royalty statement, and a check for $18.90. Should I complain? Milton got 5 pounds for *Paradise Lost.* I think most of the volumes of the limited edition were sold. I am grateful, too, Isabella, that you care so much for the book. Baudelaire, before commencing his work, prayed to the Virgin Mary, his Mother, and Edgar Poe. I pray, too, for those powers, for who knows when his Ilium will be sacked and burnt? How many well-known mediocrities I have known who spoke of their next master-piece!

I shall pass on your good greetings to Kerrigan, and tell him that you will try to get his very fine translation of Barcia's *Chronicles.* He remembers you very well, and will be exceedingly pleased. Moreover, I told him I thought you were a gifted nature, and a tender woman; what more can dust be, and if I am presumptuous enough to criticize a human being I am very fond of, and have such a high regard for, well, I do it, I hope, to enlarge letters and the soul.

Coming back in a ramshackle machine and colliding with a mechanical leviathan we by a miracle escaped death. This was outside Madrid. The Spanish driver, although at fault, first denied it, but then angry students came to our defense. Finally the Spaniard was ashamed, and promised to tell the authorities the truth, saying that if he did not he hoped that he would find his sons dead and that his wife would never sleep with him again. We parted the best of friends, embracing and forgiving.

For the past fifteen days I have hardly slept more than five hours a night. There was so much to see, to revalue. In Poitiers, France, there were in a crypt many sarcophagi of granite upon which I dropt the tears of the heart; for death is more moving and maybe more valuable than life. I do not know. I saw some churches which were immense gothic skulls, all flesh peeled away, no dross or cartilage or excess, solely pain and rapture, each column the visionary bone and principle of thought.

You have my warm love and that faith that is grounded on negation and doubt, and which somehow goes beyond it into feeling. Doubt is my chant, my petrine rock, and my love.


## To: Isabella Gardner

May 30, 1958
Palma de Mallorca, Spain

Dear Isabella:

Your good, tender words sweeten my metaphysical royalties. Thank you very much for them. I devoutly wish you could have been with me, but then all our talks and communications have more to do with First Causes, and are therefore ether, vapor, and primordial beginnings. By now, I am almost resigned to epistolary friendships and aetiological love. . . . .

You speak of your son who was 13; one of mine will be the same age in October; but if I met either of them on the street, I should not recognize them. You know, if I saw you, I might not know you, for we spoke no more than three minutes. You can say that my deep feeling for you is as pure as a man can make it.

I don't think Rago [Henry, editor of *Poetry: A Magazine of Verse*] has printed a review of *The Sorrows of Priapus*. Why I can't tell, since Robert Duncan wrote that he had read the book three times, and that Rago had asked him to do a short book review. That after Rago's letter warmly extolling my work. I am not a squalid commodity, and my vision cannot be hired! I had had a wondrous epistle from Archibald MacLeish saying that he was anxious to write about the book in the *New Republic*, but nothing happened, although he has always been very charming and kind to me..... [William Carlos] Williams' piece never appeared, nor was his twelve-page essay on *The Flea of Sodom* ever printed. How grateful was Flaubert when Baudelaire came to his rescue. Baudelaire, himself, waiting to see what a debacle his *Les Fleurs de Mal* would be, could hope for no more than a *succès d'estime*; and who paid any attention to Corbière?

It is worse in the States because the country is too big; all great civilizations were born in small lands. The Elysian Fields were no larger than a bull's hide which had been stretched out, and was as much territory as Menelaus required. Carthage was said to be of the same size. When Euripides was played in Athens, a city of 60,000 inhabitants, half of them attended the performance, and I don't believe that London, when it was muck and mire, in the days of the real, though ravening Elizabeth, had any more people in it than that.

Have you ever seen the great bull Zeus astride Europa? To live out one's life in American Suburbia is, at least for me, a wizened portion. To go into starved, eyeless streets each day, void of antique buildings, and without having a single shop or edifice or ancient monument to appease the heart and placate the blood is too hard. Every time the American sets about to improve a city or town he destroys whatever is good in it. The most characterless city in the world is Los Angeles, the visionary spa for purpled-hair dowagers who are rich. I cannot stomach the entire brutality of the American economy in which men and women are kept apart all day in order to get their miserable bread and debility. There is no American hamlet or thoroughfare which has not been dunged upon by tin and rubber. I sometimes wonder whether anybody genders or feeds any longer except the automobile? Did you ever see any of the pistachio or meringue pie bungalows in Los Angeles, or look at a picture window? The houses or *sets* are all façades, without entrails or interiors, and the pecuniary lawns are too desolate ever to be a homely and simple burial-site. Did I mention Sir Thomas Browne's *Urn Burial*; if you have read it, do so many times; also do not fail to read the *Religio Medici*, and his *Garden of Cyrus*, as well as his *Common Faults and Errors*. You must find a language for your feelings, warm and good, to transfigure them. What is known as the American tongue is stylized sloth. It requires great activity of the soul to speak coherently, and then how much more to compose one's emotions as Pindar or Propertius did. Did you ever get Christopher Smart's *Rejoice in the Lamb?* Or, again, your daughter might care a great deal for William Gilchrist's *Life of William Blake*. His widow read the *Leaves of Grass* and fell in love with the giant baby of our Muses, and he was also a baby homosexual, non-practicing of course, and when Mrs. Gilchrist proposed to come to Camden, New Jersey, to visit him, Whitman was terrified. What would he do with a woman, and a fine one at that? Imagine any woman nowadays falling in love with a man because he wrote a remarkable book. Take a look at American women, and you will see what is the matter with American Literature. Stendhal once remarked, "The reason that Turkish Literature is so mediocre is that the women are so brutish." Of course, the men are no better, and doubtless far worse. But you can't have a visionary civilization unless women and men love each other. I can't bear the cinema any more because it sickens me to watch a pansy make love to a lesbian on the screen. When I was a boy, growing up in the wild, leafy streets of Kansas City, men and women sat on porches in the summer evenings; fine, buxom lasses ran off with men to Joplin or Topeka or to Tulsa, Oklahoma. Pederasty was an underground vice, and few ever mentioned it, because no one could imagine that a man would seek another male to express his lusts when he could mingle with some wanton or chippy or girl with a carnal heart. I knew cattle ranchers, livery stable proprietors, locomotive engineers, and corrugated johnnies who were employed in the roundhouses or in the West Bottoms where all the factories were located, and Elysium for them was a Woman. Of course, I can't get my books reviewed because I believe in the old orthodoxies of sex. I am afraid of using the word, Homo sapiens, any more, which was so fashionable and erudite when I was at college.

The American Tragedy is the tragedy of separation. Have you ever asked, why don't we write amorous verse any more? Once Gorki came to America, and, naturally, he was taken to Coney Island. He looked about, and said, "My God, think what a mournful people the Americans must be to get their recreation out of mechanical amusements." When Gorki came to New York with his mistress, and at the hotel did not indulge in the usual American sex cant, by writing in the hotel register, Mr. and Mrs. Maxim Gorki, the United States Government almost collapsed. That little Socialist prig and sere eunuch who perpetrated *The Rise of Silas Lapham* sent a strong protest demanding that Gorki be deported. William Dean Howell's friend, Mark Twain, did the same. Do you know that when Margaret Fuller, a brach of Concord, heard that Elizabeth Osgood was a friend of Edgar Poe, she organized a delegation of women who came to see her and to demand that she relinquish his friendship. The mournful, obituary truth is that I don't think poor Ishmael or Israfel Poe derived any real manly advantages from this charming and consolatory attachment.

You, poor darling, must do the best you can, and as I recollect you, you are a splendid, robust woman, and can survive anything.

# To: Josephine Herbst

Josephine dear:

I earnestly pray that you are continuing to improve. Your illness troubled me deeply; for some hours my soul failed me, but when I saw you again yesterday morning I was deeply reassured. *Please* do not leave the hospital too quickly. The novel will wait, and you will have, if you have patience, far more strength to return to it.

I am writing to Elizabeth [Pollet, Mrs. Delmore Schwartz] after these words to you asking her to let me know how you are, so that I shan't worry about you. I will anyway. Look, my dearest friend, we are a vanishing tribe, but a class of people, feeling and mind, that is disappearing, maybe for a millennium. How many centuries did it take to produce Hesiod or Callimachus? How much earth must we manure to gender the father of the *Iliad*? I am grateful that you have such tender friends, Jean [Garrigue] and Elizabeth. Elizabeth is a very fine woman, and if she can garner her force, and not be pounded in the mortar by that cruel pestle we imagine is life, she should have a ripening. How many Golgothas does it take to write one good book? I go on with your own wondrous book on Bartram. Last night I spoke to Jonathan Williams. I told him you were the most remarkable woman in America. Soon as he heard that you had done a volume on Bartram he was enormously interested. He, alas, does not, and cannot pay, but he binds and prints some of his books quite beautifully. He himself is poor, and I do not know how he gets the money to do anything. Should there be something you might want him to do, believe me I should press him to do it. I think a few pages of Bartram should be enough of a tonic to quicken his blood, which

is not slow, anyway. He publishes Patchen, Zukofsky, Robert Duncan, Olson, and William Carlos Williams has done forewords to one or two of his books. I met quite a number of admirers last night through J. Williams, and even one disciple, imagine that! But I am not gulled by flattery; these talented boys imagine that they can draw an aesthetic out of sports. Why, I used to hear 80-year-old women talking about the Kansas City Blues—a baseball team— when I was a little boy. Whatever is stale and senile they think is new. God, I abhor the new and all the cult that goes with it. One who called himself a great admirer of *Do These Bones Live* picked up the *Daily Graphic* and said, "Can anybody write as well as that; this is a classic." My only simple retort was: "Please don't be foolish." Of course, everybody began to call me Edward at once. I said that I had not the least reason to be pretentious about anything, but I did not think that one should address a Worm by calling him Harry, John or Moses, until one was more certain that the Worm was friendly. My greatest foes always begin by calling me Ed. Of course, if a lovely woman feels the desire to call me by my first name, I regard that as a tribute. . . . .

You must from now on take care of your health. Darwin was an invalid and only worked three hours a day, and lived to be an old man. Please, I beg you, do not cast away your strength. Keep it for your books and for those who love you.

Since there is so little love in the world because each one seems to hoard it, as though it were a miser's secret trove, let me send you mine.

# To: Jonathan Williams

September 23, 1958
New York City

Dear Mr. Williams:

. . . . I believe you are a brave and talented man; give, if you don't think I am a pedagogue, enough time to season your own pulses with good, wise books. Try as best you can to link the past with today; otherwise you have all the raging buffoonery of Dada, which some call surrealism, existentialism, or what the vulgarians now call the "beat generation." Everybody is defeated from the moment he quits his mother's womb. Soon as you are in the world, and granting that some centuries are worse than others, and we are at the bottom of the pit of Acheron, the struggle commences. What is important then is to find examples that will nourish other people and not kill them. Let Nature do that, and the task will be accomplished soon enough.

Of course, it is wonderful of you to encourage so many people who would not have a chance with venal publishers. But must you encourage everybody?

I like you very much, and also Joel Oppenheimer, and if you will heed me, since I have no creed to offer you, but a long humiliating experience, a thousand Golgothas, I may be of some use to you as a person and a writer. I am not looking for disciples. Jesus did not even know what to do with the apostles, and they had such dull auditory nerves that they could not hear what came from his soul. It is easier to walk on water as Peter did than it is to listen to another man.

It is better to save your money and to print what is best in the land than to do many miscellaneous chapbooks which are pleasant enough but with not enough meaning to nurture and guide the lost, and we are all lost. I am absolutely nowhere in America at the age of 58. I have been in exile in this land since I was a boy. But it is the only country I know, and homeless here I somehow or other

touch the ground, a threshold, and a few people who are my kindred even if they don't recognize it. . . . .

I would, if my suggestions do not irk you, because you know how to print and bind a book with great taste, and I don't know anything about either, bring out books that do not simper or are not eccentric. When one is a poet he does not have to try to look like one. The enemy recognizes him even in the gray, deathlike double-breasted suit. All a poet nowadays has to do is to open his mouth to sow dragon's teeth, and so it is not essential that he dress like one, or that you clothe a book with upside-down photographs. Let us try to be as simple and plain as we can about what we feel. Were you a parcel of that beat genera-tion, you would not immolate your person and pocketbook in an impossibilist's effort to bring to others books. I would not go on writing either; ask yourself, what do you write for? ask yourself all the questions that press down upon your identity so that you won't do more stupid things than I did when I was your age. We are born fools and die wretches, and there is no necessity to be more clownish or miserable than we already are.

It is good to publish those who cannot find some one to do it. You also have another task, even more significant, to print the works of those who will be of use to purblind souls. We are all Cimmerians, living in some subterranean bog in our souls, and when I glance through a volume, I don't want to know whether this author cannot otherwise find someone like yourself to bring him out. What is most important is that, whatever age he is, he can be the viaticum for my own nature, and give me enough food so that my own spirit can soar for an afternoon or at least until dusk. In other words, despite the fact that it is very hard for young people, and also the older ones, to get somebody to place their sighs and constellations between boards, what is of imperial worth is what they can do for others. Otherwise, you are bringing out books by Narcis-sus. There is already too much self-love in the world. Don't encourage a man to love himself more than he already does. Do what you can to impress upon him the necessity of caring for somebody else. Every page is either a vision or Circe's sty. Somehow or other most of us can gather the acorns and the masts, and we in this respect are as agile as the sea pigs around the Pillars. What everybody requires, you and I, is a book to take us back to Isis and Osiris so that we can understand this smallest of periods we attach so much importance to, our lives. If a book is not the most acute moiety of a man's valorous pursuit for ends, then it is the devil of Gadarene.

I hope I have not been too lengthy. What I want to impress upon your own nature is that my situation is no different from yours. Maybe you think I am a successful writer. I can tell you that I loathe the word success. My dear, good friend, Josephine Herbst, is inveighing against fame when she asserts that Bartram searched for the source of streams, gathered seeds, walked through unknown fens, scrutinized the leaves of the alder and the scrub oak, not to be renowned, but because he had an overpowering love within himself which he wanted to give to others. Is a volume a seedling which may grow into an aspen, a plane tree or a birch within you? If nothing grows after you have read a book then you have had a baleful and dismembering experience. Do we have to go to books to be assassinated? How much loam, ordinary dirt, foliage, moss, and even the dead carcasses of birds that once were jubilant is in a book. Whole islands that are composed of the dead are today the loam and ground of the living. Does a book awaken you? Will it bring you closer to another lorn person? You and I know the tragedy of separation, which we won't dissolve by palaver and beer at the Cedar Bar. It is a great purgative experience to be together provided that our purpose is mirthful or earnest or both and not just to be more sodden and inert.

My God, you may think this is pedantic, I only give you that counsel that I try to follow myself, and with what luck and purpose I shall let you judge.

Be sure, please, of my genuine interest in you and of my most friendly regard for your person. I admire what you are doing, and simply urge you not to be the prey and the loot—"the expense of spirit in a waste of shame.". . . .

## To: Josephine Herbst

October 22, 1958
New York City

Dear Josephine:

. . . . I am deeply sorry that you did not see Sir Herbert [Read]. He is a beautiful nature, but is involved in these absurd journeys, giving awards to painters and sculptors (and never to writers; nobody ever thinks of that), all of which does not kindle deep sympathies in me. I have always said: "A painter hangs his paintings, but a writer can only hang himself." His real work is little known, and I have been cudgelling him for three years to do a small book on Ruskin, and now he says he will do it, and dedicate it to me. As you know, I would never have a sleepy friendship with anybody, and Herbert Read says that I am his conscience and Socratic gadfly. May it please earth and heaven that I am, because it is hard to convince anybody nowadays that someone gets himself into difficulties for no other reason than to prevent another from miring on his Holy Ghost. Last night I was at a dinner given by an eminent cardiologist who was the teacher of Bill Williams' son at the university. There was Edith Halpert of the Downtown Gallery; also present were Mr. Abe Rattner, the artist, and his wife, both very gifted natures. I tried very hard to explain that you could not translate Bosch or Velásquez into one single, valorous ideal or conception. On the contrary, whereas one looks at Delacroix with a soporific mind or none at all, it requires intellectual attention to comprehend or even misread Plato's *Ion*.

Now, my dear Josephine, I don't think you should deplete your own remarkable identity on Nathanael West or Edmund Wilson. You said that Wilson was once a very forceful critic. No; we were ignorant and callow and thought he was. It is well-nigh impossible to write well about bad books. Nietzsche said that people outside of the creative processes can never understand those within them, and that describes Wilson. Do you know he once wrote that I had the genius of the Hebrew Prophets but that he could not read either me or Burton or Sir Thomas Browne? What he was saying was that he cannot read. To return to the cardiologist. He had several walls of very expensive paintings. Maybe some were good, perhaps not. I don't know. I long since resolved to destroy one art at a time. Rattner had a canvas which is an abstract Job. I don't know what that is, but I liked the man and his wife so very much that I refused to judge it, if I could. I decided to like what I saw in their faces. . . . .

The finger is still inflamed. I have not one utensil in this apartment. My despondency has been too great for me to go out and buy these commodities. I sit here, however, with the *Memoirs* of Saint-Simon, Herzen, the letters of Coleridge, some remarkable passages from AE, and a good deal of John Ruskin. In the evenings I pore over the *Confessions* of St. Augustine, and they heal the stinging asps in my heart. *The City of God*, too, has been a great ecstasy for me. I am religious, but altogether profane and unchurchly. Coleridge dropped to his knees twice a day, and Samuel Johnson said that he would as lief kneel on Fleet Street with Kit Smart as not. But I too know what Ruskin meant when he said that gneiss in the Alps no longer moved him as it once did. God, devil, or minerals may be my First Cause; it matters not; worm that I am I shall expire in wrath against the Angels for no other cause than some day I shall be no more, and also without quiet because I know I cannot be less.

I pray, Josephine, that my vehement credos will never be mistaken by you for inhumanities. I am very acerb, and I cannot help it, but I can be blown over by one soft word.

Again, I repeat, don't waste yourself on scribblers. I abhor all the nonsense about the times, the 20's, the 30's and the 40's. My God, what do a thousand decades mean that we should neigh and sport over five lustra. . . . .

Bill Williams, you know, had another small stroke; I tremble for him, and also weep for him. He has done many things of which I disapprove, but I do not want to go on rebuking him. Poor, poor Bill, he is much too close to Nature. I would kill Nature could I save him.

## To: Anthony Kerrigan

November 10, 1958
New York City

Dear Tony:

I have genuine regard for your identity and high probity, and I should be exhilarated to hear that you are going forward with your desires to be a man of letters. You may say you are now one, and I do not gainsay it. I simply say that you are not prepared enough to satisfy me, and that it is not enough to translate Unamuno and others, but that you must know what they read too. Now, you don't translate a very gifted author solely for wages; you love some of the men and their work you have rendered in imaginative English.

I am your friend, and the friend of your fate, but I have been writing, and making infernal mistakes for eighteen years longer than you have, and you must heed me, and

READ. I want you to read Macrobius, Pausanias, Herodian, Suetonius, Clement of Alexandria, Josephus, the *Moralia* of Plutarch, the Elizabethans, the writers of the Comedy of the Restoration, Livy, Thucydides, Coleridge's *Biographia Literaria*, Dryden's *Essays*, Ruskin's *Praeterita*, Herzen, Saint-Simon, Pliny, Strabo, Dionysius of Halicarnassus, and sundry other authors and savants. How many of these have you read, and if any, what do you recollect? You must go all the way, on your journey to mountainous values. I want you to have bread, otherwise, I would not be sending out half-crazy letters in your behalf. Now no roundabout letters from you in return; you are a stubborn Celt, and I am an obdurate Jew, and I am going to win this victory, your victory, or have done with you.

I also brought to your attention that you did not act with a tender regard for my own plight in Palma, and I repeat it, though you again disregarded what I had said. You are only shunning yourself. And until your flesh is the most pitying, I don't care one straw whether you read anything or not (and nothing will make a hard man soft, not even suffering, privation, the desert, and periods of hopelessness the shades can endure better in Orcus than here) if you have no compassion. Of course, you were in a Stygian perplexity; but don't you think I haven't hungered for bread, but I did not forsake my friends, poor waifs like myself, when they were desponding, indigent or starved for human companionship. What you do when you are hindered you will also do when you are prosperous.

I am going to teach you if I can so that we will have another gifted author in the earth, and as I said I don't care how flinty you are, that is my visionary duty to you and your life. I have seen too many people fall in the dust because they were ill-read, lacking compassion, or as stiff-necked as you. Look in the mirror at those recalcitrant shoulders. God hardened Pharaoh's heart, it is said in Exodus. . . . .

Remember, please that I only fight you because I fight

for you. Look about you, and ask yourself whether there is one other soul in the earth, and cast in all your Spanish writers, too, who can be of the kind of use I can be to you as a writer. . . . .

Coleridge in writing his critical work said he wanted to spare younger authors years of waste and attrition. Did he help a single one despite his wise counsel? I don't know. Herder said the same.

If you drudge all day for your bread, when will you have your Cana wine?

A student of mine, that is, a former one whom I taught at Boston University 11 years ago, comes to see me almost every day so that I can cure his health. He is half-Jew, part Irish, English and Scotch. He now teaches at that abominable academic factory, New York University, and is always in trouble because though he is altogether male he is tender with his students, and straight with them as I was with him and others. The Dean there never forgot me, and continued to tell students long after I left that there was once a man here who tried to run my college. . . . .

## To: Karl Shapiro

November 27, 1958
New York City

Dear Karl:

. . . . Karl, you are a good man, but you say odd things. I have not the least interest in literary parochialism. There is nothing new or very virile about the apotheosis of the yokel, which we once knew as regionalism. The truth is, if you had read my book [*The Sorrows of Priapus*] with any care at all, you could hardly have avoided perceiving that what I was doing was to provide an indigenous myth for the poet. That does not appear to satisfy you.

307

I must also be hilarious, but what is there to be rhapsodic about? Or don't you live in these States and see what is occurring? Why do you imagine we have so much nihilism in literature—because the raw apprentice and the disenchanted youth see so much about them which gives them felicity? When I see a land declining I go to the Walls of Jerusalem to weep. You laugh. Well, Heraclitus wept, and Democritus of Abdera laughed. But most of the philosophers and poets are saturnine though deeply human. Some years ago, not too many, Henry Miller told me that Sir Herbert Read had written him that he was happy. Miller asked me, What reason had he to be happy? Have you forgotten some of his dismal judgments regarding America?

It was my delight to tell you that I was very pleased that you printed Miller's simple, warm prose [in *The Prairie Schooner*], but was my praise to be used as a cudgel with which to beat me on the head?

Almost the whole of literature is against your hilarity. There is none in Aeschylus, Sophocles, Sir Thomas Browne, Robert Burton, and even in so much less a scribe as Twain. If you laugh after reading *Huck Finn* or *Life on the Mississippi* or *Roughing It*, you don't know what you are laughing at.

I like you very much, Karl, but I don't think I can allow you to garble my own books. What Sir Herbert Read had written, considering many books, was that I was profoundly human. Do you take a weak affirmation when there is a strong negation that is better? Nietzsche once said: "We destroy one sanctuary in order to create another," and I am by nature an iconoclast, but one who is always in search of images, fables and proverbs— the wine for the aching heart. Many of my admirers are young men, and I have not met one who came away from my book with less merriment than he had gone to it. . . . .

The whole difficulty is that a writer is expected not to please one poet and editor, but five or six other persons besides. Can you find such unanimity when you publish a book of your verse? If you can get three people together who have a common experience and tradition, and who agree, you have translated the water in the Cana jars into wine.

I know you have been a steadfast adherent of Bill Williams, and you deserve great credit for it. I had from the first admired *In the American Grain*, but had many misdoubts regarding the poems. A man of genius, he is surrounded very often by coarse people. As he is tender he is easily duped and persuaded. I fear I share your own feelings about "Paterson 5," but I would no more think of impugning a man at 75 who has had three strokes than I would of insulting Jehovah. Bill at his best will be remembered, and I give him all honor for his perceptions. Nor is he senile as one rude person told me. We spent several hours together about ten days before he was sick, and he said: . "You are not afraid to be tender with a man." No, I am not, and I'm no pederast either.

Now, Karl, it is most gracious of you to suggest that I send you some moiety of my autobiography when I have pages ready for your eyes. Even if I am lucky enough with the Muses to please you, how many persons will find it essential to dismember your own sights as well as my writing before you dispatch it back to me and Tartarus?

Anyway, I am never unmindful of your graces; the letter killeth the spirit, and since you always seem to be in trouble with those who are around you, and do all to gainsay your own insights, I know you are no basilisk. Far from it, as I told you before, you have imperial kindnesses, but you can be unjust, as you were to me about Aiken. It is a very bad book, and Samuel Johnson has said that to attack a poor book is a benefaction to the commonwealth. . . . . By the way, Allen Tate is a very great admirer of *The Sorrows of Priapus*; is he also a negative man? I don't think so at all, and believe that what he has been fighting, and what I have been struggling for, often against malice, at the most Stygian odds, is *Ecce Homo*. . . . .

# To: Josephine Herbst

August 18, 1960
Soller de Mallorca, Spain

Dear Josephine:

How delighted I was to find your epistle; I asked for mail when I went to Palma, not expecting any, but there were two for me. We live so much in seclusion, being hermits of letters, that word from the world seems like seeds or pollen dropped by some Cherub, one of those great contemplative birds of the Old Testament.

I cannot tell you, Josephine dear, how grateful I am to you for doing the review for *Commentary*. As for being detached, who but a churl who has no attachment to a single human being in the earth feigns to be so. Of course, it is said that in the *Bhagavad-Gita*, that that is the true vision of Confucius, but we are western, and though I am deeply pierced by the Rig-Vedas, and other such sayings from old India, I have never had that kind of nature. I love, I err, I am dust, and that is what I hope to be, and alas, am. God save both of us while we vibrate, think, and imagine we have one conception worthy of the Universe or even of the smallest gnat.

Now the Majorcan house is finished; there are details to be taken care of; but we are living in it. The house is about 40 degrees cooler than it is outdoors, and I am not being mawkish or giving you foolish remarks. The old peasant rock dwelling is surrounded on three sides by those great Mountains which Atlas must have cast up out of the sea, for does not each person, dwarf or giant, make his own burdens so that he will not have a niggard fate? At dusk we beat the branches filled with almonds, and we have 8 such nut-bearing trees, and two fig trees, tender citrus saplings, plum-bearing ones which should yield their fruit in a year or two, and a well, about 15 meters when the bucket first pierces it, and I delight in drawing up the cold water furnished by some small rivulet or current that comes from these sere, prophetic mountain ranges. For I love what is dry and what is wet, the orchards and Oceanus, as well as the sweet-limbed Nereids which preside over minute brooks, wells, or even a puddle of rain-water.

I selected the furniture, all antique, tables from Aragon, Catalan, Extremadura, Madrid, and Castille, all your Spanish earth, for nothing is ours save we give our hearts to it, a wizened truth, very old, and even trite, and so little understood by occidental peoples. But you know it, and that is why I am a devoted admirer of yours.

I feared that I might have vexed you by suggesting that you be wary of employing the vernacular; I tried it in the second fragment from the *Because I Was Flesh*, and it has been a thorn in my flesh ever since, and I cannot wait to mend that, and, of course, I did not have the effrontery to send it to you. Thinking of you, as I often do, I could not refrain from feeling that the only good thing in [William Carlos] Williams' last poem [?] is your letter, and all those winged and almost bird-like delights in the honey of flowers. I should, perhaps, not praise you, while I set aside another, but poor, sick Williams, for whom I have so much compassion, although he has erred against both of us, never had any real development. That is the tragedy of the writer in terra incognita, not yours, and I pray not mine; let my sins come not from weakness or from being a poltroon of letters; the honey comes from the lion's carcass. The weak hurt us most, and it may be that though earth, clay, marl, are as we know utterly perishable, are far more stable than that other mighty element, water, regarded by Virgil as deceitful. . . . .

# To: Frank MacShane

July 9, 1961
Soller de Mallorca, Spain

Dear Mr. MacShane:

I must apologize for my meager letter to you. By the time your most courteous epistle reached me in Soller I thought it would be too late to write you about Ford Madox Ford. Such a remark places another burden upon me. Will I be able to do any better now?

I had heard a good deal about Ford's legendary renown when I met him in his apartment which, I believe, was above the Rochambeau on 6th Avenue at 11th Street. Quite callow, and gorged with Marxist boastfulness, I thought him old, flaccid and porcine. A short time later I was one of a group of speakers on the platform at the New School for Social Research. We had come there to address a large audience and to organize a committee for indigent writers and artists. I suspect that the Communist Party had gotten the various people together. Anyway, I was rather startled to hear one celebrated man, who was talking to the persons in the hall, refer to me in the most complimentary manner. It was Ford who had turned toward me as he made this assertion.

Thereafter, I saw him on various occasions on 8th Street; he had a slow, obese shuffle and his breathing was very hard. I looked at this Falstaffian bag of heaving clothes with some contempt. Could this be a demigod of letters? I had not read a single book of his. At about the same time, or maybe two or three years later, E. E. Cummings said to me: "What's the matter with Sherwood Anderson; how can a man allow his face to fall to pieces that way?" By then I was extremely vexed by such a pitiless view of hapless flesh. . . . .

Ford would stop me on 8th Street or at lower 5th Avenue and say: "When are you going to bring me your novels to read?" Imagine a man saying that to you today. He would either tell you that he was too busy to read your books because he was going abroad, beginning a volume himself or trying to finish one. Ford stopped me on several occasions and repeated his query. Was I proud or stupid or just gauche? I came to his apartment one day and gave him my first two novels, *Bottom Dogs* and *From Flushing to Calvary*. When he had completed reading these he said: "What about the third one you wrote?" I gave him that also, and he told me that I was among the very few writers of autobiographical fiction who had succeeded in moving to a far less personal form of literature. He admired *Those Who Perish*, the third one, and later wrote a piece for *Forum* Magazine on three neglected authors, William Carlos Williams, E. E. Cummings, and myself.

We had many arguments; he knew I was very passionate about books and a literary bigot, and he always did his best to raise my ire, and seldom failed. One day after one of my long iconoclastic fits, he said: "All Jews are nasty icon-breakers." What about Nietzsche? I replied. I soon learned that his last wife Biala was a Jew. He cared for many authors I could not stomach, particularly Hemingway and also Faulkner. One day, his trousers very loose and his suspenders hanging down, he said while frying a pair of eggs in a skillet: "I think most of Shakespeare's plays were potboilers; certainly *Hamlet* was, and so was *Macbeth*." I thought this was a sacrilegious statement, but I thought about it afterwards a great deal.

Ford used to have Thursday afternoon teas at his apartment, 10 5th Avenue, New York City. He had two rooms, very sparsely furnished, a few secondhand chairs, a studio couch, a sofa for people who came for tea, Sutter's cookies, and outrageous declarations. It was perhaps the last literary salon in America, before virtually all of life was in the streets. The pair of emaciated and sterile rooms were rented for $65 a month. I went to these teas quite often, and Ford never failed to ask me to be sure to appear next week.

Whether I made good or bad talk at these afternoons, he felt that if I were present there would be irascible conversation.

At the time he wrote the *March of Literature* he told me when I was in his apartment that he had not consulted a single book to do this volume. He assured me that he had relied altogether on his memory. I remember when he said to me that swifts copulate on the wing, which I believe he got from *Selborne*, that wonderful 19th century book on natural history. Ford had the reputation of being a liar. People either said he was fat or always lied. I received no other impression from Sherwood Anderson. Ford used to invite people to be a guest of his at a Southern manor which did not exist. Now what kind of lies were these? Ford had "windmills in his head!"; if life could not provide him with the manor and the lucre his heart needed, why he had to invent them. Could he not be as generous as his nature demanded why not indulge in apocryphal tales. Anderson too was a big liar, and he admitted it in his memoirs, but when he was sluggish, and far from a book, he forgot about his own inclinations. Who can impugn visionary perjuries of this sort? . . . .

. . . . One day at his apartment William Carlos Williams, Ford and I were talking . . . . Suddenly, Ford turned to me, and said: "Why don't we start a group, meet, say, once a month, in order to get Bill Williams' books published?" I replied with much exuberance, and Ford thought, and then said: "How about a name? What do you think of calling the group The Friends of William Carlos Williams?" I said I considered it a very good name.

Ford drew up a list of names of people whom he thought we should invite to join. Among these were Paul Rosenfeld, Anderson, Marsden Hartley, Stieglitz, the painter Elizabeth Sparhawk Jones, altogether about 50. I asked him to expunge some of the names as I said there is no point in getting together the enemies of literature to be the friends of the very authors they have been suppressing.

Ford smiled; he had not had so many obscure protégés whose cause he had advanced against so many philisters without appreciating my feeling. The young, valiant James Laughlin was also a member of the group. We met once a month at the Downtown Gallery on 13th Street. There were, I believe, three dinners given for three authors: Williams, Cummings, and myself. Ford presided at all these meetings, and I must say a wonderful galaxy of genuine people in the arts attended these affairs. I say this because it could have been a piece of Dada nonsense or worse, something for poeticules.

. . . . The third dinner was given for me, and I read from a MS, later to be published as *Can These Bones Live.* As a result of these felicitous evenings Ford got publishers interested in Williams. . . . . After my own reading I was told that Ford had persuaded a woman to give $1500 as a prize for the best piece of work done till that time, and that I was to receive this money.

Shortly thereafter, I brought the finished MS of *Can These Bones Live* to Ford and he read it. What I did not know then was that he was dying. One day he walked with me across the street from 10 5th Avenue to the Brevoort, and told me I had written a book of genius, and after paying me so many delightful compliments he advised me to have nothing to do with publishers. He said I was too wild, too forthright, and could only be my worst adversary. Some while before Harrison Smith had bought the *Saturday Review,* and I had urged him to employ Ford as the literary editor. Of course, he had no intention of doing this; far too shrewd, he was interested in a business sheet of letters. I antagonized him as I was quite put out when he refused to take such an opportunity.

Ford told me that day that he would be my literary agent; I was not then 39, my development had been most sluggish, and my star had already fallen into the dust. I did not know then how to thank this man whom I had once looked upon as a decayed gentleman of the quondam arts, asthmatic, obscenely gross in bulk. That day I had the occasion to look into his eyes; D. H. Lawrence, whom Ford disliked, said Ford had the "dove-gray eyes of the Shulamite." He had the large Mediterranean orbs of Astarte; but no matter. Lawrence had gotten the man, and it was the truth. One never knows where a man's genius is, in his hands, cheeks, or in that great upland forehead of Ford's, or in the eyes of Anderson, which resembled those of the cow-goddess Io.

I asked Ford whether he would write the introduction, and he told me how proud he would be to do that. He took the MS with him when he sailed for France, and three weeks later a great man had died in Deauville. I was utterly prone when I read the obituary notice in the *New York Herald Tribune*. I had lost the most steadfast friend I had ever had in literature. Most authors are a perfidious lot, weathervane critics, but not this good, stalwart man.

I telephoned William Carlos Williams and suggested that we hold another meeting at the Downtown Gallery and read fragments from some of [Ford's] books. Williams replied: "Death is a biological fact," and that terminated the conversation.

Ford had very little money, and I can say that I heard of no one who spoke of his books at all, alleging that they were either good or ill. I never heard anybody mention the Tietjens books. I must freely own that I had not read them myself. It is a hard statement for me to make since I loved Ford, and never tried to exploit his outrageously kind heart. I did not have the chance to had I been so boorish; he had already offered to do everything for me.

You doubtless know of the New Directions Memorial issue to Ford; I wrote a piece there, and maybe you saw my tender words about him in *Can These Bones Live*.

Like Sherwood Anderson at that period Ford was a fabulous name in literature, but a forsaken one. I never even recollect that Anderson ever referred to a single book that Ford had written. Despite Ford's long essay on Dreiser in *Portraits From Life* Dreiser never once spoke to me of any book by Ford.

I am almost positive that the *March of Literature* was remaindered. Again, I must be regarded as being no less base than those I mention. I had not read the volume either. For some reason or other I got the impression that it was an academic anthology of literature, and I abhor anthologies. I tell you this because I believe it conveys the apathy toward this genius.

Even when Knopf did the Tietjens books they were a failure; that is my impression. Ford represented a pleasant expatriate fable; everybody feigned to admire him, but not only was he neither read nor misread; most of his books were not known to those whom he helped. And Ford was the Archangel of every obscurian, every illuminated waif of the Muses who could not get into a magazine or into a book. I know he was poor because I used to go to see his widow, Biala, simply out of respect for Ford. I thought this was a marriage of convenience too. She did not get money out of this, but she did derive a social literary position that meant a great deal to her. She had come from the dumps of Provincetown, where she had painted and starved. Ford, of course, arranged to get her a one-man show, and it was a big affair that I attended. . . . . I doubt that even now the revenue from Ford's books could be much more than metaphysical.

He was a close friend of Allen Tate's, an intimate friend of mine, whom I did not know then. And I should find it hard to believe that he could have indulged too much in what Randolph Bourne called "the new orthodoxies of propaganda." Still, he was an ardent advocate of my own Marxist novel, *Those Who Perish*. But he associated with all sorts of people at the end, Padraic Colum, as Roman Catholic as Tate was in those days. But I cannot speak with any assurance. He detested Nazism, and I believe he wanted to die before another world war took place, before France was destroyed. He had as poor luck with his books as he

had with women in the fag-end of his great, heart-break life.
I know he had asked a fine, buxom, and rather demented
wench . . . . to marry him, but she refused. She became a
devout Communist, but I think the proposal was long before that, and she used to come to the Thursday afternoon
teas, too. . . . .

I have jotted down these things in great haste, and I
don't know whether I have said anything of use to you or
not. But you can believe that I have the most ardent love
for Ford, his works, and his life. Once Unamuno said: "I
am not a Cervantist; I am a Quixotist." It is a beautiful dis-
tinction, and it fits Ford Madox Ford; he was everybody's
warrior; as far as I am concerned he had no faults, or if
he had any I wish to God that I could borrow them, for
I could live better with his defects than I can with my alleged virtues.

You have, be sure, my deepest and friendliest sympathy
and regard. Would to heaven I could be more useful; the
truth is that we never see people at all; we imagine we do,
not even clever enough to realize that we do not know anything about ourselves, either. And that is why we are so
coarse; we are too phlegmatic to be valiant or even charitable enough to perceive a great man.

## To: Stanley Burnshaw

April 4, 1962
Soller de Mallorca, Spain

Dear Stanley:
Your good letter came to me from Palma; a word from
a friend is manna in my wild heart . . . . It was a great
pleasure for me to know that you are quite satisfied with
the *Moby-Dick* essay. Aside from the fact, dear Stanley,
that I honored all the work you had done on the essay,

and apart from my reluctance to meddle with your own emendations, I was by then too remote from the work to know what to do. We are positively automatic most of the days of our lives, and when we imagine that we have a little clear knowledge of our deeds, we are surely obscure to ourselves. I would not give a straw for any deliberate act of mine. I do what I can, and later pray that it is not horrible, and wonder how I can commit some other act of kindness or of solicitude which will not turn out evil.

I did an introduction to Sherwood Anderson's *Mid-American Chants* which the publisher [Jonathan Williams, publisher of *Jargon Books*] admires, but this was a task of love. The poems themselves are tender and slight, but I cared for the man, and now someone has asked me to do an introduction to a castaway I had known and who died alone and miserable in a furnished room. I knew him well-nigh 30 years, and had only realized toward the close of a young life, he was only about 54, that he was a poet. Now, out of feeling for him, I am going to do a preface to his poems which I have never seen! Of course, I shan't receive a nickel for this . . . . What can I do? Most of what I do is for nothing and for oblivion. What does it matter so long as I do it, as inertia is a terrible yoke, and I cannot be a bondsman in an idle and lascivious Egypt.

It was heartening to hear that your health is good, and that your own woes about that are at an end; I am grateful for that.

I earnestly hope that you will get the Guggenheim money [so that you can prepare *The Modern Hebrew Poem Itself*]; I long ago stopped applying for their pecuniary quails, as it was useless. More, I deeply hope that you will find what ritual you need for your life and apply it to your own Pisgah, and not run to and fro looking for a new translation to do. You did the remarkable task on the poems of others; now, do your own work, and let nothing be a stumbling block to that. All else, no matter how good it is, wil be thorns and thistles in your blood . . . .

I regret this epistle is nothing but woe. Even if I am sent back to the U.S. I have no way of earning a livelihood; who will hire an iconoclast who is nearly 62, and who will be regarded as a life insurance risk to the bursar and the deans? You know what luck I had with the Department of Education at New York University. You got that for me, and you know I was liked and asked back, but I was unable to earn more than $275 for a semester, and that was given me because Dean Warren was charitable, for I had only four students, all acolytes of mine, but four!

The book [*Because I Was Flesh*] should be done with in two to three weeks at the most. I am poring over the *Mishneh Torah*, the *Zohar*, the Jewish Apocalyptic works, to complete an American book. And I have not a tittle of reverence for the church or God or his archangels, or his demons in my veins. But I revere learning, and do what I can to knead it even as the baker of Asher works his dough, and to make the whole lump into a vision of my own. Well, we shall see; boasting is idle, and I have no bombastic feelings. I know nothing, and I wonder how that is even possible; for that too implies certainty of a sort. . . .

## To: Kim Taylor

June 27, 1962
Soller de Mallorca, Spain

Dear Kim Taylor:
. . . . New York is not really my terrain; it's a big, cruel, auto town, and a graveyard of many hopes. Had I known how to make a life in the Midwest I should never have gone to New York. As a child my mother and I lived in Dallas, and then for a time in Fort Worth; and about 17 years ago I thought of settling in San Antonio, but I had no way of earning my bread there. I should have been

quite satisfied to have remained in Kansas City had I found two to three congenial and pensive companions who could have told me what books to read. So quite against my will and character I have been an exile at home and abroad; the truth is I care nothing at all for the ecstasy of being an expatriate. . . . .

I simply could not write a bad book for lucre; no matter how I tried I could only compose a shabby novel or volume with the most idealistic zeal. Mr. [James] Laughlin, a gallant man, and not venal, has doutbless told you of my trials as an author; still, it is better to have windmills in one's brain than to be shrewd. Besides, we only do what we are, though I doubt that we ever know what we are doing, or even why. . . . .

A man ought to write books in order to be liked; no matter how stony his negations are that should be his motive, and if I have in some way persuaded you to have friendly feelings towards me, believe me I appreciate it. After a long and feverish solitude Prince Myshkin is so overwhelmed by the hospitality of the General and his three daughters, and nearly beside himself because he is with people again that he says: "I thank you so very much for liking me." . . . .

## To: Allen Tate

July 10, 1963
Soller de Mallorca, Spain

Dear Allen:

I have your very generous letter; no, Allen, it is I who am indebted to you. Moreover, I don't mind at all this debt of the heart which can never be paid. Is not ingratitude as great a sin as murder; to take something from a man, and then deprive him even of thanks is to spoil him of hope and trust. . . . .

Now, my connection with the unlettered street urchins in lascivious, dirty drawers, nazarite sandals and bedunged beards, is quite bizarre. How did I come by it? I don't know. The little I have read of their noisome scribblings has filled me with loathing. Still, this is the way a writer comes into notoriety. A quiet fame is well-nigh impossible to come by. Look, I live here in such obscurity that even when somebody hears that I am a writer he does not believe it. Then the universal craze to be an artist is one of the pests of our time. That reminds me, I don't think I ever thanked you enough for all the help you gave me in persuading the people at the University [of Minnesota] Press to bring out *Alms for Oblivion*. Is not the title a symptom of my feeling, the hopeless plight of an author in the world? After writing three miserable novels I resolved to be a man of letters, not too pompously phrased I pray; what has been the outcome of that resolution? Today, I am some kind of inverted saint of pederasts, bums, fools, simpletons, and rascals who know nothing about literature or have any veneration for a single master. One day I met Allen Ginsberg, who is supposed to be an admirer of mine (be sure these roaring illiterates of Cedar Bar have never done a thing for me, or mentioned me; so how I should come into this kind of *Esquire* [the July 1963 issue described Dahlberg as one of the "heroes" of the American literary underground] notice I don't know), and having read "Howl" and "Kaddish," I said that any one who described his mother's secret parts was as foul as Nero was with Agrippina. That should have endeared me to them. I met Burroughs in Paris four years ago, and he spent all his time telling me how the police had been pursuing him because of his addiction to narcotics. He acted like a fellow traveler, saying that he was a remote sympathizer but not an actual party member. Each word that fell from his mouth was stupid and I told him so. . . . .

Meantime, I am considering a book of maxims, using a good deal of North American Indian background for it, as well as many allusions to Dampier, Bandelier, Herrera, and other renowned travelers for that purpose. Of course, I am only indolently brooding now; with what strength I have I look long at the olive trees here; when I think of the cult of youth and then consider how wise a senile olive is, I know that this century can bear only unripe fruit. Have you ever thought about an olive, its trunk, as old as the living oak Agamemnon planted, and wondered how it is possible that as we decay we are far more majestic than an ever-green citrus sapling with odors that are as alluring as Solomon's bedchamber?

You have my enduring friendship and great admiration, my dear Allen, and I love both you and Isabella [Gardner; Mrs. Allen Tate]. I have nothing left but what love there is in me, and though that may be as small as the cummin seed it is what I prize most. . . . .


## To: Mrs. Michael Sands

November 15, '63
Soller de Mallorca, Spain

Dear Minnie:
. . . . A letter just arrived from my brother Michael; tell him that I love him and will reply very shortly; I owe Steve [Stephen Sands, nephew of Edward Dahlberg] an answer also, and will get that off tomorrow. Believe me, I am immensely pleased to be of any advantage to Steve. You can't obtain an education in a university; that is one certitude, and in the course of four years you are not likely to meet one human being. I have been battling the curricula of Caliban that is offered at all universities for many years, and oddly enough I get more attention and notice in the U.S.A. academies than I do in the papers which I also detest. My position in American Letters is incongruous: papers and letters and books of mine are in

more colleges than I know; above a week ago I was informed that I was well represented in the Lawrence, Henry Miller, Lawrence Durrell Collection at the University of California at Los Angeles and in other archives there. Letters of mine, many, are in the Alfred Stieglitz Memorial Collection at Yale University, and Texas University gives me enormous amount of regard. What does it all mean? . . . . As I told you or Michael the University of Minnesota is publishing this February a volume of essays, *Alms for Oblivion*, and Oxford Press in England and Unwin in Canada are buying books from them. Myself, I have not received one penny for the book. But don't imagine I am complaining. One French writer said: "If I had my life to live over again I would shoot myself." I totally agree with such a salubrious opinion, but at the same time no matter what the risks were, and they were infernal, I would only be a writer. Making a book, good or bad, is the only cure for any disorders I know. That brings us back to the other quandary: What should Steve do? I told your quick, intelligent son that what you and Michael were doing for him was marvelous, and I am grateful to hear that he thanked his father many times. And, of course, you. Tell me, how can I tell a young man, who must needs take hard-earned money from his father and mother to pursue poverty. And to decide to be an author is to resolve to be poor. I thought of a middle-way, being no man of compromises myself. It was and is my firm belief that Steve after two years of intense study of French (don't let him make a Cook's Tour of Europe and just squander your money and his life) should return to some university and get his doctorate. Sure, by then God knows what a college will have done to his mind, nature, and ethics; but what choice is there? Most work is odious; if somebody had told me that I had to be a drudge in an office or die of want, I should have preferred the latter alternative. But I cannot so advise my nephew. Assuming that courses in idiocy do not utterly deprave him, he can earn his bread as a professor and at some time or other do an honorable book on some sage of literature. I have gone all the way, but look at the ill health

I now have, and if I discovered to you the years of darksome penury I have had even after I was 40, you would wince. Meantime, be sure, I will do my best to counsel him; will he take my advice? if it is good, probably not, but I will be pertinacious.

I am very glad that both of you enjoy the strength that is needed to keep alive in this earth. Steve said quite proudly that his father is a handsome man, and of course that pleased me very much.

Meantime, you have again my thanks and affections. My one seeing eye still troubles me, and that is alarming. Suppose I cannot in the close future study learned books I am then good for nothing. But shortly I go to see another eye-surgeon in Palma, and if that is a bootless errand, I shall, after recovering more strength, arrange for a sea voyage to Barcelona.


## To: Stephen Sands

January 30, 1964
Soller de Mallorca, Spain

Dear Steve:
A just commonwealth depends upon the purity of the language of its poets. Of course, there is no justice, and I am speaking of a republic that is not dominated by the rabble. Sir Philip Sidney makes good reading for you, and so should Edmund Spenser be; both are somewhat tedious, but the language will refine your soul. Myself I prefer Sir Walter Raleigh's verse, and Wyatt's. But I am teased by Sidney, Spenser and Samuel Daniel.

I am asking my publisher to mail you a copy of *Because I Was Flesh*. . . . . You should know it, for we must try our best to understand our origins; what ancestors howl in our ribs.

Paris is brutal, but where can one go? Rousseau said that after he had been away from Paris for a fortnight he was as good as dead to his friends. If you are alone in that city it is hellebore. The reason that I suggested Alliance Française is that I thought you might have some feminine companionship. Without a woman I find any city an inferno of progress.

Sir Herbert [Read] is now in America, and I will be writing to him in a very few days, and see whether he knows some people there. Those I have met there are homosexuals, narcotic addicts and café *flâneurs*. Or you just encounter poseurs at the Dome or the Select.

I earnestly pray that you are accepted at Oxford, anything is better than the army. Should you have trouble, for God's sake return to the States so that you are beyond the talons of some brach on the draft board. I should not like to see you go so far from me, but I realize what a wretched experience military life would be for you.

Meanwhile, I do nothing, a sordid and mad occupation. I am still between books, and do not know what I shall do next, perhaps a volume on women or a book of adages à la Rochefoucauld which will bring me a hundred readers. Stendhal wrote a marvelous book, not a boudoir essay, called *L'Amour.* You should read it, so that you will make your mistake later rather than now. At 20 you know nothing about women, but you don't realize it, at 40 you know nothing about women, but imagine you are not as ignorant as you were, at 60 you have no knowledge of women and can be enchanted for no more than two to three days. After that it is ennui, two bored people staled together. . . . .

So you have moved to another room. It was Pascal who said that all of man's troubles came from his inability to remain quiet in one room.

Wish, my dear Steve, I could be more useful to you. The tragedy of being alive, or imagining that you are, is that you can do nothing for others, or almost nothing. . . . .

Your devoted uncle.

# To: Jonathan Williams

June 27, 1964
Dublin, Ireland

Dear Jonathan:

. . . . Can anybody give good counsel to another, or is the heart  absolutely surd when advice is offered? Do you want a quick reputation, or do you propose to be a poet? That is the dilemma as I see it. Your seniors never gave you a good paradigm, but you insist on copying their mannerisms. Learning is not knowledge unless it is an inward volcano that explodes into a sonnet. You cannot use pedestrian conversation, place alongside it instructions pasted on the door of a rooming house, and add to that, a line or two from the *Purgatorio*. That is the modern fraud, and it makes for outside poetry which is composed in Gaza, and not on the holy hills of Jerusalem. I know I have told you this many times, and just as many times, with rare exceptions, you have shunned my exhortations. When you come to the conclusion that the Word is First after the Void has been dissolved then you will be as good as God or as weary from going to and fro in the earth as Lucifer. Should you wish to circumnavigate your soul it is not good enough just to cite Hakluyt's *Voyages*; you yourself must make the journey, and all the pelagic meadows must be within you and not added on to an easy piece of American jargon.

Though you have a magnificent heart, and it is a miracle that we have a Jonathan Williams to republish [Sherwood] Anderson's *Mid-American Chants*, what is the good of illustrating them with photographs? Or one may wonder whether the verses of Anderson are not just the subtitles for the camera work. I think this is a parcel of your perplexities. You might ask why Ben Shahn did the drawings for *The Sorrows of Priapus*. It is the same thing we are discussing. You can't get people to read, and so you prepare as a snare for them drawings or photography, hoping that after they have glanced for a delirious minute at the camera pictures or the artist's illustrations they will then be tempted to peruse the book. I don't believe that people go from one to the other. Admiring even a great oil painting by Velasquez requires the smallest amount of intellectual attention, whereas you cannot examine Plato's *Critias* without employing all your faculties. In short, we are art-crazy because we are lazy, supine, and do not care to use our minds. Stieglitz, a wonderful nature, is responsible for this, but then seers are often charlatans. . . . .

## To: Dr. William Ryan

September 2, 1964
Dublin, Ireland

Dear Mr. Ryan:

This morning I sent you an air letter, registered, and later I went to Thomas Cook and Son and received your cable.

In my letter to you I explained why I was so tardy in answering your very kind enquiry. First, I had had word from Miss Dorothy Wilson asking me whether I would accept a visiting professorship for two months at the University of Missouri. I replied that I would, but asked what would be paid me since I should have to travel from here to Kansas City and then return to Spain.

Now I am in a perplexity. I am packing to make ready to get the boat this evening for Liverpool and from there will go to Folkstone and afterwards to France and then to Spain.

What I do not know is what you are offering me. Am I to go there as a visiting professor and what would be the salary?

Then there is another matter, and I pray that you shall understand and appreciate my reasons and not regard me as bombastic in any manner whatsoever. I should prefer to be considered as a man of letters and poet, and not give the usual academic courses. Good teaching is apocalyptic talking. I should rather speak about the life of Melville, explaining his genius and limitations, and the influence of *Timon of Athens* and *Lear* upon him, but quite informally than, say, give a course on 19th century American Literature. Or it would give me far more pleasure in describing Swift, Congreve, Pope, Wycherley, in a casual way, but with enough passion to awaken the faculties of the student, than to deliver a long and rigid peroration on that period of literature.

When my dear friends, Sherwood Anderson and Ford Madox Ford, were asked to come to a university outside of Detroit they went there as warm, pulsing writers who hoped to engage the interest of students in an easy, talkative manner and to introduce them to books by referring to the writers they had known and the books they had composed.

Had I to teach many courses I should not have the time nor the emotional strength to write a book. And I feel that I should also be an advantage to the University of Missouri, if whilst I was there, I was lucky enough to make a good and truthful book.

Meantime, I have no idea what Miss Dorothy Wilson has in mind, and whether she proposes to communicate with me, and let me know what she expects of me. I had mentioned that I would enjoy giving a course in the writing of poetry and prose, but would wish to entice those students who have an intellectual passion for literature, and whose mind would be on the contribution they might at some time make to the American commonwealth. In a word, I am not interested in scurrile dollar scribblers, and do not care to make people more corrupt or trashy than our age is. . . . .

# To: Michael Blankfort

September 29, 1964
Soller de Mallorca, Spain

Dear Mike:

Your review and note, forwarded from Dublin, arrived yesterday. You show great delicacy of the heart in asking me whether anything you have written about me has offended me. On the contrary, I thank you very much for your gracious, and manna-like words about *Alms for Oblivion*. But then I have not forgotten that you have been my defender since the early days of my novels. The making of many books is a great weariness and also a great poverty, and when one is not venal, writing to be as truthful as one's bones will allow, a friend like Michael Blankfort is very necessary. Otherwise, you lie at the bottom of limbo and each volume (and there have been times when I feel under the impression that I have been writing posthumously for years) you compose is Alms for Oblivion. Do you recall Ulysses' speech in *Troilus and Cressida?*

In spite of the attention that *Because I Was Flesh* got, lucre and I are still stout antagonists; but that is the way it has to be, and I am not sniveling about it. It's far too late for that kind of tear-bottle. I will champ honor when I receive it, and imagine it's hope, soup, and potatoes. Had I to do it over again (and who has the heart to repeat even a felicitious experience?) I should do what I am doing. Why not? What is worse and what is better?